2021 Kentucky PSI Real Estate Exam Prep. Questions and Answers

Study Guide to Passing the Salesperson Real Estate License Exam Effortlessly

Written by
Real Estate Exam Professionals, Ltd.

First Printing, 2021

Printed in the United States of America

Table of Contents

INTRODUCTION

Thank you for purchasing this Real Estate Exam Prep. book. We hope you will learn a great deal from our study guide and that you will study well and pass your exam. It is our purpose to provide you with the most up to date information for your state real estate exam. We have made every effort to present this material as the closest possible example to what you will see on your actual state exam. At times, it will appear to be exactly what you will see on the exam. We have tried very hard to make this book as error and typo free as possible. However, we are not without our faults. Real estate exam material and the real estate exams change rapidly and we are continuously updating this book as these changes occur. You may find a typo here and there, but do not be alarmed. We assure you that if you find one, it will be obvious and it will not prevent you from being able to tell what the correct answer is.

You will find that after you have studied this material as instructed in the *How to Use this Guide Effectively*, you will discover that this is all you need to pass the real estate exam. There are many real estate schools out there such as Allied Real Estate School, Anthony Real Estate School and Kaplan that, although they are good schools, also offer exam cram or exam preparation materials, but are extremely overpriced. Their materials can cost into the $100 and $300 ranges and provide a lot of extra "fluff" material that will not help you pass the exam and will waste your time. This book offers all the same materials in a condensed and precise manner with no fluff. Once you have taken the department of real estate certified classes and passed them, qualified to for a state exam date then you do not need those classroom materials anymore. All you will need are the answers to the state and national real estate exam questions. Study those, nothing else, memorize them, and you will pass your exam on the 1st try. There is no need to buy expensive materials from other schools, no need to sit in live exam cram courses, and there is no need for the Real Estate Exam for Dummies books. We have been offering this material to thousands of licensees for over 10 years with a tremendous amount of positive reviews and feedback.

How To Use This Guide Effectively

Here you will find tried and true steps to help you use this guide effectively and to get the best results while minimizing your study time. Please understand that as you go through the real estate questions we have prepared for you, you may come across a few that you have never seen before. Do not be alarmed. These are questions that are on the state exam, but were never given to you in the real estate class you took or in your class textbooks. This is why there is such a high failure rate for the real estate exam. The actual questions on the state or national real estate exams are NOT created by the same agency that created the college courses or text books. These college courses are designed by regional college accreditation agencies and the state real estate exams are created by the individual state's department of real estate or real estate commissions. It is very frustrating, we know. That is why there publishers like us who create exam cram courses and applications to "bridge the gap" of knowledge for the real estate exams.

STEP 1: Read and understand the VOCABULARY section first. These are very important terms. The key to successful knowledge of real estate is understanding and knowing the vocabulary used. Review them until you are confident to go onto the questions. Do not continue to the questions until you know these terms well.

STEP 2: Now go to the STUDY SECTION and read all the real estate questions with their correct answers and explanations in each exam. There are a lot of questions. Pace yourself and allow time to understand and memorize the correct answers.

STEP 3: Go back to the VOCABULARY section and review. Again, they are VERY important. You must know these forwards and backwards.

STEP 4: Repeat step 2 until you feel you are scoring 90% or better. Then review the VOCABULARY section again.

STEP 5: Now begin the MATH only portion of the STUDY SECTION. Read the questions with the answers and explanations until you have mastered them just as you did with the regular real estate questions. Make sure you set aside a separate time of the day to ONLY study the math. The reason for this is that the analytical/math function of the human brain works on math problems from different areas of the brain than word problems. When studying it takes approx. 10 min. for the brain to fully switch to a pure analytical/math function. If you are studying word problems and math problems in the same study session, you will be wasting a lot of time and overworking your brain. Time is key here, especially when it comes to the day of the exam, more about that later.

STEP 6: Repeat the MATH ONLY portion in the STUDY SECTION until you feel you are scoring at least 90% or better.

STEP 7: Now you are ready to go on to the TEST SECTION of this book. These questions will simulate what you will find on the actual state exam. You will have a limited time to complete the exam. Set a timer to the amount of time that your state allows for you to complete the state exam. Begin taking one of the exams and write your answers on a blank sheet of paper. When you are finished, check your answers with the correct answers shown in the same exams from the STUDY SECTION and score yourself. Now continue to Step 8.

STEP 8: Did you score 90% or better? If so, congratulations! You are ready to take the actual state exam and pass on your first try. If you did not score 90% or better, review the questions you missed using the STUDY SECTION. Study them, and retake the corresponding exam in the TESTING SECTION. Continue doing this and review the Vocabulary, if needed, until you are scoring 90% or better.

IMPORTANT!!!

REMEMBER THIS ON THE DAY YOU TAKE YOUR STATE EXAM…

DO NOT ANSWER, OR EVEN READ, THE FIRST 5 QUESTIONS OF THE EXAM. DO THOSE SECOND TO LAST AND ANY MATH RELATED QUESTIONS, VERY LAST!!!

Write the numbers to these questions on a piece of paper to remember to do them later. The reason is that they have placed the hardest questions in the first 5 spots to distract you, make you nervous and frustrated while taking the test. So, do those just before doing the math questions. Do the math questions very last because as we explained earlier, psychologically it takes the brain about 5-10 minutes to go from comprehensive thinking to analytical mathematical thinking. You only have a limited amount of time to complete the real estate exam. Therefore, your time will be very valuable. Do not leave any question unanswered. An unanswered question will be scored as a wrong answer.

Be sure to read the section *"Secrets to Passing the Real Estate Exam"* this section was developed by ex-real estate exam proctors. It will give you more detailed steps and inside information on how to use the above method on the day of your exam. It will also show you how to answer a question correctly even if you have completely forgotten the answer.

Good luck and study well!

REAL ESTATE VOCABULARY

Due to the length of this Real Estate Glossary, we have included it as a link below. Please understand these are general real estate terms used in almost every state. This is here for review purposes and reference only.

http://www.realestateabc.com/glossary/

You may also download a PDF version here:
http://tinyurl.com/realestatevocab

Study Section

In this section you will have the Real Estate Vocabulary Exam, Kentucky Real Estate Exam and Real Estate Math Exam. Read through all the questions in each exam according to the *How to Use this Guide Effectively* chapter and ONLY look at the correct answers in each exam. Start with the Vocabulary Exam and read question number one and then read ONLY the correct answer immediately. Continue to do this for each question until you have read all the questions in the first exam. If you go through each exam 3-4 times in this manner, you will then be able to recognize the correct answer right away when it comes to taking the actual exam. If your reading device has the ability to highlight the correct answer in each question, please utilize this feature. It will make it a little easier each time when reading through the exams in this section.

REAL ESTATE VOCABULARY EXAM

Please understand these are general real estate terms used in almost every state. This is here for practice and review purposes only. Some terms may not be on your exam.

1. Which of the following describes the term "appreciation"?

A.   Kind words expressed to someone about something they did
B.   An increase in the value of property
C.   An item of value owned by an individual
D.   None of the above

Answer: B. Appreciation is the increase in the value of a property due to changes in market conditions, inflation, or other causes.

2. When ownership of a mortgage is transferred from one company or individual to another, it is called

A.   an assumption
B.   an assignment
C.   an assessment
D.   all of the above

Answer: B. When ownership of a mortgage is transferred (assigned) from one company or individual to another, it is called an assignment.

3. A mortgage loan which requires the remaining balance be paid at a specific point in time is called a/an

A. balloon mortgage
B. early due mortgage
C. mortgage of convenience
D. promissory note

Answer: A. A mortgage loan that requires the remaining principal balance be paid at a specific point in time is a balloon mortgage.

4. The following reason accounts for why bridge loans are not used much anymore:

A. More second mortgage lenders now will lend at a high loan to value
B. Sellers would rather accept offers from Buyers who have already sold their property
C. Neither A or B
D. Both A and B

Answer: D. Bridge loans are not used much anymore because more second mortgage lenders now will lend at a high loan to value and sellers often prefer to accept offers from buyers who have already sold their property.

5. A title which is free of liens or legal questions as to ownership of the property is called a _____ title.

A. good
B. cloudy
C. clear
D. free

Answer: C. A title free of liens or legal questions as to ownership of the property is called a clear title. It is clear because there can be no challenges made to its legality.

6. What is the collateral in a home loan?

A.   The property itself
B.   A person's good name
C.   The amount of savings a person has
D.   The current automobile the person owns

Answer: A. The property itself is the collateral, and the borrower risks losing it if he does not repay according to the terms of the mortgage or deed of trust.

7. The adjustment date on an adjustable-rate mortgage is

A.   the date the interest rate changes
B.   the date the stock market goes up
C.   30 days from the date the mortgage was taken out
D.   all of the above

Answer: A. The adjustment date is the date the interest rate changes (adjusts).

8. What is the deposit made by a potential buyer to show he is serious about buying a house called?

A.   Serious money deposit
B.   Earnest money deposit
C.   "Nothing ventured, nothing gained" deposit

D.   Down payment

Answer: B. The deposit made by a potential buyer to show they are in earnest about purchasing a house is called an earnest money deposit.

9. A right-of-way which gives persons other than the owner access to or over a property is known as an

A.   easement
B.   ingress
C.   egress
D.   none of the above

Answer: A. An easement is a right-of-way to persons other than the owner and gives them legal access.

10. Which best describes a "subdivision"?

A.   Houses in the same neighborhood similar in style and size
B.   A housing development created by dividing a tract of land into individual lots
C.   A development which is "substandard"
D.   None of the above

Answer: B. A subdivision consists of individual lots created from a larger tract (subdivided) and are offered for sale or lease.

11. When someone contributes to the construction or rehabilitation of a property with labor or services rather than cash, that contribution is called

A. a personal contribution
B. sweat equity
C. a big help to the contractors
D. toil and labor

Answer: B. Sweat equity is the contribution to the construction of or rehabilitation of a property in the form of labor or services rather than cash.

12. A two-step mortgage is defined as

A. an adjustable rate mortgage with one interest rate for the first five or seven years and a different rate for the remainder of the term.
B. a mortgage which is both adjustable and fixed
C. a mortgage which is named after a dance step
D. all of the above

Answer: A. A two-step mortgage starts out with one rate for the first five or seven years and then changes to a different rate for the remainder of the term of the mortgage amortization.

13. A legal document evidencing a person's right to or ownership of a property is called a:

A. quitclaim deed
B. title
C. yearly lease
D. accurate appraisal

Answer: B. A title is a legal document evidencing a person's right to or ownership of a property.

14. If you were buying a house that included furnishings, you would receive a written document transferring title to the personal property. This document is called a/an

A.   title
B.   deed
C.   bill of sale
D.   evidence of payment

Answer: C. A bill of sale is a written document that transfers personal property from one owner to another.

15. An oral or written agreement that is binding in a court of law is called a:

A.   gentlemen's agreement
B.   contract
C.   business deal
D.   promissory note

Answer: B. A contract can be oral or written and is binding in a court of law.

16. The part of the purchase price of a property that the buyer pays in cash and does not finance with the mortgage is called the

A.   deposit
B.   second mortgage

C.   down payment
D.   deed of trust

Answer: C. The down payment is the amount paid down in cash as the initial upfront portion of the total amount due. It is usually given in cash at the time of finalizing the transaction.

17. A female named in a will to administer an estate is called an

A.   executor
B.   executrix
C.   individual representative
D.   able inheritor

Answer: B. The female executor named in a will to administer an estate is called an executrix.

18. The greatest possible interest a person can have in real estate is called

A.   fee complex
B.   fee simple
C.   no additional fees
D.   ownership

Answer: B. The greatest possible interest a person can have in real estate is called fee simple.

19. Required for properties located in federally designated flood areas, this type of insurance compensates for physical property damage resulting from flooding. It is called

A. water damage insurance
B. hurricane insurance
C. there's no such thing
D. flood insurance

Answer: D. Flood insurance is required in federally designated flood areas and does compensate for physical property damage resulting from flooding.

20. The following is true of a government loan:

A. It is guaranteed by the Department of Veterans Affairs (VA)
B. It is guaranteed by the Rural Housing Service (RHS)
C. It is insured by the Federal Housing Administration (FHA)
D. All of the above

Answer: D. Government loans are either insured by FHA, guaranteed by VA or RHS. Mortgages that are not government loans are called conventional loans.

21. The person conveying an interest in real property is called

A. the buyer
B. the grantee
C. the grantor
D. the mortgagor

Answer: C. The grantor is the person conveying an interest in real property to another party.

22. Insurance that covers in the event of physical damage to a property from fire, wind, vandalism, or other hazards is called

A.   act of God insurance
B.   hazardous insurance
C.   hazard insurance
D.   there is no such insurance

Answer: C. Insurance covering physical damage to a property from fire, wind, vandalism, or other hazards is called hazard insurance.

23. A liquid asset is

A.   an asset which is not in solid form
B.   an asset which cannot be frozen
C.   a cash asset or an asset easily turned into cash
D.   an asset that is hard to get to

Answer: C. A liquid asset is either cash or something easily turned into cash.

24. Another term for the lender in a mortgage agreement is the

A.   banker
B.   mortgagee
C.   mortgagor
D.   private mortgage company

Answer: B. The mortgagee is the lender.

25. If you are buying a house and asking the Seller to provide all or part of the financing, you are asking for _____ financing.

A.   special
B.   owner
C.   personal
D.   non-bank

Answer: B. When the Seller provides all or part of the financing it is called owner financing.

26. A point is

A.   the part of the pen you sign a contract with
B.   a score in a basketball game
C.   the reason for telling the story
D.   1% of the amount of the mortgage

Answer: D. A point is 1% of the amount of the mortgage.

27. What does a power of attorney grant someone?

A.   The ability to attend law school
B.   Complete or limited authority on behalf of someone else
C.   Complete control over which medical facility someone uses
D.   The right to inherit an estate

Answer: B. A power of attorney derives power from a legal document and grants someone complete or limited authority on behalf of someone.

28. The principal is

A.   the amount borrowed or remaining unpaid
B.   part of the monthly payment that reduces the remaining balance of a mortgage
C.   an ethic or value
D.   both A and B

Answer: D. The principal is the amount borrowed or remaining unpaid, as well as the part of the monthly payment that reduces the remaining balance of a mortgage.

29. A promissory note is

A.   a written promise to repay a specified amount over a specified period of time
B.   an oral promise to repay a specified amount over a specified period of time
C.   a note passed back and forth in class
D.   a note you deliver to another telling them of your intentions

Answer: A. A promissory note is a written promise to repay a specific amount over a specified period of time.

30. Which of the following best describes a real estate agent?

A.   A licensed person who negotiates and transacts the sale

of real estate
B.   The owner of a real estate firm
C.   A person who negotiates and transacts the sale of real estate but is not licensed
D.   A person who sells both property and insurance

Answer: A. A real estate agent is a licensed person who negotiates and transacts the sale of real estate.

31. When does an assumption take place?

A.   When someone believes something and it turns out to be true
B.   When the buyer assumes the seller's mortgage
C.   When the seller assumes the buyer's mortgage
D.   All of the above

Answer: B. When the buyer assumes the seller's mortgage is a transaction called an assumption.

32. A legal document conveying title to a property is called a/an

A.   sales contract
B.   option to purchase
C.   deed
D.   contract for deed

Answer: C. A deed is a legal document conveying title to property.

33. If you have a loan and transfer the title to another

individual without informing the lender, it is likely that the lender will demand payment of the outstanding loan balance. He is able to do this because of a clause in your mortgage called the

A.   due on demand clause
B.   acceleration clause
C.   amortization schedule
D.   both A and B

Answer: B. An acceleration clause allows the lender to demand payment, most commonly if the borrower defaults on the loan or transfers title to someone without informing the lender.

34. The most common type of bankruptcy is called

A.   Chapter 11 bankruptcy
B.   Chapter 11 no asset bankruptcy
C.   Chapter 7 no asset bankruptcy
D.   Chapter 7 bankruptcy

Answer: C. The most common type for an individual is a "Chapter 7 No Asset" bankruptcy, which relieves the borrower of most types of debts.

35. Which of the following best describes a "broker"?

A.   Someone who owns a real estate firm
B.   Some real estate agents working for brokers
C.   Someone who acts as an agent and brings two parties together for a transaction and earns a fee for this
D.   All of the above

Answer: D. A broker can own a real estate firm, work for another broker who owns the firm, broker loans in the mortgage industry, but basically is defined as anyone who acts as an agent, bringing two parties together for any type of transaction and earns a fee.

36. A normal contingency in a real estate contract would be that the

A.   purchaser is able to obtain a satisfactory home inspection from a qualified inspector.
B.   seller is allowed to come back and spend 2 weeks in the house each year
C.   purchaser is able to have occupancy as soon as the sales contract is signed
D.   seller is allowed to dig up some of the landscaping and take it with him

Answer: A. A normal contingency in a sales contract would be that the purchaser is able to obtain a satisfactory home inspection from a qualified inspector. This condition has to be met before the contract is legally binding.

37. If you go to a bank or mortgage company to apply for a home, what type of mortgage would you be applying for?

A.   Government
B.   Conventional
C.   American
D.   Adjustable rate

Answer: B. Home loans which are not VA or FHA are called conventional loans.

38. A report of someone's credit history which is prepared by a credit bureau and used by a lender in the loan qualification process is called a

A.   personal affidavit
B.   credit card history
C.   savings account history
D.   credit report

Answer: D. A report of an individual's credit prepared by a credit bureau and used by a lender in determining a loan applicant's creditworthiness is called a credit report.

39. If you have not made your mortgage payment within 30 days of the due date, the mortgage is considered to be in

A.   arrears
B.   default
C.   trouble
D.   bankruptcy

Answer: B. Failure to make the mortgage payment within a specified period of time, usually 30 days for first mortgages or first trust deeds, causes the loan to be in default.

40. A term used by appraisers to estimate the physical condition of a building. It may be different from the building's actual age.

A.   Estimated age
B.   Longevity
C.   Preferred age
D.   Effective age

Answer: D. An appraiser's estimate of the physical condition of a building is called effective age. Its actual age may be shorter or longer than the effective age.

41. The difference between the fair market value of a property and the amount still owed on the mortgage and other liens is the owner's financial interest in the property and is called his

A.   equity
B.   balance due
C.   indebtedness
D.   none of the above

Answer: A. A homeowner's financial interest in a property is called his equity. It is the difference between fair market value and what is still owed on the mortgage and any other liens.

42. You put in a new driveway to your property, but in the process the paving goes across your property line onto your neighbor's property a few inches. This is called an

A.   illegal driveway
B.   extra benefit for your neighbor
C.   encroachment
D.   easement

Answer: C. An improvement that intrudes illegally on another's property is called an encroachment. An easement would be a LEGAL intrusion.

43. A government loan that is not a VA loan would be a/an

A.   FHA mortgage
B.   FDA mortgage
C.   This type loan does not exist
D.   ARM mortgage

Answer: A. A mortgage which is insured by the Federal Housing Administration (FHA) and is the other type of government loan besides a VA loan is an FHA mortgage.

44. If you convey an interest in real property to a relative, that person is known as the

A.   receiver
B.   mortgagor
C.   grantee
D.   lucky relative

Answer: C. The person to whom an interest in real property is conveyed is the grantee.

45. You decide you want to buy a boat and you want to borrow against the equity in your home. You would get a mortgage loan up to a specified amount which is in second position to your first mortgage. This arrangement is called a

A.   perfectly acceptable way to buy a boat
B.   leverage against your house
C.   home equity line of credit
D.   line of credit for personal purposes

Answer: C. A mortgage loan, usually in second position, which allows the borrower to obtain cash drawn against the equity of his home, up to a predetermined amount, is known as a home equity line of credit.

46. You are your sister are joint tenants in a home your mother left you. Your sister has three children in her will and you have one. If she dies first, who does the property go to?

A.   It is divided equally between her three children
B.   It goes entirely to you
C.   It is divided equally between her three children and your one
D.   It goes into her estate

Answer: B. In the event of death in joint tenancy, the survivor owns the property in its entirety.

47. What is the best description of a lien?

A.   Something that doesn't stand up straight in a house
B.   Something that's illegal
C.   A legal claim against property that must be paid off when it's sold
D.   None of the above

Answer: C. A lien, such as a mortgage or first trust deed, is a legal claim against a property that must be paid off when it is sold.

48. What is a lock-in?

A. A gated community which locks the gate at midnight
B. An agreement from a lender guaranteeing a specific interest rate for a specific time at a certain cost
C. What parents do with wayward children
D. A type of key available at most hardware stores

Answer: B. A lock-in is a rate guaranteed by the lender for a certain period of time at a certain cost to the buyer.

49. The right of a government to take private property for public use upon payment of its fair market value. It is the basis for condemnation proceedings.

A. Eminent domain
B. Governmental domain
C. Encroachment
D. Both A and B

Answer: A. Eminent domain is the right of the government to take private property for public use upon payment of its fair market value.

50. A mortgage with a lien position subordinate to the first mortgage on a piece of property is called a

A. second mortgage

B.   first subordinate mortgage
C.   mortgage which isn't legal
D.   lien position mortgage

Answer: A. A second mortgage is a mortgage with a lien position subordinate to the first mortgage.

51. An adjustable-rate mortgage, also known as an ARM is

A.   one in which the interest rate is fixed over time
B.   one in which the interest rate changes periodically, depending on index changes
C.   one in which the interest rate changes periodically, depending on the stock market
D.   a type of mortgage that the mortgagor can adjust himself

Answer: B. An adjustable rate mortgage in one in which the interest rate adjusts periodically, according to corresponding fluctuations in an index.

52. A schedule that shows how much of each payment will be applied to principal and how much toward interest over the life of the loan is called a/n

A.   amortization schedule
B.   annual percentage rate
C.   assumption
D.   both A and C

Answer: A. An amortization schedule is a table showing how much of each payment is applied to interest and how much to principal. It also shows the gradual decrease of the loan balance until it reaches zero.

53. The term applied to a mortgage in which you make the payments every two weeks, thereby making thirteen payments a year rather than twelve. This mortgage is paid off faster than a normal mortgage.

A.   Twice-monthly mortgage
B.   Accelerated mortgage
C.   Bi-weekly mortgage
D.   None of the above

Answer: C. A mortgage in which you make payments every two weeks instead of once a month is called a bi-weekly mortgage.

54. The limitation of how much an adjustable rate mortgage may adjust over a six-month period, annual period, and over the life of the loan is called a

A.   buy-down
B.   high point
C.   top stop
D.   cap

Answer: D. The limitation on how much the loan may adjust over a period of time and for the life of the loan is a cap.

55. When is a real estate transaction considered to be "closed"?

A.   When the buyer has signed all the sales contracts

B.   When the closing documents have been recorded at the local recorder's office

C.   When all the documents are signed and money changes hands

D.   Both B and C.

Answer: D. In some states "closed" means when the documents are recorded at the courthouse, and in others it is a meeting where the documents are signed and money changes hands.

56. A record of an individual's repayment of debt, reviewed by mortgage lenders in determining credit risk is called a

A.   credit affidavit
B.   credit history
C.   there is no such record
D.   credit worthiness

Answer: B. A record of an individual's repayment of debt is called a credit history.

57. If you sell your property to a neighbor and the lender demands repayment in full, this means you have a _____ in your mortgage.

A.   seller pays all provision
B.   buyer pays all provision
C.   due-on-sale provision
D.   none of the above

Answer: C. A provision in a mortgage which allows the lender to demand repayment in full if the borrower sells the property that serves as security for the mortgage is called a due-on-sale provision.

58. The sum total of all the real and personal property owned by an individual at time of death is called their

A. estate
B. probate
C. will
D. all of the above.

Answer: A. The sum total of all the real and personal property owned by an individual at time of death is called an estate.

59. If you list your property with a real estate agent and sign a written agreement that they are the only ones entitled to a listing for a specific time you have given them an

A. exclusive listing
B. exclusive right to advertise
C. exclusive right to show
D. inclusive listing

Answer: A. A written contract giving a licensed real estate agent the exclusive right to sell a property for a specified time is called an exclusive listing.

60. Fair market value could be defined as

A. how much a property is worth, determined by a realtor's market analysis
B. the most a buyer, willing, but not compelled to buy,

would pay

C.   the least a seller, willing, but not compelled to sell, would take

D.   both B and C

Answer: D. Fair market value is the highest price that a buyer, willing but not compelled to buy, would pay, and the lowest a seller, willing but not compelled to sell, would accept.

61. If a lender agrees to make a loan to a specific borrower on a specific property, he has made a

A.   decision to make the loan

B.   statement that both the buyer and the property pass inspection

C.   firm commitment

D.   both B and C

Answer: C. A lender's agreement to make a loan to a specific borrower on a specific property is called a firm commitment.

62. If you buy a house and build cabinets into the wall, then sell that house, the cabinets stay because they have become a

A.   type of attachment

B.   fixture

C.   part of the house

D.   none of the above

Answer: B. Personal property becomes real property when attached in a permanent manner to real estate and is called a fixture.

63. A home inspection is

A.   a thorough inspection by a professional which evaluates the structural and mechanical condition of a property
B.   not required by law
C.   often a contingency in a contract that it turns out satisfactorily
D.   both A and C

Answer: D. A home inspection is a thorough inspection by a professional that evaluates the structural and mechanical condition of the property. A satisfactory home inspection is often a contingency.

64. An insurance policy which combines personal liability insurance and hazard insurance coverage for a dwelling and its contents is called

A.   homeowner's insurance
B.   buyer's insurance
C.   errors and omissions insurance
D.   all of the above

Answer: A. Homeowner's insurance combines personal liability insurance and hazard insurance coverage for a dwelling and its contents.

65. Which of the following is true of a lease-option?

A.   It is an alternative financing option
B.   Each month's rent may also consist of an additional

amount applied toward the purchase

C.   The price is already set in the beginning

D.   All of the above

Answer: D. A lease-option is an alternative financing option that allows home buyers to lease a home with an option to buy. Each month's rent payment may consist of not only the rent, but an additional amount which can be applied toward the down payment on an already specified price.

66. In simple terms, a sum of borrowed money (principal) usually repaid with interest is called a

A.   mortgage
B.   loan
C.   conventional loan
D.   alternative mortgage

Answer: B. A sum of borrowed money generally repaid with interest is simply a loan.

67. A property description which is recognized by law and is sufficient to locate and identify the property without oral testimony is known as the property's

A.   address
B.   911 address
C.   legal description
D.   identifying information

Answer: C. A legal description describes the property and is recognized by law. It is sufficient to locate and identify the property without oral testimony.

68. The date on which the principal balance of a loan, bond, or other financial instrument becomes due and payable is called

A. its due date
B. maturity
C. end of the paper trail
D. delivery

Answer: B. The date on which the principal balance of a loan, bond, or other financial instrument becomes due and payable is called maturity.

69. The person borrowing money in a mortgage agreement is called the

A. mortgagor
B. mortgagee
C. borrower
D. lessee

Answer: A. The borrower in a mortgage agreement is called the mortgagor.

70. Which of the following is true about an origination fee?

A. It applies to both government and conventional loans

B. It is usually 1% on a government loan

C.   It is usually 2% on a conventional loan
D.   Both A and B

Answer: D. Origination fees apply to government and conventional loans. A government loan origination fee is one percent of the loan amount, but additional points may be charged which are called "discount points". In a conventional loan, the origination fee refers to the total number of points a borrower has to pay.

71. Which of the following falls under the term "personal property"?

A.   A garage attached to a house
B.   A sofa
C.   The front porch of a home
D.   The windows in a home

Answer: B. Personal property is any property that is not part of the real property. A, C, an D are all parts of the house.

72. In some cases if a borrower pays off a loan before it is due he may encounter a penalty called a

A.   penalty for early withdrawal
B.   loan to value penalty
C.   prepayment penalty
D.   there is never a penalty for paying a loan off early

Answer: C. A fee that may be charged to a borrower who pays off a loan before it is due is known as a prepayment penalty.

73. Which of the following statements is true regarding the term "pre-approval"?

A.   It applies only to the property
B.   It is done before the loan application is complete
C.   It s a loosely used term
D.   None of the above

Answer: C. Pre-approval is a loosely used term generally taken to mean a borrower has completed a loan application and provided debt, income, and savings documentation which an underwriter has reviewed and approved.

74. PITI reserves applies to

A.   a cash amount the borrower must have on hand after down payment and closing Costs.
B.   an amount which is financed with the mortgage
C.   both A and B
D.   none of the above

Answer: A. PITI reserves must equal the cash amount that the borrower would have to pay for principal, interest, taxes, and insurance for a predefined number of months.

75. Why would a public auction take place?

A.   It's a good way to buy property
B.   To inform the public about property for sale
C.   To help auctioneers get employment
D.   To sell property to repay a mortgage in defaults

Answer: D. A public auction is a meeting in an announced public location to sell property to repay a mortgage that is in default.

76. The term "realtor" applies to

A.   any real estate agent who has passed the state exam
B.   any real estate agent whose license is active
C.   any real estate agent who is a member of a local real estate board affiliated with the National Association of Realtors.
D.   any real estate agent who belongs to his local board

Answer: C. A realtor is defined as an agent, broker, or associate who holds active membership in a local real estate board which is affiliated with the National Association of Realtors.

77. "Remaining term" refers to

A.   the remaining school term for a real estate class
B.   the original amortization term minus the number of payments that have been applied
C.   the months left in a pregnancy
D.   all of the above

Answer: B. The remaining term applies to the original amortization term minus the number of payments that have been applied.

78. Which of the following is not true of a "revolving debt"?

A.   It is a type of credit arrangement, like a credit card
B.   It revolves around no interest for the first six months

C.   A customer borrows against a pre-approved line of credit
D.   The customer is billed for the amount borrowed plus any interest due

Answer: B. Revolving debt is a credit arrangement, such as a credit card, which allows a customer to borrow against a pre-approved line of credit when purchasing goods and services. The borrower is billed for the amount that is actually borrowed plus any interest due.

79. Which of the following does a survey not show?

A.   Precise legal boundaries of a property
B.   Location of improvements, easements, rights of way
C.   Encroachments
D.   Location of furnishings within the dwelling

Answer: D. A survey is a drawing or map showing the precise legal boundaries of a property, the location of improvements, easements, rights of way, encroachments, and other physical features.

80. What is meant by "seller carry-back"?

A.   The seller physically carries his furnishings out of the house on the day of closing
B.   The seller agrees to be on the mortgage with the buyer
C.   the seller provides financing, often in combination with an assumable mortgage
D.   The seller carries the principal, but not the interest on a loan

Answer: C. A seller carry-back is an agreement in which the owner of a property provides financing, often in combination with an assumable mortgage.

81. A title company is one which

A.   is usually not needed in a real estate transaction
B.   is not called upon until one year after the sale is closed
C.   specializes in examining and insuring titles to real estate
D.   specializes in preparing deeds and deeds of trust

Answer: C. A title company specializes in examining and insuring titles to real estate.

82. A state or local tax which is payable when title passes from one owner to another is called a

A.   title tax
B.   transfer tax
C.   revenue stamps
D.   real estate tariff

Answer: B. State or local tax payable when title passes from one owner to another is called a transfer tax.

83. What is Truth-in-Lending?

A.   A state law requiring lenders to fully disclose in writing all terms and conditions of a mortgage
B.   A federal law requiring lenders to fully disclose in writing all terms and conditions of a mortgage
C.   A local law requiring lenders to fully disclose in writing

all terms and conditions of a mortgage
D.   None of the above

Answer: B. Truth-in-Lending is a federal law requiring lenders to fully disclose in writing the terms and conditions of a mortgage, including the annual percentage rate and other charges.

84. A VA mortgage

A.   is a conventional mortgage for the state of Virginia
B.   is guaranteed by the Department of Veterans Affairs
C.   originates in Texas but ends up in Virginia
D.   in available to anyone applying for a mortgage

Answer: B. A VA mortgage is guaranteed by the Department of Veterans Affairs.

85. Which of the following is not true of "amortization"?

A.   Over time the interest portion increases as the loan balance decreases
B.   Over time the interest portion decreases as the loan balance decreases
C.   Over time the amount applied to principal increases so the loan is paid off in the specified time
D.   None of the above

Answer: A. The loan payment consists of a portion which will be applied to pay the accruing interest on a loan, with the remainder being applied to the principal. Over time the interest portion decreases as the loan balance decreases and the amount applied to principal increases so that the loan is paid off (amortized) in the specified time.

86. The valuation placed on property by a public tax assessor for taxation purposes is called

A.   real value
B.   fair market value
C.   assessed value
D.   predicted value

Answer: C. The valuation placed on property by a public tax assessor for purposes of taxation is called assessed value.

87. If a veteran is eligible for a VA loan, he or she would receive a document from the VA called

A.   Certificate of Authenticity
B.   Certificate of Approval
C.   Certificate of Met Requirements
D.   Certificate of Eligibility

Answer: D. A certificate of eligibility is a document issued by the Veteran's Administration that certifies a veteran's eligibility for a VA loan.

88. Which of the following usually earns the largest commissions in a real estate transaction?

A.   Attorneys
B.   Realtors
C.   Loan officers

D.   Home warranty companies

Answer: B. Realtors generally earn the largest commissions, followed by lenders.

89. An unwritten body of law based on general custom in England and used to an extent in some states is called

A.   common law
B.   uncommon law
C.   casual law
D.   it isn't law if it's not written down

Answer: A. An unwritten body of law based on general custom in England and used to an extent in some states is called common law.

90. If a real estate agent is trying to determine the market value of a property, one thing they would use is recent sales of similar properties or

A.   neighbors' estimates of the value of the property
B.   records from several years back in the same neighborhood
C.   comparable sales
D.   sales they estimate to happen in the future

Answer: C. Recent sales of similar properties in nearby areas and used to help determine the market value of a property are called comparable sales, or "comps."

91. A person to whom money is owed is known as a

A. debtor
B. creditor
C. mortgagee
D. lender

Answer: B. A creditor is a person to whom money is owed.

92. Discount points refer to

A. a system of figuring out how much the property will be discounted
B. points paid in addition to the one percent loan origination fee
C. usually only FHA and VA loans
D. both B and C

Answer: D. This term is usually used in reference to only government loans (FHA and VA). Discount points are any points paid in addition to the one percent loan origination fee.

93. Which of the following can the Equal Credit Opportunity Act (ECOA) not discriminate against?

A. Race, color or religion
B. National origin
C. Age, sex, or marital status
D. All of the above

Answer: D. ECOA is a federal law requiring lenders and other creditors to make credit equally available without discrimination based on race, color, religion, national origin, age, sex, marital status, or receipt of income from public assistance programs.

94. An exclusive listing is one which gives a licensed real estate agent the exclusive right to sell a property

A. until it sells
B. until the owner takes it off the market
C. for a specified period of time
D. none of the above

Answer: C. An exclusive listing gives a licensed real estate agent the exclusive right to sell a property for a specified period of time.

95. Which of the following is true about Fannie Mae's Community Home Buyer's Program?

A. It is an income-based community lending model
B. It has flexible underwriting guidelines to increase low to moderate income family's buying power
C. Borrows who participate must attend pre-purchase home-buyer education sessions
D. All of the above

Answer: D. Fannie Mae's Community Home Buyer's Program is an income-based community lending model, under which mortgage insurers and Fannie Mae offer flexible underwriting guidelines to increase a low or moderate income family's buying power and to decrease the total amount of cash needed to purchase a home. Participating borrows are required to attend pre-purchase home-buyer education sessions.

96. The mortgage that is in first place among any loans recorded against a property and usually refers to the date in which loans are recorded, but not always, is called a

A.   primary mortgage
B.   first in line mortgage
C.   first mortgage
D.   both A and B

Answer: C. The mortgage that is in first place is a first mortgage.

97. The legal process by which a borrower in default under a mortgage is deprived of his or her interest in the mortgaged property is called a

A.   takeover by the mortgage company
B.   public auction
C.   foreclosure
D.   proceeds sale

Answer: C. The legal process by which a borrower in default under a mortgage is deprived of his or her interest in the mortgaged property is called a foreclosure.

98. Loans against 401K plans are

A.   not allowed for down payments on property
B.   an acceptable source of down payment for most types of loans

C.   too great a risk for most people to take
D.   only allowed if you're accumulated $50,000 in the plan

Answer: B. Some administrators of 401(k)/403B plans allow for loans against the monies you have accumulated in these plans. Loans against 401k plans are an acceptable source of down payment for most types of loans.

99. A late charge is

A.   the penalty a borrower pays when a payment is late a stated number of days
B.   usually put into play when the payment is fifteen days late on a first mortgage
C.   usually not applicable to most people
D.   both A and B

Answer: D. A late charge usually kicks in after fifteen days on a first mortgage and is a penalty a borrower must pay.

100. A person's financial obligations are known as his

A.   payments
B.   assets
C.   liabilities
D.   credit risks

Answer: C. A person's financial obligations are called liabilities and include long-term and short-term debt and any other amounts owed to others.

101. Which of the following is not true of annual percentage rate (APR)?

A.   It is the note rate on your loan
B.   It is not the note rate on your loan
C.   It is a value created according to a government formula intended to reflect the true cost of borrowing and expressed as a percentage
D.   It is always higher than the actual note rate on your loan

Answer: A. Annual percentage rate is not the note rate on your loan. It is a value created according to a government formula intended to reflect the true annual cost of borrowing, expressed as a percentage. The APR is always higher than the actual note rate on your loan.

102. An individual qualified by education, training, and experience to estimate the value of real property and personal property and who usually works independently is called an

A.   estimator of value
B.   appraiser
C.   on-site inspector
D.   underwriter

Answer: B. An appraiser is an individual qualified by education, training, and experience to estimate the value of real and personal property. Some work for lenders, but most are independent.

103. Which of the following best describes a "balloon

payment"?

A. Payment delivered with a "bang"
B. First of many payments on a mortgage
C. The final lump sum payment due at the termination of a balloon mortgage
D. Payments which go higher and higher each year

Answer: C. A balloon payment is the final lump sum payment due at the termination of a balloon mortgage.

104. When a borrower refinances his mortgage at a higher amount than the current loan balance with the intention of pulling out money for personal use, it is referred to as a

A. refinance extra
B. cash-out refinance
C. home equity refinance
D. adjustable lump sum refinance

Answer: B. A cash-out refinance is when a borrow refinances his mortgage at a higher amount than the current loan balance because he wants to pull our money for personal use.

105. A certificate of deposit is

A. the same as a down payment
B. a liquid asset
C. a deposit held in a bank paying a certain amount of interest to the depositor over a certain time
D. a deposit held in a bank which pays double the amount of normal interest over time

Answer: C. A certificate of deposit is a time deposit held in a bank which pays a certain amount of interest to the depositor.

106. Common area assessments are

A.   sometimes called Homeowners Association Fees
B.   paid by individual owners of condominiums or planned unit developments
C.   used to maintain the property and common areas
D.   all of the above

Answer: D. Common area assessments are also sometimes called Homeowners Association Fees and are paid by the individual owners of condos or planned unit developments and are used to maintain the property and common areas.

107. A short-term interim loan for financing the cost of construction is called a

A.   flexible loan
B.   convertible loan
C.   construction loan
D.   not a loan, but a promissory note

Answer: C. A short-term interim loan for financing the cost of construction is called a construction loan. The lender makes payments to the builder at periodic intervals as the work progresses.

108. In simple terms, debt is

A.   credit extended to someone
B.   an amount owed to another
C.   an amount owed to another with interest
D.   repayable

Answer: B. Debt is an amount owed to another

109. Which of the following is not true of the term "depreciation"?

A.   It is a decline in the value of property
B.   It is an accounting term showing the declining monetary value of an asset
C.   It is a true expense where money is actually paid
D.   Lenders add back depreciation expense for self-employed borrowers and count it as income

Answer: C. Depreciation is not a true expense where money is actually paid. It is a decline in the value of property and an accounting term showing the declining monetary value of an asset. Lenders add back depreciation expense for self-employed borrowers and count it as income.

110. Which of the following would not be paid by escrow disbursements?

A.   Real estate taxes
B.   Hazard insurance
C.   Mortgage insurance
D.   Personal property taxes

Answer: D. Personal property taxes are not a typical escrow disbursement, but real estate taxes, hazard insurance and mortgage insurance are.

111. The lawful expulsion of an occupant from real property is called

A.   conviction
B.   divorce from bed and board
C.   eviction
D.   there is no way to lawfully remove an occupant from real property

Answer: C. The lawful expulsion of an occupant from real property is called eviction.

112. If you have a loan in which the interest rate does not change during the term of the loan you have a _____ mortgage.

A.   fixed-rate
B.   conventional fixed-rate
C.   owner financing
D.   all of the above

Answer: A. A loan in which the interest rate does not change during the term is called a fixed-rate mortgage.

113. The following is true of a Home Equity Conversion Mortgage (HECM).

A.   It is also known as reverse annuity mortgage
B.   You don't make payments to the lender, the lender

makes payments to you

C.   It enables older homeowners to convert their equity into cash

D.   All of the above

Answer: D. Usually called a reverse annuity mortgage, this mortgage is unique in that instead of making payments to a lender, the lender makes payments to you, allowing older homeowners to convert their equity to cash. The loan does not have to be repaid until the borrower no longer occupies the property.

114. A written agreement between property owner and tenant stipulating the conditions under which the tenant may possess the property for a specified period of time and the payment due is called a/an

A.   contract
B.   option
C.   lease
D.   lease-option

Answer: C. A written agreement between property owner and tenant laying out the terms of the agreement including payment and period of time is called a lease.

115.   A lender is

A.   the firm making the loan
B.   the individual representing the firm making the loan
C.   the individual offering owner financing
D.   both A and B

Answer: D. A lender is the firm making the loan or an individual representing the firm making the loan.

116. A margin is

A.   a measurement of error
B.   an artificial line not to write in on a loan document
C.   both A and B
D.   the difference between the interest rate and the index on an adjustable rate mortgage

Answer: D. A margin is the difference between the interest rate and the index on an adjustable rate mortgage which remains stable over the life of the loan.

117. Which of the following is the best definition of a mortgage broker?

A.   A mortgage company which originates loans, then places with other lending institutions
B.   A mortgage company which originates loans, then keeps them in house
C.   An individual which originates loans, then sells on the secondary market
D.   Much like a real estate broker, receives a commission on loans

Answer: A. A mortgage broker is a mortgage company which originates loans, then places with a variety of other lending institutions with whom they usually have pre-established relationships.

118. The term "note rate" refers to:

A.   the speed at which a musician plays scales
B.   the interest rate stated on a mortgage note
C.   the interest rate stated on a personal loan
D.   the rate at which a note is amortized

Answer: B. Note rate means the interest rate stated on a mortgage note.

119. If you have not made your mortgage payment, you are likely to receive which of the following?

A.   Notice of non-payment
B.   A written eviction notice
C.   Notice of default
D.   A letter from an attorney

Answer: C. You are likely to receive a formal written notice, called a notice of default, that a default has occurred and legal action may be taken.

120. A payment that is not sufficient to cover the scheduled monthly payment on a mortgage loan is called a

A.   late payment
B.   partial payment
C.   "too little, too late" payment
D.   a drop in the bucket

Answer: B. A payment insufficient to cover the scheduled monthly payment on a mortgage loan is a partial payment, normally not accepted by the lender, but in times of hardship a borrower can make a request of the loan servicing collection department.

121. PITI stands for

A.   principal, interest, taxes and insurance
B.   principle, interest, taxes and insurance
C.   prepayment, interest, tariff and insurance
D.   none of the above

Answer: A. PITI is principal, interest, taxes and insurance.

122. Which of the following describes "prepayment"?

A.   An amount paid to reduce the interest on a loan before the due date
B.   An amount paid to reduce the principal on a loan before the due date
C.   Can result from a sale, owner's decision to pay off the loan, or foreclosure
D.   Both B and C

Answer: D. A prepayment reduces the principal on a loan before the due date and can result from a sale, the owner's decision to pay off the loan early, or foreclosure.

123. What is private mortgage insurance?

A. Mortgage insurance that is arranged for by the buyer privately

B. Mortgage insurance provided by a private mortgage insurance company

C. Insurance required for loans with a loan-to-value percentage in excess of 80%

D. Both B and C

Answer: D. A prepayment reduces the principal on a loan before the due date and can result from a sale, the owner's decision to pay off the loan early, or foreclosure.

124. If you were trying to buy a home you and the seller would need to sign a written contract called a/an

A. purchase agreement
B. down payment agreement
C. option to purchase
D. all of the above

Answer: A. A written contract signed by buyer and seller stating the terms and conditions under which a property will be sold is called a purchase agreement.

125. What is a recorder?

A. A public official who keeps records of real property transactions

B. The county clerk

C. The registrar of deeds

D. All of the above.

Answer: D. A recorder is a public official who keeps records of real property transactions in their area and is also known by the names "county clerk" and "registrar of deeds".

126. The principal balance on a mortgage is

A.   the outstanding balance of principal and interest
B.   the outstanding balance of principal only
C.   the amount the mortgage has been paid down
D.   none of the above

Answer: B. The principal balance is the outstanding balance of principal only on a mortgage and does not include interest or any other charges.

127. Which of the following is not true about qualifying ratios?

A.   There are two types of ratios—"top" or "front" and "back" or "bottom"
B.   The "top" ratio is a calculation of the borrower's monthly housing costs (principal, taxes, insurance, mortgage insurance, homeowners' association fees) as a percentage of monthly income
C.   the "back" ratio includes all monthly costs as well as "back" taxes
D.   Both calculations are used in determining whether a borrower can qualify for a mortgage

Answer: C. The "back" or "bottom" ratio includes housing costs as well as all other monthly debt.

128. The definition of "real" property is

A.   property that has nothing artificial on it, only natural materials
B.   land and appurtenances, including anything of a permanent nature such as structures, trees and minerals
C.   things located within houses such as furniture, accessories, appliances, and clothing
D.   all of the above

Answer: B. Real property is defined as land and appurtenances, including anything of a permanent nature such as structures, trees, minerals, and the interest, benefits, and inherent rights thereof.

129. In joint tenancy, if one person dies and the other inherits the property, this is called

A.   tenants in common
B.   whatever is stated in the will
C.   following the wishes of the deceased
D.   right of survivorship

Answer: D. In joint tenancy the right of survivors to acquire the interest of a deceased joint tenant is called right of survivorship.

130. A secured loan is

A.   backed by collateral
B.   when the borrower promises something of value to the

lender
C.   when the bank is not in danger of failing
D.   when the bank has been bailed out

Answer: A. A secured loan is backed by security, also called collateral.

131. A mortgage or other type of lien that has a priority lower than that of the first mortgage is called

A.   a second mortgage
B.   subordinate financing
C.   first subordinate financing
D.   all of the above

Answer: B. Subordinate financing is any mortgage or other lien that has a priority lower than the first mortgage.

132. If you were buying a house and wanted to protect yourself against any loss arising from disputes over ownership of your property, you would purchase

A.   hazard insurance
B.   errors and omissions insurance
C.   title insurance
D.   deed insurance

Answer: C. Insurance that protects the lender (lender's policy) or the buyer (owner's policy) against loss arising from disputes over ownership of a property is title insurance.

133   Which of the following is true of the Veteran's Administration (VA)?

A.   It encourages lenders to make mortgages to veterans
B.   It is an agency of the federal government which guarantees residential mortgages made to eligible veterans
C.   The guarantee protects the lender against loss
D.   All of the above

Answer: D. An agency of the federal government, the VA guarantees residential mortgages made to eligible veterans of the military services. This guarantee protects the lender against loss and thus encourages lenders to make mortgages to veterans.

134. The form used to apply for a mortgage loan, which contains information about a borrower's income, savings, assets, debts, and more is called a/an

A.   application for funds
B.   income documentary
C.   both A and B
D.   application

Answer: A. The form used to apply for a mortgage loan containing information about a borrower's income, savings, assets, debts, and more is called an application.

135. An assessment does which of the following?

A.   Places a value on property for the purpose of real estate sales
B.   Is the same as a competitive market analysis

C.   Places a value on property for the purpose of taxation

D.   Is usually carried out by the mayor of a town

Answer: C. An assessment places a value on property for the purpose of taxation.

136. Which of the following is not true about the "bond market"?

A.   It refers to the daily buy and selling of thirty-year treasury bonds

B.   Lenders do not usually follow this market closely

C.   The same factors that affect the bond market affect mortgage rates at the same time

D.   Fluctuations in this market cause mortgage rates to change daily

Answer: B. Lenders actually do follow this market closely because the same factors that affect the Treasury Bond market also affect mortgage rates at the same time.

137. What does the term "buydown" mean?

A.   Usually refers to a fixed rate mortgage where the interest rate is "bought down" for a temporary period, usually one to three years.

B.   A lump sum is paid and held in an account used to supplement the borrower's monthly payment

C.   These funds can sometimes come from the seller to induce someone to buy their property

D.   All of the above

Answer: D. A buy-down refers to a fixed rate mortgage where the interest rate is "bought down" for a temporary period. The funds for this can come from the seller, the lender, or some other source. The lump sum is paid and held in an account used to supplement the borrower's monthly payment for a time and after that time the borrower's payment is calculated at the note rate.

138. Certificate of Reasonable Value (CRV) applies to

A. an FHA loan
B. a conventional loan
C. a VA loan
D. a car loan

Answer: C. Once the appraisal has been done on a property being bought with a VA loan, the VA issues a CRV.

139. If you are buying a piece of property and have someone else who is obligated on the loan and is on the title to the property, that person is called a

A. spouse
B. family member or friend who shares the property and payments with you
C. co-borrower
D. none of the above

Answer: C. An additional individual who is both obligated on the loan and is on the title to the property is called a co-borrower.

140. How would you define "collection"?

A.   A plate, usually at church, where money is donated
B.   It goes into effect when a borrower falls behind
C.   It applies to several or many things in the same category on a loan application
D.   It only applies to trash

Answer: B. When a borrower falls behind, the lender contacts them in an effort to bring the loan current. The loan then goes to "collection" and the lender must mail and record certain documents in case they have to foreclose on the property.

141. Which of the following is true of "condominium"?

A.   It applies to ownership, not to construction or development
B.   It is a type of ownership where all of the owners own each other's interior units
C.   It is an ownership where owners own the property, common areas, and buildings together
D.   both A and C

Answer: D. A condominium is real property where all the owners own the property, common areas and building together, with the exception of the interior of the unit to which they have title. Mistakenly referred to as a type of construction or development, it actually refers to type of ownership.

142. An organization which gathers, records, updates, and stores financial and public records information about the payment records of individuals being considered for credit is

called a

A.　credit repository
B.　credit reporting agency
C.　mortgage company
D.　bank

Answer: A. A credit repository is an organization which gathers, records, updates, and stores financial and public records information about the payment records of individuals being considered for credit.

143. In some states a recorded mortgage is replaced by a

A.　contract for deed
B.　promissory note
C.　deed of trust
D.　deed

Answer: C. Some states do not record mortgages but do record a deed of trust which is essentially the same thing.

144. If you have failed to pay mortgage payments when they are due, it is called

A.　delinquency
B.　foreclosure
C.　collections
D.　no big deal

Answer: A. Failure to make mortgage payments when they are due is called delinquency. Most are due on the first day of the month, and even though they may not charge a "late fee" for a number of days, the payment is considered to be late and the loan delinquent.

145. Which of the following would not be considered an "encumbrance", limiting the fee simple title, on a piece of property?

A.   Leases
B.   Mortgages
C.   Easements or restrictions
D.   Furniture not paid for

Answer: D. Encumbrances include mortgages, easements, leases, or restrictions.

146. An earnest money deposit is put into this until delivered to the seller when the transaction is closed.

A.   the realtor's bank account
B.   the attorney's bank account
C.   the buyer's bank account
D.   an escrow account

Answer: D. An earnest money deposit is put into escrow until delivered to the seller when the transaction is closed.

147. Which of the following is true of the Federal National Mortgage Association (Fannie Mae)?

A.   It is the nation's largest supplier of mortgages
B.   It is congressionally chartered, shareholder owned

C.   It is the same as Freddie Mac
D.   both A and B

Answer: D. Fannie Mae is a congressionally chartered, shareholder-owned company that is the nation's largest supplier of home mortgage funds.

148. An employer-sponsored investment plan allowing individuals to set aside tax-deferred income for retirement or emergency purposes is called a _____ plan.

A.   436(k)/401B
B.   339(k)/372B
C.   401(k)/403B
D.   both A and B

Answer: C. 401(k)/403B plans are employer-sponsored investment plans allowing individuals to set aside tax-deferred income for retirement or emergency purposes. Private corporations provide 401(k) plans; 403B plans are provided by not for profit organizations.

149. Which of the following is true of the Government National Mortgage Association, also known as Ginnie Mae?

A.   It is government owned
B.   It was created by Congress on September 1, 2002
C.   Provides funds to lenders for making home loans
D.   Both A and C

Answer: D. Ginnie Mae is government owned, created by

Congress on September 1, 1968. Ginnie Mae performs the same roles as Fannie Mae and Freddie Mac in providing funds to lenders for home loans, but it provides funds for government loans (FHA and VA).

150. At what amount is a loan considered to be a "jumbo" loan, which exceeds Fannie Mae's and Freddie Mac's loan limits? It is also known as a non-conforming loan.

A. $417,000
B. $227,150
C. $300,000
D.   Jumbo refers to the percentage borrowed, not the amount

Answer: A. A jumbo loan is anything over $417,000.

151. Usually part of a homeowner's insurance policy, this type insurance offers protection against claims alleging that a property owner's negligence or inappropriate action resulted in bodily injury or property damage to another party.

A.   Malpractice insurance
B.   Liability insurance
C.   Hazard insurance
D.   Collision insurance

Answer: B. Liability insurance protects against claims against a property owner for negligence or bodily injury or property damage to another party.

152. A lender refers to the process of getting new loans as

A.   selling his product
B.   loan origination
C.   his bread and butter
D.   more than just a job

Answer: B. A lender refers to the process of getting new loans as loan origination.

153. The percentage relationship between the amount of the loan and the appraised value or sales price (whichever is lower) is called

A.   value to loan
B.   first-time homebuyer's loan
C.   loan to value
D.   both B and C

Answer: C. The percentage relationship between the amount of the loan and the appraised value or sales price is called loan to value.

154. If you are applying for a loan, the lender gives and guarantees you a specific interest rate for a specific time. This period of time is called the

A.   period of no return
B.   rate-freeze period
C.   lock-in period
D.   period at which you cannot seek other financing

Answer: C. The time during which the lender has guaranteed a certain rate is called the lock-in period.

155. A credit report which reports the raw data pulled from two or more of the major credit repositories is called a

A.   multi-credit report
B.   merged credit report
C.   this is not legal
D.   none of the above

Answer: B. A merged credit report reports the raw data pulled from two or more of the major credit repositories.

156. Sometimes, called a first trust deed, this is a legal document pledging a property to the lender as security for payment of a debt.

A.   promissory note
B.   deed of trust
C.   owner financing document
D.   mortgage

Answer: D. A mortgage is a legal document pledging a property to the lender as security for payment of a debt.

157. Which of the following is not true of mortgage insurance?

A.   It covers the lender against some of the losses incurred resulting from default on a home loan
B.   It is sometimes is mistakenly referred to a PMI (private mortgage insurance)

C.   It is required on all loans having a loan to value of more than 90%

D.   No "MI" loans are usually made at higher rates

Answer: C. Mortgage insurance is required on all loans having a loan to value of more than 80%.

158   A no-point loan has an interest rate

A.   lower than if you pay one point
B.   the same as if you pay one point
C.   higher than if you pay one point
D.   a no-point loan does not exist

Answer: C. The interest rate on a "no points" loan is approximately a quarter percent higher than on a loan where you pay one point.

159. The total amount of principal owed on a mortgage before any payments are made is called the

A.   total amount due
B.   original principal balance
C.   a lot less than you'll actually pay
D.   your down payment times ten

Answer: B. The total amount of principal owed on a mortgage before any payments are made is called the original principal balance.

160. A planned unit development (PUD) is different from a condominium because

A. a condominium usually has more amenities
B. there are fewer units in a condominium development
C. in a condominium the individual owns the airspace of the unit
D. all of the above

Answer: C. A planned unit development is a type of ownership where individuals actually own the building or unit they live, but common areas are owned jointly with the other members of the development or association. In a condominium, an individual owns the airspace of his unit, but the buildings and common areas are owned jointly with the others in the development.

161. The term that means a limit on the amount that the interest rate can increase or decrease over the life of an adjustable rate mortgage is

A. term cap
B. life cap
C. ARM cap
D. none of the above

Answer: B. A life cap limits the amount the interest rate can increase or decrease over the life of the mortgage.

162. If a commercial bank or other financial institution extends you credit up to a certain amount for a certain time, you are receiving a

A. line of credit

B.   personal loan
C.   unsecured loan
D.   both B and C

Answer: A. A line of credit is given by a commercial bank or other financial institution for a certain time and certain amount.

163. The term "modification" means

A.   a change in your mortgage without having to refinance
B.   a change in house plans before building begins
C.   the right of the bank to modify the interest rate without telling you
D.   both B and C

Answer: A. Occasionally a lender will agree to modify the terms of your mortgage without requiring you to refinance.

164. Which of the following is true of the term "mortgage banker"?

A.   They are generally assumed to originate and fund their own loans
B.   It is a loosely applied term to those who are mortgage brokers or correspondents
C.   They usually sell loans on the secondary market to Fannie Mae, Freddie Mac, or Ginnie Mae.
D.   All of the above.

Answer: D. A mortgage banker is generally assumed to originate and fund their own loans, which are then sold on the secondary market. Firms loosely apply this term to themselves, whether they are true mortgage bankers or simply mortgage brokers or correspondents.

165. Which of the following describes "prime rate"?

A.   It is the interest rate banks charge to their preferred customers
B.   The same factors that influence the prime rate also affect interest rates of mortgage loans
C.   Changes in the prime rate are usually not widely publicized in the news media
D.   Both A and B

Answer: D. Prime rate is the interest rate banks charge to their preferred customers. Changes in the prime rate are widely publicized in the news media and the same factors that influence prime rate also affect interest rates of mortgage loans.

166. A no cash-out refinance is

A.   intended to put cash in the hands of the borrower
B.   calculated to cover the balance due on the current loan and any costs associated with obtaining the new mortgage
C.   often referred to as a "rate and term refinance"
D.   both B and C

Answer: D. A no cash-out refinance is not intended to put cash in the hands of the buyer, but the new balance is calculated to cover the balance due on the current loan and any costs associated with obtaining the new mortgage. It is often referred to as a "rate and term refinance".

167. A legal document requiring a borrower to repay a mortgage loan at a stated interest rate during a specified period of time is called a

A.   note
B.   deed of trust
C.   mortgage
D.   both B and C

Answer: A. A note is a legal document requiring a borrower to repay a mortgage loan at a stated interest rate during a specified period of time.

168. The date when a new monthly payment amount takes effect on an adjustable-rate mortgage or graduated-payment mortgage is called the

A.   new payment date
B.   payment change date
C.   new payment due date
D.   change payment date

Answer: B. The date when a new monthly payment amount takes effect on an adjustable-rate mortgage or graduated-payment mortgage is called the payment change date.

169. A quitclaim deed does which of the following?

A.   Transfers with warranty whatever interest or title a grantor may have at the time the conveyance is made
B.   Transfers without warranty whatever interest or title a grantor may have at the time the conveyance is made

C.   Does not transfer interest at all
D.   Quitclaim deeds are no longer used

Answer: B. A quitclaim deed transfers without warranty whatever interest or title a grantor may have at the time the conveyance is made

170. In a refinance transaction, what happens?

A.   One loan is paid off with the proceeds from a new loan using the same property as security
B.   An additional loan is added to the present loan
C.   The loan's interest rate changes
D.   The term of the loan is increased

Answer: A. A refinance transaction is the process of paying off one loan with the proceeds from a new loan using the same property as security.

171. The amount of principal that has not yet been repaid is called the

A.   amount owed
B.   balance of the loan
C.   remaining balance
D.   all of the above

Answer: C. The amount of principal that has not yet been repaid is called the remaining balance.

172. If you made an arrangement to repay delinquent installments or advances, you would be setting up a

A. good faith payment plan
B. repayment plan
C. another loan to pay off
D. oral contract

Answer: B. A repayment plan is an arrangement made to repay delinquent installments or advances.

173. Your neighbor has given you a right of first refusal on a piece of land he plans to sell. What does this mean?

A. He has given you the first opportunity to purchase it before he offers it for sale to others
B. He expects you to refuse to buy it
C. He expects you to pay more for it than anyone else
D. None of the above

Answer: A. A right of first refusal is a provision in an agreement that requires the owner of a property to give another party the first opportunity to purchase or lease the property before he offers it for sale or lease to others.

174. You are selling the house you live in, but the house you're moving to is not completed. You need to stay on in the house a while after closing. You work out a deal with the new purchaser called a

A. no-rent lease agreement
B. delayed possession for the new purchaser
C. sale-leaseback
D. lease for one year past closing

Answer: C. A sale-leaseback is a technique in which a seller deeds property to a buyer for a consideration, and the buyer simultaneously leases the property back to the seller.

175. In a tenancy in common

A. ownership passes to the survivors in the event of death
B. ownership does not pass to the survivors in the event of death
C. there are no provisions made for the death of the owners
D. when one person dies, the others have to move

Answer: B. In a tenancy in common ownership does not pass to the survivors in the event of death.

176. The duties of a "servicer" include

A. collecting principal and interest payments from borrowers
B. managing borrowers' escrow accounts
C. usually a servicer services mortgages purchased by an investor in the secondary mortgage market
D. all of the above

Answer: D. A servicer is an organization that collects principal and interest payments from borrowers and manages borrowers' escrow accounts. The servicer often services mortgages that have been purchased by an investor in the secondary mortgage market.

177. In "third-party origination"

A.   an independent political party originates a loan
B.   a lender uses another party to completely or partially originate, process, underwrite, close, fund, or package the mortgages it plans to deliver to the secondary mortgage market.
C.   three parties are involved in the loan process
D.   all of the above

Answer: B. A lender uses another party to completely or partially originate, process, underwrite, close, fund, or package the mortgages it plans to deliver to the secondary mortgage market.

178. A title search of a property would show the following to be true:

A.   the seller is the legal owner of the property
B.   there are no liens or other claims against the property
C.   the previous owners came over on the Mayflower
D.   both A and B

Answer: D. A title search would show that the seller is the legal owner and there are no outstanding liens or other claims against the property.

179. A trustee

A.   is known to be trustworthy
B.   is someone who has a great deal of trust in others
C.   is a fiduciary who holds or controls property for the benefit of another

D.   is usually a job for relatives

Answer: C. A trustee is a fiduciary who holds or controls property for the benefit of another.

180. When a person is "vested" he can

A.   use a portion of a fund such as an individual retirement fund
B.   use a portion of a fund without paying taxes on it
C.   have access to a bulletproof vest when in dangerous situations
D.   both A and C

Answer: A. A person who is "vested" can use a portion of a fund such as an individual retirement fund, but must pay taxes on funds that are withdrawn. If someone is 100% vested, they can withdraw all the funds set aside for them in a retirement fund.

181. Which of the following is not true of the term "appraised value"?

A.   It usually comes out lower than the purchase price when using comparable sales
B.   It is an opinion of a property's fair market value
C.   It is based on comparable sales
D.   None of the above

Answer: A. The appraised value usually comes out at the purchase price because the most recent sale is the one on the property in question.

182. If a buyer qualifies and is able to take over the seller's mortgage when buying his home, this type of mortgage is called

A.   "pass on down" mortgage
B.   assumable mortgage
C.   owner financing
D.   both B and C

Answer: B. A mortgage that can be assumed by the buyer when a home is sold is called an assumable mortgage. Usually the borrower must qualify in order to assume.

183. A call option is most similar to

A.   a lifetime cap
B.   a buy-down
C.   an acceleration clause
D.   all of the above

Answer: C. A call option is most similar to an acceleration clause.

184. A "chain of title" would show

A.   the transfers of title to a piece of property over the years
B.   members of the "chain gang" who had previously owned the property
C.   neither A nor B
D.   both A and B

Answer: A. A chain of title is an analysis of the transfers of title to a piece of property over the years.

185. Which of the following is true of a cloud on title?

A.   It usually cannot be removed except by deed, release, or court action
B.   It is the result of conditions revealed by a title search that adversely affect the title to real estate
C.   both A and B
D.   neither A nor B

Answer: C. A cloud on title is any condition revealed by a title search that adversely affects the title to real estate. Usually clouds cannot be removed except by deed, release, or court action.

186. Which of the following applies to "closing costs"?

A.   They are divided into two categories—"non-recurring closing costs" and "pre-paid items"
B.   Lenders try to estimate the amounts of non-recurring and pre-paids on a Good Faith Estimate shortly after receiving the loan application
C.   Pre-paids are items which recur over time, such as property taxes and homeowners insurance
D.   All of the above

Answer: D. Closing costs are either "non-recurring" or "pre-paids." "Pre-paids" occur over time, like property taxes and homeowners insurance. Lenders try to estimate both categories and give a Good Faith Estimate within three days of receiving a home loan application.

187. What is "community property"?

A.   Property that is owned by an entire condominium development
B.   Property that is owned by an entire subdivision of single-family homes
C.   Property acquired by a married couple during the marriage and considered to be jointly owned
D.   Both A and B

Answer: C. Community property, an outgrowth of the Spanish and Mexican heritage of the area, determines that property acquired by a married couple during their marriage is considered to be jointly owned.

188. If an apartment complex is converted to a condominium, this is called

A.   a condominium conversion
B.   an apartment conversion
C.   either an apartment or condominium conversion
D.   fewer options for people to rent

Answer: A. Changing the ownership of an existing building (usually a rental project) to the condominium form of ownership is called a condominium conversion.

189. This is an adjustable rate mortgage that allows the borrower to change the ARM to a fixed rate mortgage

within a specific time.

A.   due-to-change ARM
B.   convertible ARM
C.   fixed rate ARM
D.   two-fold mortgage

Answer: B. A convertible ARM is an adjustable rate mortgage that allows the borrower to change the ARM to a fixed rate mortgage within a specific time.

190. If someone gives you "credit," you are

A.   agreeing to receive something of value in exchange for a promise to repay the lender at a later date
B.   getting something you deserve for something you did
C.   very lucky, because this doesn't happen often
D.   both B and C

Answer: A. Credit is an agreement in which a borrower receives something of value in exchange for a promise to repay the lender at a later date.

191. In an effort to avoid foreclosure (which may or may not happen), you might give the lender

A.   the payments he is due, all at one time
B.   your car and any other valuable personal property you have
C.   a "deed in lieu" (of foreclosure)
D.   a "deed in lieu" (of foreclosure), which then will not affect your credit badly

Answer: C. A "deed in lieu of foreclosure" conveys title to the lender when the borrower is in default and wants to avoid foreclosure. The lender may or may no stop foreclosure proceedings. Regardless, the avoidance and non-repayment of debt will most likely show on a credit history. The "deed in lieu" may prevent having the documents preparatory to a foreclosure becoming a matter of public record by being recorded.

192. When a lender performs this calculation annually to make sure the correct amount of money for anticipated expenditures is being collected, the lender is performing

A. checks and balances
B. an escrow analysis
C. a detailed loan analysis
D. lenders don't do this

Answer: B. Once a year your lender will perform an "escrow analysis" to make sure they are collecting the correct amount of money for the anticipated expenditures.

193. The report on the title of a property from the public records or an abstract of the title is called

A. a title report
B. an examination of title
C. an examination of deed, survey and title
D. title insurance

Answer: B. The report on the title of a property from the public records or an abstract of the title is called an examination of title.

194. A consumer protection law that regulates the disclosure of consumer credit reports by consumer/credit reporting agencies and establishes procedures for correcting mistakes on one's credit record is called the

A.   Credit Reporting Act
B.   Fair Credit Reporting Act
C.   Consumer Protection Act
D.   Truth-in-Lending Act

Answer: B. The Fair Credit Reporting Act is a consumer protection law that regulates the disclosure of consumer credit reports by consumer/credit reporting agencies and establishes procedures for correcting mistakes on one's credit record.

195. If you inherit from someone, the best type of estate to inherit is called

A.   a fee simple estate
B.   general, all-encompassing estate
C.   life estate
D.   none of the above

Answer: A. A fee simple estate is an unconditional unlimited estate of inheritance that represents the greatest estate and most extensive interest in land that can be enjoyed and is of perpetual duration.

196. A homeowner's association does which the following?

A.   It manages the common areas of a condominium project or planned unit development
B.   It owns title to the common elements in a condominium development
C.   It doesn't own title to the common elements in a planned unit development
D.   All of the above

Answer: A. A homeowner's association manages the common areas of a condominium project or planned unit development, owns title to the common elements in a planned unit development but doesn't in a condo development.

197. In simple terms a judgment is

A.   a personal opinion about real estate
B.   an individual's way of making decisions about legal matters
C.   a decision made by a court of law
D.   an opinion of an attorney

Answer: C. A judgment is a decision made by a court of law. In repayment of a debt, the court may place a lien against the debtor's real property as collateral for the judgment's creditor.

198. This is a way of holding title to a property wherein the mortgagor does not actually own the property but rather has a recorded long-term lease on it.

A.   contract for deed
B.   rent-to-own contract

C.   long-term lease
D.   leasehold estate

Answer: D. A leasehold estate is a way of holding title to a property when the mortgagor does not actually own the property but rather has a recorded long-term lease on it.

199. Which of the following are duties of a loan officer?

A.   The solicitation of loans
B.   Representation of the lending institution
C.   Representation of the borrower to the lending institution
D.   All of the above

Answer: D. A loan officer, sometimes called a lender, loan representative, loan "rep," or account executive solicits loans, represents the lending institution, and represents the borrower to the lending institution.

200. The amount paid by a mortgagor for mortgage insurance, either government or private is called

A.   mortgage insurance premium
B.   private mortgage insurance premium
C.   FHA insurance premium
D.   VA insurance premium

Answer: A. The mortgage insurance premium is paid by a mortgagor for mortgage insurance, either to a government agency such as the Federal Housing Administration (FHA) or to a private mortgage insurance (MI) company.

201. Which of the following statements is not true of mortgage life and disability insurance?

A.   It begins immediately after someone becomes disabled

B.   It pays off the entire debt if someone dies during the life of the mortgage

C.   It is a type of term life insurance often bought by borrowers

D.   In this type insurance, the amount of coverage decreases as the principal declines

Answer: A. Be careful to read the terms of coverage because often it does not start immediately upon the disability, but after a specified period, sometimes forty-five days.

202. Which is the best definition of "multi-dwelling units"?

A.   They are properties that provide separate housing units for more than one family with several different mortgages

B.   They are properties that provide separate housing units for more than one family, but with a single mortgage

C.   They are properties that provide separate housing units for more than one family, but are leased rather than owned

D.   They are properties that provide separate housing units for more than one family on a lease-option basis

Answer: B. Multi-dwelling units provide separate housing units for more than one family, although they secure only a single mortgage.

203. Which of the following is true of "negative amortization"?

A.   It is also called "deferred interest"
B.   Because some ARM's allow the interest rate to fluctuate, the borrower's minimum payment may not cover all the interest
C.   The unpaid interest is added to the balance of the loan and the loan balance grows larger instead of smaller
D.   All of the above

Answer: D. Because some adjustable rate mortgages allow the interest rate to fluctuate independently of a required minimum payment, if a borrower makes the minimum payment it may not cover all the interest. The borrower is deferring the interest payment, called "deferred interest." It is then added to the balance, making it grow larger, and thus the term "negative amortization.

204. For someone to be determined to be "pre-qualified" for a loan, what has taken place?

A.   The person has given a written statement saying he can afford the loan
B.   A loan officer has given a written opinion of the borrower's ability to qualify based on debt, income, or savings
C.   The loan officer has reviewed a credit report on the borrower
D.   The information given to the loan officer is in the form of written documentation

Answer: B. Pre-qualification usually refers to the loan officer's written opinion of the ability of a borrower to qualify for a home loan, after the loan officer has made inquiries about debt, income, and savings. This information provided to the loan officer may have been presented verbally or in the form of documentation, and the loan officer may or may not have reviewed a credit report on the borrower.

205. The four components of a monthly mortgage payment on impounded loans are

A. principal, interest, taxes, maintenance
B. principal, interest, insurance, bank fees
C. principal, interest, taxes, miscellaneous charge
D. principal, interest, taxes, insurance

Answer: D. The four components of a monthly mortgage payment on impounded loans are principal, interest, taxes and insurance (PITI). While taxes and insurance are usually paid into an escrow account until they're due, principal refers to the part of the monthly payment that reduces the remaining balance and interest is the fee charged for borrowing money.

206. The term "periodic rate cap" refers to

A. an adjustable rate mortgage
B. a limit on the amount the interest rate can increase or decrease during any one adjustment period
C. conventional fixed-rate loans
D. both A and B

Answer: D. For an adjustable rate mortgage, a limit on the amount that the interest rate can increase or decrease during any one adjustment period, regardless of how high or low the index might be is called a periodic rate cap.

207. The acquisition of property through the payment of money or its equivalent is called

A.   a purchase money transaction
B.   having a down payment and mortgage
C.   simply, buying property
D.   a sales transaction

Answer: A. The acquisition of property through the payment of money or its equivalent is called a purchase money transaction.

208. What is a recording?

A.   A sound file of music to study real estate by
B.   Details of a properly executed legal document noted in the registrar's office
C.   A document, such as a deed or mortgage note which becomes public record
D.   Both B and C

Answer: D. The noting in the registrar's office of the details of a properly executed legal document, such as deed, mortgage note, satisfaction of mortgage, or extension of mortgage, thereby making it a part of the public record is called a recording.

209. If a landlord wants to protect himself against loss or rent or rental value due to fire or other casualty that would render the premises unusable for a time he would purchase

A.   hazard insurance
B.   fire insurance
C.   rent-loss insurance

D.   there is no such insurance

Answer: C. Rent loss insurance protects a landlord against loss or rent or rental value due to fire or other casualty that renders the leased premises unavailable for use and as a result of which the tenant is excused from paying rent.

210. The right to enter or leave designated premises is called

A.   the right of ingress or egress
B.   the right to enter or leave
C.   the right of non-trespass
D.   an easement

Answer: A. The right to enter or leave designated premises is called the right of ingress or egress.

211. "Secondary market" means

A.   a market which is not as important as the primary market
B.   the buying and selling of existing mortgages, usually as part of a "pool" of mortgages
C.   a market of lower real estate values
D.   none of the above

Answer: B. The buying and selling of existing mortgages, usually as a "pool," is called the secondary market.

212. The property that will be pledged as collateral for a loan is called

A.   the back-up plan

B.   the credit
C.   security
D.   the borrower's former home

Answer: C. Security is the property that will be pledged as collateral for a loan.

213. If you were purchasing a piece of property, either you or your bank would want to know if you were paying a fair price and would order

A.   a market analysis by a realtor
B.   an appraisal
C.   survey
D.   termite inspection

Answer: B. An appraisal is a written justification of the price paid for a property, primarily based on an analysis of comparable sales of similar homes nearby.

214. Which of the following is an example of "transfer of ownership"?

A.   The purchase of property "subject to" the mortgage
B.   Joint tenancy
C.   The assumption of the mortgage debt by the property purchaser
D.   Both A and C

Answer: D. Lenders consider the following to be a transfer of ownership: the purchase of a property "subject to" the mortgage, the assumption of the mortgage debt by the property purchaser, and any exchange of possession of the property under a land sales contract or any other land trust device.

215. Which of the following does not apply the Treasury index?

A.   An index used to determine interest rate changes for certain fixed-rate loans
B.   It is based on the results of auctions that the U. S. Treasury holds for its Treasury bills and securities
C.   derived from the U. S. Treasury's daily yield curve
D.   None of the above

Answer: A. The Treasury index is an index used to determine interest rate changes for certain adjustable rate loans.

216. What are assets?

A.   Items of value owned by an individual
B.   Items that can be quickly converted into cash are called "liquid assets"
C.   Real estate, personal property, and debts owed to someone by others
D.   All of the above.

Answer: D. Assets are items of value owned by an individual. Assets quickly converted to cash are considered "liquid assets" and include bank accounts, stocks, bonds, mutual funds, etc. Other assets include real estate, personal property, and debts owed to an individual by others.

217. One who establishes the value of a property for taxation purposes is called

A.   a government tax appraiser
B.   an assessor
C.   an appraiser
D.   all of the above

Answer: B. A public official who establishes the value of a property for taxation purposes is called an assessor.

218. A certificate of deposit index is

A.   one of the indexes used for determining interest rate changes on some adjustable rate mortgages
B.   is an average of what banks are paying on certificates of deposit
C.   both A and B
D.   neither A nor B

Answer: C. A certificate of deposit index is used for determining interest rate changes on some adjustable rate mortgages. It is an average of what banks are paying on certificates of deposit.

219. Which of the following is true of "common areas"?

A.   They include swimming pools, tennis courts, and other recreational facilities
B.   They are portions of a building, land, and amenities owned or managed by a planned unit development or condominium project's homeowners' association

C.   They have shared expenses by the project owners for the operation and maintenance
D.   all of the above

Answer: D. Common areas include portions of a building, land, and amenities owned by or managed by a planned unit development or condo project's homeowners' association (or a cooperative project's cooperative corporation) that are used by all of the unit owners, who share in the common expenses of their operation and maintenance. They include swimming pools,, tennis courts, and other recreational facilities, as well as common corridors of buildings, parking areas, means of ingress and egress, etc.

220. In a condominium hotel you would find the following:

A.   Rental or registrations desks
B.   Daily cleaning services
C.   No individual ownership
D.   Both A and B

Answer: D. Often found in resort areas, this is a condominium project with rental or registration desks, short-term occupancy, food and telephone services, and daily cleaning services. It is operated like a commercial hotel even though the units are individually owned.

221. A type of multiple ownership where the residents of a multi-unit housing complex own shares in the cooperative corporation that owns the property and gives each resident the right to occupy a specific apartment or unit is called

A.   an investment condominium
B.   an investment planned unit development
C.   a cooperative
D.   a government-run housing project

Answer: C. A cooperative (co-op) is a type of multiple ownership where the residents of a multi-unit housing complex own shares in the cooperative corporation that owns the property and gives each resident the right to occupy a specific unit.

222. Which is true of the cost of funds index (COFI)?

A.   It represents the weighted-average cost of savings, borrowings, and advances of the financial institutions such as banks and savings & loans in the 11th District of the Federal Home Loan Bank
B.   It is one of the indexes used to determine interest rate changes for certain government fixed rate mortgages
C.   It is an index used to determine interest rate changes for certain adjustable-rate mortgages
D.   Both A and C

Answer: D. The cost of funds index is one of the indexes used to determine interest rate changes for certain adjustable-rate mortgages. It represents the weight-average cost of savings, borrowings, and advances of the financial institutions such as banks and savings and loans, in the 11th District of the Federal Home Loan Bank.

223. Once you buy a house, the amount you pay each month includes an extra amount above principal and interest. This

extra money is held in a special account to pay your taxes and homeowners insurance when it comes due. This account is called

A.   an escrow account
B.   a savings account
C.   a regular checking account
D.   both B and C

Answer: A. Once you close your transaction, you probably have an escrow account with your lender which is composed of extra money taken from your monthly payments to be put in escrow and pay your taxes and insurance when they come due. The lender pays them with your money instead of you paying them yourself.

224. Which of the following does the Federal Housing Administration do?

A.   Lends money and plans and constructs housing
B.   Insures residential mortgage loans made by government lenders
C.   Sets standards for construction and underwriting
D.   None of the above

Answer: C. The main activity of the FHA is the insuring of residential mortgage loans made by private lenders. It sets standards for construction and underwriting but does not lend money or plan or construct housing.

225. If you purchase a type of insurance called homeowner's warranty, you would do so because

A.   It will cover repairs to certain items, such as heating or air conditioning if they break down within the coverage period
B.   The seller will sometimes pay for it
C.   Both A and B
D.   Neither A nor B

Answer: C. Homeowner's warranty will cover repairs to certain items like air conditioning or heating during the coverage period. The buyer often requests the seller to pay for this, but either party can pay.

226. A type of foreclosure proceeding used in some states that is handled as a civil lawsuit and conducted entirely under the auspices of a court is called

A.   a legal foreclosure
B.   a court-appointed foreclosure
C.   a judicial foreclosure
D.   a civil foreclosure

Answer: C. A type of foreclosure proceeding used in some states that is handled as a civil lawsuit and conducted entirely under the auspices of a court is called a judicial foreclosure.

227. Which of the following is not part of loan servicing?

A.   Processing payments, sending statements
B.   Managing the escrow account
C.   Handling pay-offs and assumptions
D.   Sending a monthly statement to the owner

Answer: D. The company you make your loan payments to is "servicing" your loan by processing payments, sending statements, managing the escrow account, providing collection efforts on delinquent loans, making sure insurance and property taxes are made, handling pay-offs and assumptions and other services.

228. A period payment cap applies to

A.   any mortgage taken out in the U.S.
B.   adjustable rate mortgages
C.   fixed-rate loans
D.   government loans

Answer: B. The period payment cap applies to an adjustable-rate mortgage where the interest rate and the minimum payment amount fluctuate independently of one another. It is a limit on the amount that payments can increase or decrease during any one adjustment period.

229. The commitment issued by a lender to borrower or other mortgage originator guaranteeing a specified interest rate for a specified period of time at a specific cost is called

A.   a rate lock
B.   under lock and key
C.   a promissory note
D.   a deed of trust

Answer: A. A rate lock is a commitment from a lender to the borrower or other mortgage originator guaranteeing a specific rate for a specific time at a specific cost.

230. A fund set aside for replacement of common property in a condominium, PUD, or cooperative project, particularly that which has a short life expectancy, such as carpet or furniture is called

A.   a capital improvements fund
B.   a replacement reserve fund
C.   a savings fund
D.   a contingency fund

Answer: B. The fund set aside for replacement of common property in a condominium, PUD or cooperative project is called a replacement reserve fund.

231. The term "servicing" describes

A.   the collection of mortgage payments from borrowers
B.   what the mechanic does to your car
C.   duties of a loan servicer
D.   both A and C

Answer: D. Servicing is the collection of mortgage payments from borrowers and related responsibilities of a loan servicer.

232. A two- to-four family property

A.   consists of a structure that provides living space for two to four families and ownership is evidenced by two to four deeds
B.   consists of a structure that provides living space for two to four families and ownership is evidenced by a single deed

C.   is not a deeded property
D.   is an illegal form of ownership

Answer: B. A two-to-four family property consists of a structure that provides living space for two to four families and ownership is evidenced by a single deed.

1. Many states determine the order of water rights according to which users of the water hold a recorded beneficial use permit. This allocation of water rights is determined by:

A. accretion.
B. riparian theory.
C. littoral theory.
D. the doctrine of prior appropriation.

Answer: D. All terms relate to water rights, with "riparian" -- the right to use water adjacent to one's property -- being the most common in sections of the U.S. where water is abundant. However, in states where water is more scarce, a form of "prior appropriation" applies. Also known as "first in time is first in right," it grants water rights to divert a specific amount of water from a specific source to irrigate a specific piece of property. Those rights are then assigned a priority based on when the right was first used or applied for. In periods of peak demand, they give those whose claim is the oldest the right to get their water first.

2. The right to control one's property includes all of the following EXCEPT:

A. the right to invite people on the property for a political fund-raiser.
B. the right to exclude the utilities meter reader.
C. the right to erect "no trespassing" signs.
D. the right to enjoy pride of ownership.

Answer: B. This right to enter and work on a property is granted to utility companies (water, sewer, gas and electric) as well as telephone and cable companies. Essentially, if a company provides a service and owns the equipment (e.g., phone and cable lines), they are usually granted an easement.

3. Which of the following types of ownership CANNOT be created by operation of law, but must be created by the parties' expressed intent?

A. community property
B. tenancy in common
C. condominium ownership
D. tenancy by the entireties

Answer: D. Tenancy by the entireties is a form of ownership that husbands and wives can choose or create by deciding to do so and declaring it as such in contracts and deeds. Tenancy in common is put in motion by state law. Community Property is a law of ownership that exists in Arizona, California, Idaho, Kentucky, Nevada, New Mexico, Texas, Washington and some other states. Tenancy by the Entireties is an estate that is recognized in some states between husband and wife, who have equal right of possession and enjoyment during their joint lives and with the right of survivorship--that is when one dies, the property goes to the surviving tenant. (In many states, if couples do not specify "Joint Tenancy," this form of ownership will be automatically assumed.) Tenancy in Common is a type of joint ownership by parties NOT married, that allows a person to sell his share or leave it in a will without the consent of the other owners. If a person dies without a will, his share goes to his heirs, not to the other owners.

4. Which of the following is/are considered to be personal property?

A. wood-burning fireplace
B. furnace
C. bathtubs
D. patio furniture

Answer: D. The concept of personal property typically comes into play at the time of sale. Things that are part of the house-- bathroom fixtures, fireplaces, carpeting and such-- go with the sale. (Unless specifically excluded, as can happen in the case of a dining room chandelier or one or two other objects with which the owners have an emotional attachment.) Furniture, rugs, lamps and other portable items that are not "nailed down" constitute personal property and are not included in the sale.

5. The word "improvement" would refer to all of the following EXCEPT:

A. streets.
B. a sanitary sewer system.
C. trade fixtures.
D. the foundation.

Answer: C. The term "trade fixture" refers to an item installed by a tenant in a rented commercial property that he or she removes at the end of the occupancy. More on this topic follows.

6. All of the following are physical characteristics of land EXCEPT:

A. indestructibility.
B. uniqueness.
C. immobility.
D. scarcity.

Answer: D. Scarcity is a fundamental economic concept that holds that the rarer and more desirable something is, the more valuable it will be. For example, professional athletes are highly paid because only the smallest percentage of people have the ability to perform at that level. Land is "scarce" because there is a finite amount available and, as Will Rogers once said, "They ain't making any more of it."

7. Certain items on the premises that are installed by the tenant and are related to the tenant's business are called:

A. fixtures.
B. emblements.
C. trade fixtures.
D. easements.

Answer: C. The term is usually applied to a commercial tenant and refers to items installed in connection with his or her business, such as stoves and refrigerators in a restaurant or display cases in a retail shop.

8. Personal property includes all of the following EXCEPT:

A. chattels.
B. fructus industriales.
C. emblements.
D. fixtures.

Answer: D. "Chattel" is a legal term that means personal property. Emblements and fructus industriales refer to profit from crops that are grown as a result of a person's labor, such as corn, as opposed to those that occur naturally, such as grass or minerals. By the custom of English common law, they are considered personal property. By contrast, a fixture is considered attached to a property and thus part of the structure.

9. A person who has complete control over a parcel of real estate is said to own a:

A. leasehold estate.
B. fee simple estate.
C. life estate.
D. defeasible fee estate.

Answer: B. All the other options have conditions attached. A leasehold estate is, as the name implies, leased property. Similarly, a life estate gives a person ownership or control of a property only for the duration of his or her natural life.

"Defeasible estates" give a person or entity control over a property only so long as certain conditions are met or avoided. For example, a community might be deeded a property on the condition that it be used only for building a school, or land willed to a child on the condition it never be used for commercial development. If the community tries to use the property for a recreation complex or the heir tries to sell to a retail developer, control would automatically revert to another party and the deed would become void.

10. A portion of Wendell's building was inadvertently built on Ginny's land. This is called an:

A. accretion.
B. avulsion.
C. encroachment.
D. easement.

Answer: C. The principal attributes of an encroachment are: 1) It is accidental and 2) it involves only part of a structure. Typically, the issue would be resolved by selling Wendell an easement or a lease or, if practical, actually moving the structure.

11. The purchase of a ticket for a professional sporting event gives the bearer what?

A. an easement right to park his car
B. a license to enter and claim a seat for the duration of the game

C. an easement in gross interest in the professional sporting team

D. a license to sell food and beverages at the sporting event

Answer: B. Easements grant access, not use. Commercial licenses, such as those required to sell beverages, souvenirs or services, cover extended periods. Although tickets to sporting events, concerts, shows and the like are technically licenses, they differ from most in their degree of restriction. For example, a concert ticket does not give the bearer the right to sit anywhere he or she chooses or wander backstage to meet the performers.

12. If the owner of the dominant tenement becomes the owner of the servient tenement and merges the two properties, what happens?

A. The easement becomes dormant.
B. The easement is unaffected.
C. The easement is terminated.
D. The properties retain their former status.

Answer: C. "Dominant" and "servient" tenements involve two adjacent properties in which an easement is involved. For example, let's say Bridle Creek Farms and Barnstable Farms are separate parcels divided by a country lane that provides access to the county road system. The lane is owned by Bridle Creek, but the deeds of both properties stipulate that Barnstable Farms shall have unrestricted access for the purpose of accessing county roads. That access is an easement. Thus, if the owner of Barnstable Farms buys Bridle Creek Farms, the need for the easement disappears.

13. Homeowner Ginny acquired the ownership of land that was deposited by a river running through her property by:

A. reliction.
B. succession.
C. avulsion.
D. accretion.

Answer: D. Accretion means the addition to a parcel of land by sand or soil deposits due to the action of a river or other body of water over time. Avulsion refers to the loss of land as a result of its being washed away by sudden or unexpected action of nature, such as a flash flood that re-routes a river.

14. The rights of the owner of property located along the banks of a river are called:

A. littoral rights.
B. prior appropriation rights.
C. riparian rights.
D. hereditament.

Answer: C. "Littoral" and "prior appropriation" are different kinds of water rights: in the first case, navigation rights to an ocean or other large body of water; in the second, the right to use a water source for irrigation. A hereditament is any inheritable property.

15. The local utility company dug up Frank's garden to install a natural gas line. The company claimed it had a valid easement and proved it through the county records. Frank claimed the easement was not valid because he did not know about it. The easement:

A. Was valid even though the owner did not know about it.
B. Was an appurtenant easement owned by the utility company.
C. Was not valid because it had not been used during the entire time that Frank owned the property.
D. Was not valid because Frank was not informed of its existence when he purchased the property.

Answer: A. Easements grant only access, not ownership, use or occupancy rights. Further, that access is generally for the benefit of the property owner, such as maintaining utilities or sidewalks. As such, they Attach" to a deed or lease and remain in effect, until specifically lifted.

16. Jim and Sandy are next-door neighbors. Sandy tells Jim that he can store his camper in her yard for a few weeks until she needs the space. Sandy did not charge Jim rent for the use of her yard. Sandy has given Jim a(n) what?

A. easement appurtenant
B. easement by necessity
C. estate in land license
D. License

Answer: D. Granting the use of property for a defined period for a specific purpose is almost always a form of licensing.

Easements grant only access, not ownership, use or occupancy rights. Further, that access is generally for the benefit of the property owner, such as maintaining utilities or sidewalks.

17. Your neighbors use your driveway to reach their garage on their property. Your attorney explains that the ownership of the neighbors' real estate includes an easement appurtenant giving them the driveway right. Your property is the:

A. leasehold interest.
B. dominant tenement.
C. servient tenement.
D. license property.

Answer: C. An "easement appurtenant" allows the holder of one property to benefit from another's. In this case, your property is "servient" because it is the one burdened by the easement while your neighbor's is Dominant" since it is the one that benefits.

18. Quintin owned two acres of land. He sold one acre to Frank and reserved for himself an appurtenant easement over Frank's land for ingress and egress. Frank's land:

A. Is the dominant tenement.
B. Is the servient tenement.
C. Can be cleared of the easement when Quintin sells the withheld acre to a third party.
D. Is subject to an easement in gross.

Answer: B. Frank's land interest is the one burdened by the easement; therefore it is the servient property.

19. Ginny owns 50 acres of land with 500 feet of frontage on a desirable recreational lake. She wishes to subdivide the parcel into salable lots, but she wants to retain control over the lake frontage while allowing lot owners to have access to the lake. Which of the following types of access rights would provide the greatest protection for a prospective purchaser?

A. an easement in gross
B. an appurtenant easement
C. an easement by necessity
D. a license

Answer: B. Appurtenant easements afford the most protection since they are generally a permanent feature of the property. Thus, in the case of sale, the lake access passes to any new owners. By contrast, an "easement in gross" is between two individuals, which would severely limit the attractiveness and value of the property if the original owner wished to sell.

20. Sam and Nancy bought a store building and took title as joint tenants. Nancy died testate. Sam now owns the store:

A. as a joint tenant with rights of survivorship.
B. in severalty.
C. as a tenant in common with Nancy's heirs.
D. in trust.

Answer: B. Joint tenancy means that two parties have an undivided interest in a particular property and, upon the death of one party, full ownership automatically goes to the survivor. Despite the way it sounds, "in severalty" means as sole owner.

21. When real estate under an estate for years is sold, what happens to the lease?

A. It expires with the conveyance.
B. It binds the new owner.
C. It is subject to termination with proper notice
D. It is valid but unenforceable.

Answer: B. Tenancy for years is the common form of rental agreements and binds all future owners for the term of the lease.

22. Evan lives in an apartment building. The land and structures are owned by a corporation, with one mortgage loan covering the entire property. Like the other residents, Evan owns stock in the corporation and has a lease on his apartment. This type of ownership is called a(n):

A. condominium.
B. planned unit development.
C. time-share.
D. cooperative.

Answer: D. This is the distinguishing characteristic that differentiates cooperative from condominium ownership.

Although often confused, a condominium owner holds title to his individual unit. A co-op owner, on the other hand, is technically a renter. It's his stock in the corporation holding title to the property that gives him the right to lease the unit as well as sell that right to another.

23. Tom leases store space to Kim for a restaurant, and Kim installs her ovens, booths, counters, and other equipment. When do these items become real property?

A. when they are installed
B. when Kim defaults on her rental payments
C. when the lease takes effect
D. when the lease expires, if the items are not taken by the tenant

Answer: D. im is free to move these fixtures at the end of her lease. However, if she chooses to leave them behind, they are considered a permanent part of the structure (just like a dining room chandelier in a home) and revert to Tom.

24. Jim, Manny and Harry are joint tenants owning a parcel of land. Harry conveys his interest to his long-time friend Wendell. After the conveyance, Jim and Manny:

A. become tenants in common.
B. continue to be joint tenants with Harry.
C. become joint tenants with Wendell.
D. remain joint tenants owning a two-thirds interest

Answer: D. Because joint tenancy must be declared, Jim and Manny remain joint tenant with a two-thirds interest while Wendell, because of his passive acquisition of his share of the property, becomes a tenant in common with Jim and Manny. The difference between the two forms is that Jim and Manny's share retains the right of survivorship provisions but Wendell's does not.

25. In a gift of a parcel of real estate, one of the two owners was given an undivided
60 percent interest and the other received an undivided 40 percent interest. The two owners hold their interests as what?

A. cooperative owners
B. joint tenants
C. community property owners
D. tenants in common

Answer: D. In order to create joint tenancy, some form of relationship must exist between the parties involved, whether business, spousal or other. Because their interests were acquired as a gift, the parties in this instance become tenants in common, with all the ownership benefits of joint tenancy, but not the survivorship rights.

26. To create a joint tenancy relationship in the ownership of real estate, there must be unities of:

A. grantees, ownership, claim of right, and possession.

B. title, interest, encumbrance, and survivorship.

C. possession, time, interest, and title.

D. ownership, possession, heirs, and title.

Answer: C. This essentially means that all parties to the agreement share equally in all aspects of the property, including the length of time it's been held. That means if one party sells or transfers interest in a joint tenancy relationship, his or her place is taken by another in the same capacity.

27. What is a Schedule of Exceptions on a title policy?

A. encumbrances

B. tax liens

C. list of things not insured in the policy

D. defects

Answer: C. Almost no title insurance policy protects against all conceivable events. As the name suggests, the Schedule of Exceptions is a specific list of items not covered and can include things such as unrecorded mechanic's liens, assessments, water rights and mining claims.

28. When a company furnishes materials for the construction of a house and is subsequently not paid, it may file a(n):

A. deficiency judgment.

B. lis pendens.

C. estoppel certificate.

D. mechanic's lien.

Answer: D. A mechanic's lien is the first, and usually most cost-effective, step for a person providing labor and/or materials to a homeowner to recover monies owed—in large part because of the pressure it puts on the homeowner to settle quickly and without costly court involvement.

29. Which of the following liens does not need to be recorded to be valid?

A. materialman's lien
B. real estate tax lien
C. judgment lien
D. mechanic's lien

Answer: B. The requirement for individuals to record liens is due in part to the necessity of correctly identifying the complainant. For example, not just "Jones Contracting," but the specific Jones Contracting that performed the work and is owed the money. Because they bear the authority of government and are easily identified, liens by taxing authorities do not need to be recorded.

30. The system of ownership of real property in the United States is what?

A. incorporeal
B. allodial
C. inchoate

D. feudal

Answer: B. "Allodial" is the modern form of ownership and is often contrasted with "feudal" in which land is held on the condition of rent or service due the government. For example, a medieval knight held property subject to coming to his baron's service when called. Similarly, the baron's land holdings were conditional on his raising an army and fighting for the king in times of conflict. Failure of any party to "perform as promised" was cause for holdings to be confiscated, often as a preliminary step to more extreme actions.

31. A mechanic's lien would be properly classified as a(n):

A. equitable lien.
B. voluntary lien.
C. general lien.
D. statutory lien.

Answer: D. A "statutory lien" is one that arises out of specific law (otherwise known as statutes). By contrast, an "equitable lien" has its roots in common law or custom. A "voluntary lien" is one entered with the property owner's knowledge and consent, such as a mortgage. A "general lien" grants a creditor the right to file a claim against all of a debtor's assets, not just a particular property.

32. Under which of the following types of liens can both the real property and the personal property of the debtor be sold to pay the debt?

A. real estate tax lien
B. mechanic's lien
C. judgment lien
D. assessment lien

Answer: C. Most liens are against a specific property, such as a primary residence. Thus, a contractor seeking payment for a new deck cannot have a homeowner's car attached in settlement. A judgment lien, however, is a decision directed by the courts and can apply to whatever assets it deems appropriate.

33. A homeowner owned a house on a lot. The front ten feet of the lot were taken by eminent domain for a sidewalk. Would the homeowner be entitled to compensation?

A. Yes. The land was taken for public use by eminent domain.
B. Yes. He must be paid for the use of the sidewalk.
C. No. He still had use of the house and lot.
D. No. Compensation is not given on land taken for public use.

Answer: A. Governments and municipalities can only seize property (other than in criminal cases) for the public good and through eminent domain, which is a process, not an arbitrary action. Part of that process involves determining fair compensation to the owner.

34. The covenant in a deed which states that the grantor is the owner and has the right to convey the title is called:

A. covenant of further assurance.
B. covenant of warranty forever.
C. covenant of seisin.
D. covenant against encumbrances.

Answer: C. Another outgrowth of the feudal system, "seisen" derives from the French meaning to "sit upon or own" and gives owners the right to sell or transfer property at will.

35. The recording of a deed:

A. Is all that is required to transfer the title to real estate.
B. Gives constructive notice of the ownership of real property.
C. Insures the interest in a parcel of real estate.
D. Warrants the title to real property.

Answer: B. Recording a deed does not convey, insure or warrant ownership. However, it does protect the owner's interest in a property by serving notice that the recorded owner is the only recognized holder of title. This places a larger burden of proof and process on someone trying to assert a prior ownership interest and/or claiming a deedholder's title is clouded.

36. Which of the following provides a buyer with the best assurance of clear, marketable title?

A. certificate of title
B. title insurance
C. abstract of title
D. general warranty deed

Answer: B. Title insurance provides the best assurance of marketable title.

37. What do liens and easements have in common?

A. Both are encumbrances.
B. Both must be on public record to be valid.
C. Neither can be done without the consent of the owner.
D. Both are money claims against the property.

Answer: A. Liens are, of course, serious in that they indicate the owner has failed to pay a debt secured directly or indirectly by the property. Easements, on the other hand, are generally a practical necessity for most residential properties.

38. The title to real estate passes when a valid deed is:

A. signed and recorded.
B. delivered and accepted.
C. filed and microfilmed.
D. executed and mailed.

Answer: B. Fundamentally, real estate transactions only involve two parties--the buyer and the seller. All that's necessary to create a legal sale is for one party to make an offer the other accepts. Recording, escrow, real estate licensees, mortgage companies and the like facilitate and support the transaction process but are not requirements of a legal sale.

39. The primary purpose of a deed is to:

A. Prove ownership.
B. Transfer title rights.
C. Give constructive notice.
D. Prevent adverse possession.

Answer: B. A deed is the instrument by which ownership of a property is transferred from one person to another, while a title is evidence of that ownership.

40. A special warranty deed differs from a general warranty deed in that the grantor's covenant in the special warranty deed:

A. Applies only to a definite limited time.
B. Covers the time back to the original title.
C. Is implied and is not written in full.
D. Protects all subsequent owners of the property.

Answer: A. The more common deed in most states is the general warranty, because it establishes the ownership trail and validity of title going back to the original recorded ownership (for example, the purchase of Manhattan Island and all subsequent divisions, subdivisions and resales). Under a special warranty deed, an owner transfers property guaranteeing the quality of title only during the period of his or her ownership, leaving subsequent buyers vulnerable to prior claims.

41. Which of the following deeds contains no expressed or implied warranties?

A. a bargain and sale deed
B. a quitclaim deed
C. a warranty deed
D. a grant deed

Answer: B. A "quit claim" deed means what it implies: The seller gives up any claims he or she may have to the property but makes no warranties whatsoever about the possibility of other claims.

42. When the grantor does not wish to convey certain property rights, he or she:

A. must note the exceptions in a separate document.
B. may not do so, since the deed conveys the entire premises.
C. may note the exceptions in the deed of conveyance.
D. must convey the entire premises and have the grantee reconvey the rights to be retained by the grantor

Answer: C. Most commonly known as "restrictive covenants," such deed restrictions are often used to maintain the consistency of a neighborhood by, for example, stipulating that only traditional home styles of a particular size and painted in traditional colors may be constructed and occupied within the subdivision. These are encumbrances on the property since they limit current and future owners in how they use the property.

43. A partition suit is used for which of the following?

A. determination of party fences
B. to allow construction of party walls
C. to force a division of property without all the owners' consents
D. to change a tenancy by entireties to some other form of ownership

Answer: C. Partition suits are typically pursued when a co-owner of a property wants to sell his or her share and the other owners are opposed. Since it is a legal action involving the courts, it is an expense with often unsatisfactory results.

44. The condemnation of private property for public use is exercised under which government right?

A. taxation
B. escheat
C. manifest destiny
D. eminent domain

Answer: D. As noted previously, eminent domain actions are generally reserved for "public good" projects such as highway expansion. However, there have been recent instances of municipalities using this power to condemn well-kept neighborhoods of middle-class housing to make way for high-end properties that will provide a higher tax base.

45. When a claim is settled by a title insurance company, the company acquires all rights and claims of the insured against any other person who is responsible for the loss. This is known as what?

A. caveat emptor
B. surety bonding
C. subordination
D. subrogation

Answer: D. For example, let's say Amanda Livingstone buys a property and the seller provides a general warranty deed stipulating clear title. However, that turns out not to be the case and a third party provides a valid claim to a share of the property. Since Amada took out title insurance, the title insurance company negotiates and pays a settlement with the claimant on Amanda's behalf. Amanda's right to sue the seller then transfers to the
title insurance company, which will take action to recover the amount they paid on Amanda's behalf.

46. Which of the following would be used to clear a defect from the title records?

A. a lis pendens
B. an estoppel certificate
C. a suit to quiet title
D. a writ of attachment

Answer: C. A owner might bring a "quiet title" action to correct a minor mistake in the property description or to remove an easement that's been unused for years. Additionally, they are used when a third party tries to asset some right to the property through a dubious claim. The suit "quiets the mouth" of that person and establishes a clear title.

47. A bill of sale is used to transfer the ownership of what?

A. real property
B. fixtures
C. personal property
D. appurtenances

Answer: C. Personal property differs from "real property" in a number of respects, most importantly its portability. Cars, furniture, clothing, paintings, jewelry, appliances and just about any other non-food item one buys are examples of personal property.

48. A written summary of the history of all conveyances and legal proceedings affecting a specific parcel of real estate is called a(n):

A. affidavit of title.
B. certificate of title.
C. abstract of title.
D. title insurance policy.

Answer: C. An "Abstract of title" is a written summary that traces every change of ownership and claim against a property (such as mortgages, liens, and easements). In some cases, the abstract goes back to the last change of title, in others to the first recorded owner. It is part of the title report required by virtually all lenders.

49. When the preliminary title report reveals the existence of an easement on the property, it indicates that the easement is a(n):

A. lien.
B. encumbrance.
C. encroachment.
D. tenement.

Answer: B. Anything that limits a person's use of a property is an encumbrance. Easements limit use in that they generally prohibit any kind of permanent structure on the area in question. For example, if a homeowner wanted to build a swimming pool in an area of his back yard and the local sewer company had an easement for pipes running under that area, he would have to find another location for his pool, even if it was not as desirable.

50. The list of previous owners of conveyance from whom the present real estate owner derives his or her title is known as the:

A. chain of title.
B. certificate of title.
C. title insurance policy.
D. abstract of title.

Answer: A. The "Chain" links together the successive owners of a property from the most recent to the original recorded title holder. In addition, it notes other relevant information such as mortgages, judgments, liens, death of title holders, inheritors and so forth.

51. A person agrees to sell a property for $500,000. The buyer gives the seller $150 as valuable consideration for a six-month option. Which of the following statements is true?

A. The $150 is valuable consideration if the seller accepted it.
B. The buyer must have at least 5% down as valuable consideration.
C. The buyer must have at least 20% down.
D. The seller cannot accept money for the option.

Answer: A. "Valuable consideration" is a necessary component of all contracts. It is the benefit one party receives in exchange for granting benefit to the other. Generally it is money in any amount both parties agree to, though it can take other forms such as personal property, work or refraining from an act.

52. Which of the following activities is a violation of the Federal Fair Housing Act?

A. a nonprofit church that denies access to its retirement home to any person because of race
B. a nonprofit private club that gives preference in renting units to its members at lower rates

C. the owner of a single-family residence selling his/her own home who gives preference to a buyer based on his/her sex
D. discrimination in the sale of a warehouse based on the prospective purchaser's gender

Answer: A. The private club is exempt because its preferential treatment is based on its membership; the home owner is exempt, so long as he is selling his home without a broker; the warehouse is exempt because it's not a housing unit.

53. A Savings & Loan institution would be violating the Federal Fair Housing Act by denying a loan to Mr. and Mrs. Happy Borrower for which of the following reasons?

A. low earnings
B. too old
C. too many loans
D. minority background

Answer: D. Fair Housing and other anti-discrimination legislation doesn't force lenders or others to abandon sound business practices (such as denying loans to unqualified borrowers), merely to be fair and equally accessible to all people.

54. The Civil Rights Act of 1866 prohibits discrimination in housing based on which of the following reasons?

A. race
B. religion

C. sex
D. marital status

Answer: A. Although surprising to many, the original civil rights legislation was passed in 1866--by one vote over the veto of President Andrew Johnson.

55. An agent working as a subagent of the seller would suggest that the buyer hire an inspector from an outside service in all of the following cases EXCEPT:

A. when they smell gas in the basement.
B. when there is a slow drain in the toilet.
C. when a hinge is off the door.
D. when there is sawdust in the kitchen cabinets.

Answer: C. Home inspectors are hired to find significant and often hidden property defects, such as signs of a leaking roof, termites, foundation cracking and so forth. Hinges and other "wear and tear" items are obvious and not among the reasons for hiring an inspector.

56. The federal anti-discriminatory laws apply to which of the following?

A. a broker selling a single-family home
B. a private club not open to the general public
C. office building sales
D. the rental of industrial property

Answer: A. Civil rights laws apply to owners of residential property, rental units, hotels and virtually any other building offering housing or accommodations to the general public.

57. A tenant complained to HUD about his landlord's discriminatory practices in his/her building. A week later the landlord gave the tenant an eviction notice. Under which of the following situations would the Federal Fair Housing Act be violated?

A. when the tenant is two months behind in his/her rent
B. when the landlord evicts the tenant for reporting him to HUD
C. when the tenant has damaged the premises
D. when the tenant is conducting an illegal use on the premises

Answer: B. Anti-discrimination laws do not apply to situations that are in violation of generally accepted policies such as paying rent on time, maintaining the premises and abiding by use agreements.

58. The Federal Fair Housing Act states that a prima facie (at first view) case against a broker for discrimination be established after a complaint has been received because the broker has failed to do which of the following?

A. The broker has failed to display a HUD Equal Opportunity poster.
B. The broker has failed to join an affirmative marketing program.

C. The broker has failed to join the HUD anti-discriminatory task force.
D. The broker has failed to attend mandatory classes on fair housing.

Answer: A. Included among Fair Housing regulations is the requirement that the HUD Equal Opportunity signage be prominently displayed.

59. A broker is discussing a new listing with a prospective Mexican American buyer. The buyer wants to inspect the property immediately, but the owner of said property has instructed the broker, in writing, not to show the house during the owner's three-week absence. The buyer insists on viewing the property. The broker should:

A. Show the property to avoid a violation of the Federal Fair Housing Act.
B. Request the Real Estate Commission arbitrate the problem.
C. Inform the buyer of the seller's instructions.
D. Notify the nearest HUD office.

Answer: C. Following an owner's lawful instructions is not only allowable, but a responsibility of the licensee. However, if the owner instructed the broker to tell minority buyers that he was out of town when he was not in order to avoid selling to a minority, the broker would be in violation of the law if he acted as the owner requested.

60. A three-story apartment complex built in 1965 does not meet with the handicapped access provisions for the 1988 Fair Housing Act. The owner must:

A. Make the ground floor handicapped accessible.
B. Make the 1st and 2nd floors accessible.
C. Make the entire building accessible.
D. The owner doesn't have to comply since it's less than 4 stories.

Answer: A. Because the building was constructed before the 1991 standards went into effect, only the first floor needs to be modified.

61. What type of a listing agreement allows the owner to appoint an exclusive agent to sell his property, but retains the right to sell the property himself?

A. open
B. exclusive right to sell
C. multiple listing
D. exclusive agency

Answer: D. Open listings mean that if the owner or any other broker or salesperson produces the buyer, the broker will lose his or her commission. Exclusive Right to Sell gives the broker his or her commission regardless of who actually sells the property, even if it is the owner. Exclusive Agency allows the seller to appoint an exclusive agent, but retain the right to sell the property himself.

62. Under an Exclusive Right to Sell Listing agreement, if the seller produces a ready, willing and able buyer he:

A. will not have to pay a commission since he produced the buyer.
B. will only have to pay the broker half the commission since he produced the buyer.
C. owes the listing broker a full commission.
D. will not be able to turn the buyer over to the listing agent since the agent has the exclusive right to sell the property.

Answer: C. In contrast to exclusive agency, the exclusive right to sell entitles the broker to his or her commission regardless of who actually sells the property.

63. Which of the following would not terminate an agency relationship?

A. abandonment by the agent
B. revocation by the principal
C. submission by the agent of two offers at the same time
D. fulfillment of the agency purpose

Answer: C. Submitting offers doesn't end the relationship--only the owner's acceptance of one and ultimately closing on the transaction.

64. The buyer of an apartment complex is told that the refrigerator in one of the apartments goes with the sale.

After taking title, he discovered that the refrigerator belonged to the tenant. Which is true about this situation?

A. Since the refrigerator was in the apartment, it automatically belongs to the new owner.
B. The refrigerator is the personal property of the tenant. The seller had no right to offer it to the buyer.
C. The refrigerator was plugged into the wall and that makes it real property.
D. The tenant will have to get permission from the new owner to remove the refrigerator.

Answer: B. Plugging in an appliance does not constitute installation. Thus it is personal property that belongs to the tenant.

65. The illegal process of a banker refusing to approve loans for a neighborhood based on the racial composition of the area is:

A. blockbusting.
B. steering.
C. redlining.
D. panic peddling.

Answer: C. Loans may only be approved or denied on the basis of whether a specific individual and property meet established standards. Thus lenders are well within their rights to deny a loan to a particular person because he or she lacks sufficient income or has poor credit. Additionally, a loan for a partially completed home or one that doesn't meet code can also be denied. However, "macro" issues such as race or neighborhood cannot be considered.

66. The illegal practice of directing minorities to areas populated by the same race or religion is called:

A. steering.
B. blockbusting.
C. redlining.
D. panic peddling.

Answer: A. Steering" is driving people towards particular neighborhoods, and is the correct answer to this question. On the other hand, Blockbusting" is the opposite side of the same coin. Synonymous with "panic peddling," it refers to trying to generate panic selling in a neighborhood dominated by one race or ethnic group by representing that another group is about to start moving in.

67. Carl Chauvinist, the owner of an apartment complex, lives in one unit of a triplex and routinely refuses to rent either of the other two units to a female. Can he do this?

A. Yes. He may do this if he does not use a broker or discriminate in advertising.
B. Yes. He may do this if he doesn't ask the tenant's age.
C. No. Carl can never discriminate on sex.
D. No. Carl must live in a single family home to discriminate.

Answer: A. Although laws vary by state as to number of units that fall under this type of provision, if a person owns and lives in a unit, he or she is entitled to practice a certain measure of discrimination. The view is that a person's dwelling (which includes units such as duplexes and triplexes) enjoys a degree of "sanctity" and the person may choose whom he or she brings into their "home."

68. An aggrieved party with a Fair Housing violation claim has how long to file a complaint with the Department of Housing and Urban Development?

A. 1 month
B. 1 week
C. 1 year
D. 7 years

Answer: C. If the complaint is not filed within one year, a person may still file a civil suit in a Federal Court.

69. Jim Jones, the landlord, rents a property to Tom Smith, a handicapped person. Mr. Smith, with Mr. Jones' permission, modifies the house to suit his needs. When the lease expires, which of the following requirements would not have to be met by Mr. Smith?

A. Mr. Smith must remove the "grab rails" in the bathroom that were installed for his use.
B. Mr. Smith must raise the kitchen cabinets that were lowered for his use.
C. Mr. Smith must repair the walls where the "grab rails" in the bathroom were removed.

D. Mr. Smith must restore the wide doorways, that were installed for him, to the original size.

Answer: D. Since the width of the door will not in any way be detrimental to future tenants, there is not a requirement for the original width of the doors to be replaced by the handicapped tenant. All of the other issues must be restored to original status.

70. All of the following are duties of the property manager EXCEPT:

A. reporting to the owner all notices of building violations.
B. providing upkeep and maintenance on the property.
C. maintaining financial records and accounts.
D. securing tenants of a particular ethnic origin in accordance with the owner's wishes.

Answer: D. Except in certain circumstances regarding the rental of space within one's personal residence or unit, owners, landlords and their agents are not permitted to discriminate against people based on race, gender, creed, handicap and other personal characteristics.

71. A mobility impaired person was renting a unit in an apartment complex. Half the units had been assigned parking spaces near the door; the other half had not. The owner:

A. may charge extra money to the handicapped person for providing the parking space near the door.

B. must take a vote of all tenants to see if they want to allow the handicapped person a parking space.

C. must give a parking space near the door to the handicapped person, if one is available and a need is demonstrated.

D. must allow the handicapped person to live there for a month and if a space becomes available during that time, give the parking space to the handicapped person.

Answer: C. The "equal access" aspects of fair housing legislation do not necessarily mean equal treatment. "Reasonable accommodation" must also be made to meet the needs of handicapped people, including exceptions to standard policies such as convenient parking and guide dogs.

72. A salesperson is involved in a transaction where an individual wishes a six month lease with an option to buy. What is true about this situation?

A. The individual must go to an attorney since it is too complicated a transaction for a salesperson.

B. This transaction is too complicated for a salesperson. Only a person with a broker's license should handle this transaction.

C. A salesperson could use two standard forms, fill in the blanks and request that his or her broker review the forms before signing.

D. The salesperson should write the purchase offer. A lease for 6 months does not need to be in writing.

Answer: C. Generally speaking, salespeople may complete standard forms so long as they are reviewed by and with the approval of their broker.

73. A void contract is one that is:

A. not in writing.
B. not legally enforceable.
C. rescindable by agreement.
D. voidable by only one of the parties.

Answer: B. In order to be enforceable, real estate contracts must meet the legal requirements for contracts in general. For example, a contract signed by a minor or a "seller" who doesn't own the property in question was never legal to begin with and is thus "void."

74. The essential elements of a contract include all of the following EXCEPT:

A. offer and acceptance.
B. notarized signatures.
C. competent parties.
D. consideration.

Answer: B. A contract sets forth the terms and conditions of a real estate transaction, but does not itself transfer ownership. Thus it does not need to be notarized.

75. If, upon the receipt of an offer to purchase his property under certain conditions, the seller makes a counteroffer, the prospective buyer is:

A. bound by his original offer.
B. bound to accept the counteroffer.
C. bound by whichever offer is lower.
D. relieved of his original offer.

Answer: D. Offers are "one-time-only" events that must be accepted or rejected. Once the seller made a counter-proposal, he rejected the buyer's offer and no contract exists. The buyer is under no obligation to continue and is entitled to have any earnest money that accompanied the offer returned immediately.

76. The amount of earnest money deposit is determined by:

A. the real estate licensing statutes.
B. an agreement between the parties.
C. the broker's office policy on such matters.
D. the acceptable minimum of 5 percent of the purchase price.

Answer: B. Earnest money is a demonstration of sincerity on the part of the purchaser and provides preliminary evidence that he or she is financially capable of completing the transaction. While it should be substantial enough to meet these two criteria, there is no set or customary amount or percentage.

77. If the buyer defaulted some time ago on a written contract to purchase a seller's real estate, the seller can still sue for damages, if he is not prohibited from doing so by the:

A. statute of frauds.
B. law of agency.

C. statute of limitations.
D. broker-attorney accord.

Answer: C. Statutes of limitations exist to keep the legal system from getting bogged down in old disputes and allow for evidence and recollections to remain reasonably fresh. Civil limitations typically range from one to six years, though in some cases up to twenty-five years.

78. A competent and disinterested person who is authorized by another person to act in his or her place and sign a contract of sale is called:

A. an attorney in fact.
B. a substitute grantor.
C. a vendor.
D. an agent.

Answer: A. "Disinterested" means being able to act in an objective manner without any hidden motivation or prospect of gain. For example, a person who made a secret deal to sign a contract contrary to his client's best interests in exchange for an under-the-table payment would not be disinterested.

79. An option:

A. requires the optionor to complete the transaction.
B. gives the optionee an easement on the property.
C. does not keep the offer open for a specified time.
D. makes the seller liable for a commission.

Answer: A. It is up to the optionor (seller)to finish the transaction. The optionee (buyer) does not have to complete (close) on the property, but would lose whatever option monies that have been deposited.

80. When a prospective buyer makes a written purchase offer that the seller accepts, then the:

A. Buyer may take possession of the real estate.
B. Seller grants the buyer ownership rights.
C. Buyer receives legal title to the property.
D. Buyer receives equitable title to the property.

Answer: D. "Equitable title" means that the prospective buyer has obtained the right to acquire ownership of a property currently owned and occupied by another.

81. H agrees to purchase V's real estate for $230,000 and deposits $6,900 earnest money with Broker L. However, V is unable to clear the title to the property, and H demands the return of his earnest money as provided in the purchase contract. Broker L should:

A. Deduct his commission and return the balance to H.
B. Deduct his commission and give the balance to V.
C. Return the entire amount to H.
D. Give the entire amount to V to dispose of as he decides.

Answer: C. Brokers and salespeople only earn their commission when a transaction closes. Since the transaction was never completed, no commission is owed. Additionally, H is entitled to have all his earnest money returned since it was the seller, not he, who defaulted on the contract.

82. A buyer makes an earnest money deposit of $1,500 on a $15,000 property and then withdraws her offer before the seller can accept it. The broker is responsible for disposing of the earnest money by:

A. turning it over to the seller.
B. deducting the commission and giving the balance to the seller.
C. returning it to the buyer.
D. returning it to the buyer.

Answer: C. A contract only exists when it is both offered by the buyer and accepted by the seller. Since the second part of this requirement was never fulfilled, the buyer is entitled to have his earnest money returned.

83. Broker K arrives to present a purchase offer to Mrs. D, an 80 year old invalid who is not always of sound mind, and finds her son and her daughter-in-law present. In the presence of Broker K, both individuals persistently urge D to accept the offer, even though it is much lower than the price she has been asking for her home. If D accepts the offer, she may later claim that:

A. Broker K should not have brought her such a low offer for her property.
B. She was under undue duress from her son and daughter-in-law, and, therefore, the contract is voidable.
C. Broker K defrauded her by allowing her son and daughter-in-law to see the purchase offer he brought to her.
D. Her consumer protection rights have been usurped by her son and daughter-in-law.

Answer: B. "Duress" is the application of coercion or pressure to influence a person to act in a way contrary to his/her best interests. Further, since voluntary participation is a key condition of any contract, Mrs. D could well be successful in such an action. A voidable contract is one that is able to be voided because Mrs D was under duress or undue influence.

84. The law that requires real estate contracts to be in writing to be enforceable is the:

A. law of descent and distribution.
B. statute of frauds.
C. parole evidence rule.
D. statute of limitations.

Answer: B. Contrary to popular belief, the statute of frauds is not about specific actions defined as fraud, but the requirement in every state that certain documents be in writing, especially those pertaining to real estate. It's called the statute of frauds because it was first enacted in England in 1677 to prevent fraudulent claims of title.

85. A(n) _____ is when an owner takes his property off the market for a definite period of time in exchange for some consideration, but he grants the right to purchase the property within that period for a stated price.

A. option
B. contract of sale
C. right of first refusal
D. installment agreement

Answer: A. It's important to note that options generally give flexibility to only one side of the transaction. For example, let's say Barney is expecting a big promotion in six months and wants to buy Fred's house for $300,000 if it comes through. In exchange for keeping his home off the market for six months and agreeing to sell it to Barney for $300,000 at Barney's option, Barney gives Fred $3,000. The $3,000 is Fred's to keep no matter what. However, Barney is not obligated to buy Fred's house; it's his choice. Further, if he does get the promotion and wants to exercise his option, Fred must sell Barney his home for $300,000, even if market conditions have now made it worth more.

86. A breach of contract is a refusal or a failure to comply with the terms of the contract. If the seller breaches the purchase contract, the buyer may do all of the following EXCEPT:

A. Sue the seller for specific performance.

B. Rescind the contract and recover the earnest money.
C. Sue the seller for damages.
D. Sue the broker for non-performance.

Answer: D. While brokers and salespeople are responsible for bringing people together, they cannot be expected to know every detail of their circumstances or intent. Thus, if a buyer cannot get clear title or a seller is unexpectedly transferred, it is not the broker's fault the transaction failed and he or she bears no responsibility or liability.

87. To assign a contract for the sale of real estate means to:

A. Record the contract with the county recorder's office.
B. Permit another broker to act as agent for the principal.
C. Transfer one's rights under the contract.
D. Allow the seller and the buyer to exchange positions.

Answer: C. Assigning a contract means to transfer it to another.

88. The property manager suspects that the tenants in a property are engaging in illegal drug trafficking. What should the property manager do?

A. Cancel the property management agreement.
B. Observe the property for 30 days and then tell the owner.
C. Notify the owner immediately of the suspicious activity.
D. Don't worry. It's the owner's problem.

Answer: C. The property manager is the owner's agent, but not his "proxy." That is, he must inform the owner but not act on his behalf without authorization. For example, while calling the police to investigate might be appropriate, if the manager's suspicions were groundless and he called the authorities without authorization, the tenants might be able to sue the owner.

89. A zoning change has been announced that will result in the loss of value of the property to a property owner. What should a property manager do?

A. Advise the owner immediately.
B. Terminate the property management agreement.
C. Follow the owner's instructions that were previously given.
D. Keep his/her mouth shut.

Answer: A. Again, the property manager is the owner's "eyes and ears" for protecting the owner's best interests. Anything that can impact the property's value in either a positive or negative way should be communicated immediately.

90. A broker and seller terminate the listing contract. An offer is received in the mail by the broker after the termination of the listing contract. The offer is for full price and includes all of the terms and conditions of the seller. Why is this NOT a valid contract?

A. There is no consideration involved.
B. No acceptance has been given.
C. No earnest money has been enclosed.

D. There is no current listing agreement.

Answer: B. It has not been presented to or accepted by the owner. Remember, contracts aren't valid until both parties agree. However, even though the listing agreement has expired, the offer should be presented. If it's accepted and the transaction closes, the broker will generally be entitled to his or her full commission.

91. Which of the following is true if, after accepting an offer in writing, a seller withdraws acceptance and cancels the transaction?

A. The broker, having facilitated a written acceptance of an offer, is entitled to a commission and may deduct it from the deposit.
B. The broker, having facilitated a written acceptance of an offer, is entitled to compensation and may sue the seller for the commission.
C. The broker, in failing to successfully facilitate the transaction, is not entitled to any compensation.
D. The seller, having accepted an offer in writing, is bound by the offer and must proceed with the transaction.

Answer: B. Since the seller accepted the offer, the broker earned his or her commission and is entitled to sue the seller for that commission.

92. Grand Rapids Realty has entered agency agreements with both the McFaddens (sellers) and Jeanie Powers (a

buyer). Jeanie Powers is interested in making an offer on the McFaddens' ranch house. Is this allowable?

A. Yes, as long as both the McFaddens and Ms. Powers agree, in writing, to the dual agency.
B. Yes, as long as the McFaddens agree to be responsible for the commission.
C. Yes, as long as Grand Rapids Realty has written agency agreements on file for both the McFaddens and Ms. Powers.
D. No, dual agency is not allowable.

Answer: A. As long as both parties give written consent to the dual agency, the brokerage can represent both parties.

93. After a seller's listing agreement with ABC Realty expires, what restrictions exist if the seller decides to list with a different agency and ABC Realty has an interested buyer?

A. ABC Realty is barred from working with the seller due to previous client-agency confidentiality agreements and must refer the buyer to another agency.
B. ABC Realty may represent the buyer but may not disclose any information about the physical condition of the property.
C. ABC Realty may represent the buyer but may not disclose any information about offers made on the property when it was listed with ABC Realty.
D. ABC Realty may only represent the buyer if at least 60 days have passed since the termination of the listing agreement with the seller.

Answer: C. ABC Realty may certainly represent the buyer now that the listing agreement with the seller is terminated. Any information about physical condition of the property must be disclosed, but other information, such as knowledge of previous offers on the property, must remain confidential.

94. Which of the following is true in the case where a real estate salesperson refers buyers to a particular lender knowing that the lender pays a fee for referrals?

A. The salesperson has acted injudiciously.
B. The salesperson is well within the bounds of good business practice if a written buyer agency agreement exists.
C. The salesperson has acted in the best interests of the buyers if the lender offers a competitive interest rate and reasonable terms.
D. The salesperson may do so only upon informing the buyers of the referral fee.

Answer: A. The salesperson acted unwisely in this instance because only the employing broker can provide compensation.

95. For which of the following actions must an agency agreement exist between buyer and real estate office?

A. To provide a buyer with specifications of available properties
B. To explain agency relationships
C. To negotiate a reasonable price on a property
D. To provide information about prospective lenders' mortgage interest rates

Answer: C. In order to negotiate a transaction, an agency agreement must exist between the real estate office and the buyer; explanations of agency relationships, and information about available properties and mortgage interest rates may be provided before an agency agreement is entered.

96. Which of the following is true of buyer-brokerage contracts in Kentucky?

A. The appropriate form must be used for the contract to be valid.
B. The contract must be in writing to be enforceable.
C. Such contracts are not regulated.
D. Such contracts are illegal.

Answer: B. The buyer-brokerage agreement is an employment contract and must be in writing to be enforceable in Kentucky.

97. A broker serving as a dual agent may collect a commission from both parties if which of the following criteria is met?

A. If both the buyer and seller are represented by attorneys who have explained the dual agency
B. If both the buyer and the seller given informed consent to the dual compensation
C. If the broker is licensed to serve as a dual agent
D. If the buyer and the seller are related by blood.

Answer: B. If both the buyer and the seller give informed consent to the dual compensation, then a broker serving as a dual agent may collect compensation from both parties; neither attorney representation nor blood relationships are required.

98. Which of the following type of agency relationships is recognized in Kentucky?

A. Designated agency
B. Disclosed dual agency
C. Subagency
D. All of the above

Answer: D. Single agency (on behalf of either buyer or seller) and disclosed dual agency are the only types of agency relationships recognized in Kentucky.

99. According to the Kentucky Board of Real Estate Brokers and Salespersons, which of the following is NOT a required element of a listing agreement?

A. Exact expiration date
B. Signatures of both broker and seller
C. Qualified expert's report of property condition
D. True copy forwarded to the seller after signing

Answer: C. The rules regarding listing agreements call for an exact expiration date, signatures of both the broker and the seller, and a true copy to be made for the seller after signing; a qualified expert's report of property condition is not necessary.

100. In which of the following circumstances is a seller's disclosure statement NOT required?

A. If the property is a commercial property
B. If the seller is listing the property as "for sale by owner"
C. If the seller has not resided on premises for at least one year
D. If the buyer has resided on the property as a tenant

Answer: A. Seller property disclosure forms are mandatory in the sale of one-to-four dwelling units, whether or not the buyer or seller has resided on the premises recently; however, seller property disclosure forms are not required in the sale of commercial properties.

101. The seller's disclosure statement should be delivered to the buyer before which of the following events?

A. Before the buyer sees the property
B. Before the seller accepts an offer in writing
C. Before the home inspection
D. Before the closing

Answer: B. Before becoming obligated to an offer, the buyer should have the disclosure statement.

102. To whom may a real estate agent divulge confidential information about a client?

A. To no one; confidential information must be safeguarded in all cases

B. To the supervising broker for the purposes of obtaining advice or assistance for the client

C. To any associate working under the same supervising broker

D. To another client with whom a dual agency has been established and who has an established need for such information

Answer: B. An agent may only disclose a client's confidential information to a supervising broker for purposes of gaining advice or assistance for the client.

103. Which of the following is true regarding disclosure of deaths in the state of Kentucky?

A. Violent deaths must be disclosed.

B. Suicides must be disclosed.

C. AIDS-related deaths may not be disclosed.

D. Deaths from natural causes may never be disclosed

Answer: C. Federal fair housing laws prohibit disclosure of AIDS-related deaths, and Kentucky law absolves agents from liability for nondisclosure of stigmatized properties.

104. Which of the following conditions applies to a salesperson who is interested in purchasing a property listed with his or her supervising broker?

A. The salesperson must receive permission, in writing, from the Kentucky Board of Real Estate Brokers and Salespersons in order to make an offer on a listing held by the supervising broker.

B. The salesperson must resign his or her affiliation with the sponsoring broker and obtain a new sponsoring broker before becoming eligible to make an offer on the property.

C. The salesperson must inform the property owner, in writing, that he or she is a licensee in order to make an offer on the property.

D. The salesperson may not make an offer on a property listed by the supervising broker because Kentucky law forbids an agent with special knowledge of a transaction (i.e. access to confidential information) from personally benefiting from a transaction within 2 years of affiliation with an office.

Answer: C. Before making an offer, the agent must specify, in writing, to the owner that he or she is a licensee.

105. Cody Rand bought a house in January which was found to have a leaky basement during spring rainstorms five months later. Although the sellers had discussed the basement leaks with the listing agent, they had agreed not to divulge those details to prospective buyers. The broker claims that Cody did not specifically ask about the basement. As a result, which of the following options is open to Cody?

A. Since he did not specifically ask about the basement before buying the property, Cody has no legal redress in this situation.

B. Cody can sue the broker for nondisclosure of necessary information on the condition of a property.
C. Cody can sue the seller for nondisclosure of necessary information on the condition of the property.
D. Cody can sue the inspector for failure to detect a substantial flaw in the condition of the property.

Answer: B. Kentucky state law requires brokers to disclose all known material facts that affect a buyer's decision to make an offer, so Cody can sue the broker

106. At which point in proceedings would an agent be considered particularly remiss in their responsibilities if a written disclosure regarding agency relationships had not yet been distributed to a prospective buyer?

A. At an open house
B. At the time of showing properties
C. Upon first meeting
D. At the closing table

Answer: D. To wait until closing is considered irresponsible; an agent should provide the prospective buyer with information regarding agency relationships before the buyer shares any confidential details.

107. The Bormans (sellers) accept an offer from the Rodins (buyers) before providing the seller's disclosure statement. Which of the following actions may the Rodins take?

A. The Rodins may withdraw from proceedings any time prior to the closing.

B. The Rodins may sue the Bormans for not providing the mandatory disclosure statement.

C. The Rodins may sue the broker after closing for failure to provide the disclosure statement.

D. The Rodins must request a seller's disclosure statement within 72 hours of the seller's acceptance of their offer or the Rodins will have no legal grounds to terminate the agreement.

Answer: A. If the sellers did not provide the buyers with a seller's disclosure statement before accepting the buyers' offer, the buyers have the right to back out of the agreement at any time before the closing.

108. A buyer receives a seller's disclosure statement immediately after the seller accepts the offer. The statement discloses a crack in the foundation. Which of the following is true?

A. The buyer may require the seller to satisfactorily correct the crack in the foundation before the closing.

B. The buyer may void the offer on the property within 48 hours.

C. The buyer may void the offer on the property within 72 hours.

D. The buyer may make an addendum offer requesting reasonable compensation to cover the expense of correcting the foundation crack.

Answer: C. The buyer has 72 hours to void the offer based on information learned from the seller's disclosure statement.

109. Which of the following pieces of information is NOT considered confidential in a dual agency relationship?

A. The buyer's financial situation
B. That the buyer's offer exceeds the seller's minimum price
C. That the buyer would actually be willing and able to pay more than they offered
D. Comparable market data for the seller after the buyer has requested and received such information

Answer: D. Any information about the buyer's or seller's finances or minimum/maximum acceptable price is to be kept confidential, but comparable market data may be shared with the seller after the buyer has requested and received such information.

110. At which point must an agency relationship be formally established between the broker and a buyer or seller?

A. Prior to receiving any information that is considered confidential
B. Prior to showing any properties or making a substantial business contact
C. At least by the time that a written offer is tendered and accepted
D. At any time before the closing

Answer: A. The brokerage relationship with a buyer or seller must be determined before receiving any type of information that could be considered confidential.

111. Which of the following entities administers the real estate license law in Kentucky?

A. Kentucky Association of REALTORS®
B. Kentucky Board of Real Estate Brokers and Salespersons
C. Kentucky Department of Civil Rights
D. Department of Housing and Urban Development (HUD)

Answer: B. The Kentucky Board of Real Estate Brokers and Salespersons administers the license law while the Department of Civil Rights deals with fair housing complaints and HUD (federal agency) oversees housing issues. The state associate of REALTORS® is a trade association.

112. Who selects the members of the Kentucky Board of Real Estate Brokers?

A. Real estate licensees
B. State association of REALTORS®
C. The governor
D. The state house of representatives

Answer: C. The governor appoints members to the Kentucky Board of Real Estate Brokers and salespersons with the advice and consent of the senate.

113. Which of the following is required under Kentucky law?

A. Sellers must divulge all known material defects that might affect the sale.
B. Brokers must reveal any material defects that might affect the sale even if the seller has already done so in the seller's disclosure statement.
C. The broker must keep all information shared by the seller confidential.
D. The broker must share all relevant information provided by the seller.

Answer: A. The state of Kentucky requires sellers to reveal any known material defects that might affect the sale.

114. Which of the following actions is under the authority of the Kentucky Board of Real Estate Brokers and Salespersons?

A. Writing rules and regulations for real estate licensees to follow
B. Administering licensing exams at the testing sites
C. Enacting the laws that real estate licensees must follow
D. Composing examination questions for the state licensing exam

Answer: A. The Kentucky Board of Real Estate Brokers and Salespersons has the authority to write the rules and regulations that have the force of law while the legislature is charged with enacting law. An independent testing service writes test questions and administers the exams for state licensure.

115. In the following situations, which is NOT grounds for the Kentucky Board of Real Estate Brokers and Salespersons to initiate an investigation of a licensee?

A. The Board votes to investigate a random selection of licensees on an annual basis in an attempt to uncover illegal practices.
B. Mira Token has written a letter to the Board complaining about dissatisfaction with practices at Cartwright Brokerage, including their failure to appropriately advise her of agency relationships and to represent her interests adequately. Based on the letter, the Board decides to investigate the supervising broker.
C. By its own initiative the Board decides to investigate a licensee rumored to be in violation of license laws requiring disclosure statements.
D. Based on rumors of unfair and illegal practices, a member of the Board makes a motion to investigate a licensee suspected of corrupt practice.

Answer: A. The Board may investigate for any legitimate reason based on a motion passed by members, their own initiative, or a written complaint from a disgruntled customer but not based on random selection.

116. In Kentucky, which of the following individuals needs a real estate license?

A. Miller Reeve and his partner, Don Brock, are selling an apartment they own jointly.
B. Patty Lehmann is a leasing agent who employs 2 other leasing agents.
C. Hayley Jones is a tenant of Somerset Village Apartments who receives half off her monthly rent for the referral of prospective tenants.
D. Brent Hughes is a licensed attorney acting under a power of attorney to convey real estate to the nephew of a deceased client.

Answer: B. Neither someone selling their own property nor a tenant receiving a consideration of half of one month's rent or less nor anyone holding a power of attorney needs to be a licensed real estate agent. A person who employs any apartment leasing agents, however, is required to be a licensed real estate broker or salesperson.

117. All of the following individuals are exempt from having a real estate license EXCEPT which one?

A. Home Hunters, a non-profit real estate referral service
B. Coast-2-Coast, a company that charges a flat fee to match business people from across the country who wish to exchange properties and assists them in doing so
C. Myles Lewis, executor of his uncle's will, who is selling his deceased uncle's house per terms of the will
D. Jewel Morton, a full-time student who refers prospective tenants in exchange for $100 off her monthly rent of $400

Answer: B. Any company that matches individuals and properties for a fee is required to have a real estate license, but non-profits, court-appointed designees, and tenants who receive consideration of one-half month's rent or less for referrals are exempt from needing a real estate license.

118. All of the following activities are considered to be "engaging in the real estate business" EXCEPT which one?

A. Collecting apartment rent
B. Building residential homes
C. Selling residential homes
D. Reselling manufactured houses

Answer: B. Builders of residential homes fall under the jurisdiction of residential builders licensing requirements, but selling real estate, reselling manufactured homes, and collecting rent for use of real estate are all considered real estate business activities.

119. An applicant for the real estate licensing exam in Kentucky must submit which of the following along with an application?

A. A current photo
B. A sworn statement attesting to the applicant's character
C. An appropriate fee
D. A recommendation letter from a real estate education instructor

Answer: C. The appropriate fee must accompany all applications for the licensing exam in Kentucky.

120. Is an office manager in violation of the license law if she performs the following activities without a salesperson's license: coordinating the flow of paperwork, preparing advertising copy, hiring and supervising clerical support staff.

A. Yes, the office manager is in violation of the license law because she is performing duties that require a real estate license.
B. Yes, all people working in a broker's office in direct contact with confidential information are required to hold a salesperson's license.
C. No, she is not in violation of the license law because she is performing non-real estate activities that do not require licensure.
D. No, she is not in violation of the license law because she is not showing properties to clients or interacting with them outside the agency office.

Answer: C. The office manager is not in violation of the license law because all of the activities specified are non-real estate activities which do not require licensure.

121. Which of the following is NOT a requirement for obtaining a broker's license in Kentucky?

A. Upstanding moral character

B. Active employment as a licensed salesperson for at least 3 years (or equivalent)
C. Completion of 90 hours of approved post-license real estate education coursework
D. Minimum age of 21

Answer: D. The minimum age for a broker candidate is at least 18 years of age, and broker candidates must show evidence of completion of 90 hours of approved real estate courses after receiving the salesperson's license, active status as a licensed salesperson for at least three years (or equivalent), and good moral character.

122. For what period of time will a passing score on a licensing examination be valid?

A. 90 days
B. 6 months
C. 1 year
D. 2 years

Answer: C. A passing examination score is valid for a period of one year from the date of examination.

123. None of the following transactions requires a real estate license EXCEPT which one?

A. The daughter of a couple living abroad has written authorization to sell her parents' home.

B. An entrepreneur negotiates the sales of businesses, including equipment and buildings, for a fee.

C. An apartment superintendent shows units to prospective tenants as part of his general duties.

D. An individual owns and personally manages a six-unit apartment building including collecting rents, showing available units, and providing maintenance.

Answer: B. A real estate license is required to sell a building but not to negotiate a sale for which written authorization is given or to manage one's own building.

Superintendents who show units in the course of normal work are specifically exempt from the requirement to hold a license.

124. An applicant for a real estate license in Kentucky must meet which of the following requirements?

A. Demonstrate good moral character

B. Show proof of passing the license examination within a two-year period prior to date of application for licensure

C. Be at least 21 years old

D. Provide evidence of at least two years of college (or equivalent work experience)

Answer: A. An applicant for licensure must be of good moral character, at least 18 years old, and must have passed the licensing exam within one year of the date of application.

125. What penalty may an unlicensed individual who engages in activities deemed to constitute real estate business face for a first-time offense?

A. A fine not to exceed $250
B. Imprisonment of not more than 30 days
C. A fine not to exceed $500
D. Community service of 90 hours

Answer: C. An unlicensed individual charged with a first-time misdemeanor of performing activities requiring a license may be subject to a penalty of a fine not to exceed $500, imprisonment not to exceed 90 days, or both.

126. On what date do real estate salespersons' licenses expire in Kentucky?

A. January 31 of each year
B. October 31 of each year
C. January 31 of every odd-numbered year
D. October 31 of every even-numbered year

Answer: B. Real estate salespersons' licenses expire annually on October 31.

**127. What is the renewal requirement for a salesperson's or broker's license in
Kentucky?**

A. The licensee must have completed six hours of continuing education during each year of the three year license cycle for a total of 18 hours of class time.
B. The licensee need only remit a fee of $250.
C. The licensee must show documentation of active status as a real estate agent.
D. The licensee must have completed a prescribed sequence of continuing education courses in fair housing, real estate law, and finance management in the past three years of licensure.

Answer: A. 6 clock hours every renewal year; 18 hours per 3 year cycle

128. What is the deadline to renew an expired license without financial penalty?

A. There is no grace period without financial penalty after the expiration date.
B. 30 days
C. 60 days
D. 90 days

Answer: A. A licensee with an expired license has 60 days to remit both the required license fee and a late renewal fee in order to renew the expired license.

129. Which of the following is true of continuing education coursework required for license renewal?

A. There are no mandatory continuing education requirements.

B. A minimum of 6 hours of approved continuing education courses must be completed every renewal year.
C. Specified classes in listing, ethics, and fair housing must be completed on a biennial basis for license renewal.
D. Of the 6 hours of continuing education required during each license period, at least 3 hours must be from a list of core real estate classes specified by the Board.

Answer: B. To renew a salesperson's or broker's license in Kentucky, the licensee must have completed six hours of continuing education every renewal year, and 18 hours per the 3 year license cycle.

130. Besides remitting the appropriate fee, a salesperson who has failed to renew her license for three full years must take all of the following steps EXCEPT:

A. Take a 40-hour salesperson prelicense class.
B. Take and pass the state salesperson's licensing exam.
C. Complete a new application for licensure.
D. Submit a written appeal to the Kentucky Board of Real Estate Brokers and Salespersons petitioning for reinstatement of the expired license.

Answer: D. A salesperson who fails to renew her license within three full years is required to make a new application, remit the appropriate fee, complete a 40-hour prelicensure course, and take and pass the salesperson's licensing exam.

131. Barbara Walker, a real estate salesperson, has let her license lapse for 27 months. What must she do to renew her license at this point?

A. Complete 6 hours of approved continuing education for the licensing year and submit a new application along with the appropriate fee.
B. Submit an application, the appropriate fee, and a letter explaining the licensee's reasons for allowing the license to lapse for a prolonged period of time.
C. Retake the state licensing exam and submit a new application with the appropriate fee.
D. Remit the required licensing fee along with a late renewal fee of $75 for each full or partial twelve-month period since license expiration.

Answer: A. To renew her license at this point, Barbara must complete six hours of approved continuing education coursework and submit a new application with the required fees.

132. Which of the following activities is an unlicensed real estate assistant unable to perform?

A. Assemble and collate legal documents for a closing
B. Prepare and distribute promotional flyers and materials
C. Compute commission checks for active agents
D. Clarify the details of simple contract documents for prospective buyers

Answer: D. An unlicensed real estate assistant in Kentucky may not explain simple contract documents to a buyer but may perform a range of secretarial duties under the supervision and approval of the licensee for whom they work.

133. According to Kentucky law, which of the following statements about personal real estate assistants applies?

A. A personal real estate assistant must hold a real estate license.
B. A personal real estate assistant may not be licensed.
C. An unlicensed personal real estate assistant may perform general secretarial duties such as inserting factual information into contracts under the supervision of the employing broker.
D. An unlicensed personal real estate assistant may host open houses and staff booths at home shows independently with the employing broker's knowledge and authorization.

Answer: C. The duties of an unlicensed personal real estate assistant are limited to ministerial duties performed under the guidance and approval of the employing broker; however, an assistant may become licensed to perform a wider range of services for the employing licensee.

134. Ron Sidwell is an Indiana resident who wishes to obtain a Kentucky real estate broker's license. What must he do?

A. Establish a principal place of business in Kentucky or be licensed under a resident
Kentucky broker
B. File an irrevocable consent agreement in Indiana
C. Be a licensed salesperson or broker in any state

D. Complete all education course requirements in Indiana

Answer: A. As a nonresident who wishes to be licensed in Kentucky, Ron must establish a principal place of business in Kentucky or be licensed under a resident Kentucky broker; he must also file an irrevocable consent agreement in Kentucky.

135. Cara, an unlicensed real estate assistant for a successful broker, has been indispensable in facilitating a recent transaction. She put in many extra hours working closely with the prospective buyers, explaining transaction details, and encouraging them to accept the seller's counteroffer. At the culmination of the sale, the broker wishes to compensate Cara for her efforts. Which of the following is true under Kentucky law?

A. The broker may not pay a commission to Cara because they are both in violation of the license law regarding unlicensed assistants.
B. The broker may reward Cara with a commission only if she is working as an independent contractor.
C. The broker may compensate Cara with a gift of tangible personal property but is not permitted to pay a commission for services provided as an unlicensed assistant.
D. The broker may compensate Cara for her services by paying her a percentage of the broker's commission for the sale.

Answer: A. Unlicensed assistants are not permitted to perform such services as explaining contractual details to clients, so the broker and Cara are in violation of the license law.

136. An on-site apartment manager negotiates apartment leases in the normal course of business. Which of the following statements is true?

A. The apartment manager is violating apartment law.
B. The apartment manager must hold a real estate license.
C. The apartment manager must hold a property manager's license.
D. The apartment manager is exempt from real estate licensing requirements because he/she lives on site.

Answer: B. An on-site manager who negotiates apartment leases must hold a real estate salesperson's or broker's license.

137. Which of the following individuals is NOT exempt from the provisions of the Kentucky Real Estate License Act?

A. An apartment tenant who receives half off her monthly rent for referring a new tenant to the owner.
B. A resident property manager responsible for maintenance
C. A property owner engaged in selling or leasing his own property
D. An individual who accepts fees to recruit prospective buyers or renters of real estate

Answer: D. Anyone who receives a fee for finding prospective buyers or renters of real estate must hold a real estate license.

138. Milton Wesley wants to list his single-family home for sale. Which of the following statements is applicable to him?

A. If he is a licensed attorney, he may list his property himself without engaging the services of a real estate licensee.
B. He does not need a real estate license to sell his house on his own.
C. He must first obtain a real estate license to be eligible to sell real estate, including his own home.
D. He must apply for and receive a temporary license from the Kentucky Board of Real Estate Brokers and Salespersons to legally sell his house.

Answer: B. In Kentucky, any property owner may sell or rent his own house without obtaining a real estate license.

139. Which of the following steps is required of an applicant for a real estate salesperson's license in Kentucky?

A. Demonstrate United States citizenship
B. Provide evidence of an associate degree or equivalent in real estate from an approved school
C. Complete a 40-hour course in the general principles of real estate
D. Complete an application for licensure and submit it, along with a statement of goals and a recommendation from a sponsoring broker

Answer: C. The first step an individual must take in obtaining a Kentucky real estate salesperson's license is to complete an approved 40-hour course in general real estate principles.

Neither a college degree nor United States citizenship is a requirement for licensure.

140. The annual continuing education requirement in Kentucky can be satisfied by which of the following?

A. 6 hours of coursework offered by an approved CE sponsor
B. A 4-hour course on real estate office management software offered through the local community college
C. An approved professional internship of at least 15 hours with a broker other than the sponsoring broker
D. Documentation of weekly supervision with the sponsoring broker over the course of
52 weeks to discuss professional issues related to the licensee's development

Answer: A. To renew a Kentucky salesperson's license, the licensee must complete a 6- hour course offered by an approved CE sponsor.

141. Which of the following is true of Kentucky real estate licenses?

A. They expire on October 31 after a three-year period of licensure.
B. They expire on October 31 after a two-year period of licensure.
C. They are renewed automatically unless a licensee is on probation or holds a license that has been previously suspended or revoked.

D. They expire annually on the anniversary date of the individual salesperson's license.

Answer: A. All Kentucky real estate licenses expire on October 31 after a three-year period of licensure.

142. Barry Gordon holds a Kentucky broker's license but claims Illinois as his home state. Which of the following is true?

A. He is exempt from the requirement to maintain a place of business in Kentucky as long as he has an office in Illinois.
B. He must maintain a physical office in Kentucky regardless of whether or not he operates an office in Illinois.
C. He need not maintain a physical office in Kentucky as long as he employs at least one Kentucky licensee as a salesperson or associate broker.
D. As long as he concurrently maintains an active broker's license in Illinois, he is exempt from any requirement to maintain physical office space in Kentucky.

Answer: B. Barry must maintain a physical office in Kentucky to retain his Kentucky broker's license.

143. Which one of the following circumstances would NOT warrant revocation of a broker's license in Kentucky?

A. Acceptance of a commission rate above the average amount
B. Felony conviction
C. Intermingling escrow funds with personal accounts

D. Incomplete or misidentification of status as a real estate licensee in advertising materials

Answer: A. Since commission rates are always negotiable, acceptance of an above average commission rate does not warrant revocation of a license; however, intermingling funds, felony conviction, and failure to identify licensee status in advertising materials may all result in revocation of a licensee's license.

144. In which of the following circumstances must an individual be licensed as a real estate salesperson or broker?

A. To construct houses
B. To buy a house for personal use
C. To sell one's own property
D. To sell 30 newly constructed homes in a popular subdivision

Answer: D. Individuals may buy, sell, rent, or build their own homes without a license, but builders who sell more than 4 homes a year need to be licensed or employ a licensed broker.

145. A salesperson's license may be revoked in which of the following circumstances?

A. She establishes an exclusive-right-to-sell listing contract with sellers.
B. She sells her primary residence without engaging a broker's aid.

C. She represents a buyer in a transaction after providing information on agency relationships.
D. She deposits a buyer's earnest money into her personal savings account.

Answer: D. Commingling escrow funds with personal funds is grounds for revocation of the salesperson's license.

146. Which of the following actions performed by a licensee is NOT a violation of the license law?

A. Placing a For Sale sign before receiving the owner's consent
B. Assisting a co-worker with illegally passing the licensing examination
C. Placing a newspaper ad that identifies the licensee as such
D. Being declared mentally incompetent

Answer: C. Identifying one's status as a licensee in advertising is required, so such an action will not result in revocation of a salesperson's license; however, being declared mentally incompetent, helping someone cheat on a licensing exam, and placing a For Sale sign without the owner's permission are all grounds for revocation of the salesperson's license.

147. All of the following are violations of the license law EXCEPT which one?

A. Shawn Birk, a broker, offers employment to successful new licensees on site at a testing center.

B. Amelia Lands, a licensed salesperson, publicizes an open house attendance prize drawing to entice attendees.
C. Wayne Janson discourages a seller from accepting an offer based on the fact that the prospective buyer is a practicing Catholic.
D. Myra Wells places a For Sale sign on the Lohmans' property after receiving written permission to do so.

Answer: D. A broker must have permission before placing a For Sale sign, so Myra is following the license law. Brokers are not permitted to solicit information or offer employment at a testing site, to use a promotion involving a game of chance, or to encourage client decision-making based on religious grounds.

148. What information must be included in a real estate salesperson's directory listing along with his name?

A. Roy Walters, Real Estate Salesperson, Residential Property Specialist. Sponsoring broker: Willie James.
B. Roy Walters, Real Estate Salesperson, Residential Property Specialist. 505 Waters St., Suite B.
C. Roy Walters, Real Estate Salesperson, Residential Property Specialist. Licensed since
January 1999.
D. Roy Walters, Real Estate Salesperson, Residential Property Specialist. License valid through October 31 of current year.

Answer: A. All advertising must be done in the sponsoring broker's name, but the licensee need not specify street address or license information (including license number, year licensed, or license expiration date).

149. Real estate licensees must include which of the following pieces of information when advertising real estate?

A. The licensee's phone number and street address
B. The name of a licensed real estate broker
C. The property owner's name and address
D. Nothing more than a phone number to call for information

Answer: B. All advertising must include the name of the employing broker. The licensee does not need to indicate her address or identify the owner of the property, but listing nothing more than a phone number would be considered a blind ad and is impermissible.

150. What specific content is required for a web site developed by a broker's office?

A. Nothing governs the content of web sites for brokerage offices.
B. Names of active licensees working for the broker must be listed.
C. Information about agency relationships must be prominently placed on the home page.
D. The name and addresses of the office and any states in which the brokerage holds licenses must be specified.

Answer: D. Brokerage web sites must include the brokerage's name, office address, and states of licensure on each screen of the web site.

151. A real estate licensee has a buyer agency agreement. What is the seller in this situation?

A. a customer
B. a client
C. a fiduciary
D. an agent

Answer: A. There's an important distinction between client and customer. Unless there is a specific agreement to the contrary, licensees represent only one side in a transaction. In this case, it's the buyer who is the client and it's the licensee's obligation to negotiate a deal that's in that person's best interests, not the one that's fairest to both parties.

152. An optionor and an optionee make a contract for an option on a commercial piece of property. If the optionee decides to exercise his option, when must he perform?

A. He must exercise his option within 6 months under state law.
B. He must exercise his option under the terms of the option contract.
C. He must exercise his option under the terms of the option contract.
D. He can exercise his option whenever he wants.

Answer: B. Options are generally concerned with only two things: time and price. Whatever the parties agree to in those regards defines the terms of the option and the obligations of the parties.

153. When can a landlord evict a disabled blind or disabled tenant from the premises?

A. If the tenant gets a dog and the apartment policy does not allow pets
B. If the tenant insists on a handicapped parking place
C. If the tenant makes modifications to his unit at his expense
D. If the tenant has loud parties and makes too much noise

Answer: D. The law requires reasonable accommodation--for example, allowing a guide dog for a blind person even if there's a no pets policy. However, that does not mean that all rules are suspended. Noise, safety, and use of premises policies may still be enforced.

154. Broker Carr, with ABC Real Estate Company, listed the property with a seller. Broker Smith, with XYZ Real Estate Company, called Broker Carr, and disclosed that he was a Buyer Agent. Broker Smith wrote a contract with a buyer for the sale of the property. What, if any, is the relationship between the buyer's broker, the seller and the listing broker?

A. There is not a relationship between the parties. Broker Carr represents the Seller and Broker Smith represents the Buyer.
B. customer
C. agency

D. dual agency

Answer: A. Since each broker represents separate sides in the transaction, no relationship exists.

155. A buyer bought a property without telling the seller of his intended purpose for the property. The contract contains no contingency clauses and it is a properly executed contract. After the closing, the buyer is unable to obtain the zoning he needs for his commercial project. What is the contract at this stage?

A. void
B. voidable
C. breach
D. enforceable

Answer: D. Since there were no contingency clauses, and no restrictive covenants of record. If the buyer cannot secure a change of zoning , the contract is perfectly valid as stands and is enforceable between the parties.

156. The seller and the buyer finally agreed to a purchase price of $203,500 with the closing to occur on June 15, 2011. The taxes for the year 2011 in the amount of $2,500 have not been paid by the seller. (Taxes are paid in arrears). How much would the tax proration amount to, and how would it appear on a full settlement statement? Base your answer on a 365 day year, and the buyer is responsible for the day of settlement.

A. $1,130.14 debit the seller and credit the buyer
B. $1,130.14 debit the buyer and credit the seller
C. $2,500 credit the seller and debit the buyer
D. Nothing. The seller does not owe since the buyer is buying

Answer: A. The seller would owe money, and the buyer would receive money, because the seller has not paid the taxes. $2,500 divided by 365 is $6.849315 times the actual days of 165 is $1,130.14.

157. A seller listed his home for six months on February 26. On April 29, a buyer made an offer on the property. The listing broker presented the offer to the seller on April 30. The seller accepted the offer on May 1, with the closing to occur on June 15. Assuming the closing took place on June 15, when did the listing expire?

A. 26-May-04
B. 15-Jun-04
C. 26-Aug-04
D. 15-Dec-04

Answer: B. Listing contracts set forth the terms and conditions under which a broker will sell a property for his or her client. When the closing takes place, the terms of the contract have been fulfilled and it expires automatically.

158. The sellers listed their property for six months on February 26 for $104,500. They agreed to pay the listing

broker a 7% commission at closing on the agreed upon sale price. A buyer made an offer on the property on March 29 for $102,000. The seller countered the offer on April 1 at $103,500, and the buyer accepted the counter offer with the closing to occur on June 15. How much commission did the seller owe the listing broker, and how would it appear on the settlement statement?

A. $3,622.50. Debit the seller.
B. $7,140. Credit the seller.
C. $7,315. Debit the seller.
D. $7,245. Debit the seller.

Answer: D. Commissions are paid based on the actual selling price, not the listing price. Additionally, since the broker represented the sellers in this transaction, the commission is debited from their side of the ledger.

159. The seller and the buyer agreed to a purchase price of $103,500 with the closing to occur on June 15. The seller's loan balance after the June 1 payment was $39,440. with an interest rate of 10%.The monthly payment was $440 principal and interest. What was the loan balance the day of closing, and how much interest did the seller owe the bank?

A. loan balance $39,440; interest due $10,350
B. loan balance $39,000; interest due $3,944
C. loan balance $39,000; interest due $862.50
D. loan balance $39,440; interest due $164.33

Answer: D. Although many types of loans can become more complex in their calculations of remaining principal and interest at a particular point in time, in this case the interest portion of the payment is calculated simply by multiplying $39,440 by 10% and dividing by twelve. That results in monthly interest of $328.66, with half that amount, or $164.33 added to the principal payment at closing.

160. The buyer and seller agreed to a purchase price of $103,500. The buyer received an 80% loan. How much was the buyer's loan and how did it appear on the settlement statement?

A. $103,500. Credit the buyer and debit the seller.
B. $100,000. Debit both the seller and the buyer.
C. $ 95,000. Credit both the seller and the buyer.
D. $ 82,800. Credit the buyer only.

Answer: D. Mortgage monies are credited to the buyer's side of the ledger as a portion of the funds he or she will use to complete the transaction. Once all the funds have been accounted for, the monies (less appropriate deductions) transfer to the seller.

161. A home improvement company was negotiating with a homeowner to add on two rooms to a home. The company agreed to take a second mortgage as long as the homeowner also included the rest of the property in the loan. The company and the homeowner agreed to a price and the company provided the necessary disclosure form on Monday

and the homeowner signed the agreement at noon the following day. Assuming that the week had five business days, until what time could the homeowner rescind the loan?

A. Tuesday, midnight
B. Thursday, midnight
C. Friday, midnight
D. There is no rescission on a house.

Answer: C. Because agreement was reached and SIGNED documents were provided on TUESDAY, Friday midnight ends the THREE-business-day period

162. The seller under a land contract is called:

A. the grantor.
B. the grantee.
C. the vendor.
D. the vendee.

Answer: C. Land contracts are also known as installment contracts. In this type of arrangement, the buyer occupies the property, but the title is held in the name of the seller until some future point in time--often when the last payment is made.

163. On an 8% straight term loan of $6,071, the borrower paid total interest of $1,700. How long did he have the loan?

A. 30 months
B. 36 months

C. 42 months
D. 48 months

Answer: C. Eight percent of $6,071 is $486 per year or $40.50 per month. $1,700 divided by $40.50 means the borrower held the loan for forty-two months.

164. The finance charges recorded on the Truth in Lending statements would include all of the following EXCEPT:

A. loan fees charged by the lender.
B. insurance premiums for mortgage insurance payment.
C. discount points and service fees.
D. recording fees and title insurance premiums.

Answer: D. These are considered legal, not financing fees and therefore are not part of the Truth in Lending statement.

165. A mortgage broker:

A. arranges loans between borrowers and investors.
B. is a lender.
C. buys mortgages in the secondary mortgage market.
D. buys mortgages and resells them at a profit.

Answer: A. Mortgage brokers function much like independent insurance agents and represent a variety of lenders. Their role is to match the circumstances of individual buyers with the mortgage program best suited to their needs.

166. The Smiths' purchased a residence for $75,000. They made a down payment of $15,000 and agreed to assume the seller's existing mortgage, which had a current balance of $23,000. The Smiths' financed the remaining $37,000 of the purchase price by executing a second mortgage whereby the seller became a mortgagee. This type of loan is called a:

A. wraparound mortgage.
B. package mortgage.
C. balloon note.
D. part purchase mortgage.

Answer: D. Also known as a purchase money second, this is a streamlined and often cost-effective financing option.

167. On a $50,000 loan the borrower is required to pay two points. How much does the borrower have to pay the lender?

A. $49,000.00
B. $50,000.00
C. $51,000.00
D. $52,000.00

Answer: C. One point equals one percent; thus two points are two percent of $50,000, or $1,000, which becomes part of the buyer's total obligation to the lender.

168. The discount points charged by a lender on a federal VA or FHA loan are a percentage of the:

A. sales price.
B. appraised price.
C. loan amount.
D. down payment.

Answer: C. Like points, discount points are one-time charges equal to one percent of the loan amount for each point charged.

169. An increase in the availability of money would lead to which effect?

A. Interest rates would go up.
B. Interest rates would go down.
C. Interest rates would NOT be affected due to RESPA guidelines.
D. Interest rates would NOT be affected due to TRUTH IN LENDING.

Answer: B. Just like most things in a free market economy, mortgage loans are subject to the laws of supply and demand. Thus, when there is more mortgage money in the market place looking for a home, borrowers have more choices, which leads to increased competition among lenders, which leads to lower interest rates.

170. When the amortized payment of a mortgage remains constant over the period of the loan but leaves an

outstanding balance to be paid at the end, this payment is called:

A. an escalation payment.
B. a balloon payment.
C. a satisfaction payment
D. an acceleration payment.

Answer: B. Typically, mortgages with balloon payments are used as a creative financing tool in which buyers plan to refinance the balance in three to five years with better terms than they can qualify for now.

171. In an installment land contract, what type of title did the seller retain?

A. joint
B. legal
C. equitable
D. record

Answer: B. In this type of contract, the BUYER doesn't receive legal title to the property until the final payment is made. The BUYER receives equitable title at closing, and upon final payment to the seller receives legal title.

172. Which of the following is true of a second mortgage?

A. It has priority over a first mortgage.
B. It cannot be used as a security instrument.

C. It is not negotiable.
D. It is usually issued at a higher rate of interest.

Answer: D. Second mortgages carry higher risk for lenders because they're second in line after the first mortgage holder. In case of foreclosure, that means the first mortgage holder is paid in full before any remaining monies are distributed. This added exposure typically results in higher interest rates.

173. Usury MOST nearly means:

A. making loans without the benefit of co-signors.
B. lending money at fluctuating interest rates.
C. being capable of multiple usage.
D. illegal interest.

Answer: D. Each state sets its own ceiling for the maximum interest rate lenders may charge. Rates above that ceiling are considered usurious and illegal. No reputable lender exceeds those rates and those that make a practice of it are commonly known as loan sharks.

174. A borrower bought a $74,000 house with no down payment. The loan was probably:

A. a conventional insured loan.
B. a VA loan.
C. an FHA loan.
D. a conventional loan.

Answer: B. VA loans are zero-down instruments, while FHA loans permit low down payments in the 5% range.

175. A house sold for $42,000. The buyer made a 20% down payment. Monthly interest on the loan was $252. What was the interest rate on the loan?

A. 5%
B. 7%
C. 9%
D. 11%

Answer: C. With a 20% down payment of $8,400, the buyer had a mortgage of $33,600. Since interest is expressed in annual terms, multiply the monthly payment of $252 times twelve. That yields an annual interest cost of $3,024, divided by the principal balance of $33,600, yields an annual rate of 9%.

176. Which of the following describes a mortgage that requires principal and interest payments at regular intervals and is called the liquidation of debt by periodic installment until the debt is satisfied?

A. amortized loan
B. annuity loan
C. acceleration loan
D. assemblage loan

Answer: A. This question is a formal description of amortized loans--the most common form of mortgage where monthly payments include both principal and interest (as opposed to balloon or interest-only seconds). Typically, monthly payment amounts remain constant, while the interest portion is higher in the earlier years, giving homeowners a larger tax deduction with higher percentages of principal paid in the later years.

177. Under RESPA, a copy of REAL ESTATE SETTLEMENT COSTS AND YOU must be given:

A. within one day before closing.
B. at the time of loan application, or within 3 days of application.
C. within 5 days of application.
D. at closing.

Answer: B. The intent of RESPA--the federal Real Estate Settlement Procedures Act—is to make borrowers more aware of costs and charges. Accordingly, it should be given at the time of application and no later than three days after that.

178. The clause in a trust deed or mortgage which permits the mortgagee to declare the entire unpaid sum due upon a default by a mortgagor is called:

A. a judgment clause.
B. an acceleration clause.
C. an escalator clause.
D. a forfeiture clause.

Answer: B. Acceleration clauses are stipulations that if certain events occur, such as not making payments, the entire amount of the mortgage can become due. Most typically, this is seen in Due on sale clauses that require the mortgage balance be paid in full at the time the house is sold.

179. An impound or reserve account MOST benefits whom?

A. the borrower
B.1 the lender
C. the trustee
D. the trustor

Answer: B. Also known as escrow accounts, impound accounts accumulate funds from closing costs and monthly payments to ensure that property taxes and homeowner's insurance are kept current.

180. The lender is not insured or guaranteed against a loss, by reason of the borrower's default in repayment, under which type of loan?

A. FHA
B. Conventional
C. VA
D. GI

Answer: B. Government-sponsored loan programs such as FHA are not actually loans, but guarantees to lenders to encourage them to make favorable mortgages available to qualifying individuals.

181. A VA loan may be granted for the purchase of a one-family to four-family property if:

A. The veteran certifies the rent collected will equal the mortgage payments.
B. The loan will be amortized for not more than 20 years.
C. The down payment will be at least 10%.
D. The veteran agrees to live there.

Answer: D. Although the rules and terms can fluctuate, the low down payment and below market interest features of VA loans come with the condition that the borrower live in the property.

182. Which of the following would usually occur in a sale-and-leaseback transaction?

A. The seller gets a return on the purchase in the form of rental payments.
B. The property is sold on the condition that the new owner lease it back to the seller at the time title passes.
C. The buyer keeps capital in inventories rather than in realty.
D. The rent that the seller pays is not income-tax deductible.

Answer: B. A sale-leaseback is usually used for the purpose of creating cash flow from a commercial property. As the name implies, the owner transfers title to the buyer in exchange for cash, then leases the property back at a monthly rate while continuing to run his business from that location or otherwise use the property.

183. A standardized yardstick expressing the true annual cost of borrowing is expressed as the what?

A. ECOA
B. Regulation Z
C. APR
D. RESPA

Answer: C. APR stands for Annual Percentage Rate and expresses the true cost of the loan by factoring fees such as points, recording fees, appraisal fees and such into the interest rate. For example, a mortgage that showed an interest rate of 4.85% on the promissory note might have an APR of 5% when associated costs are factored in.

184. RESPA would prohibit which of the following acts?

A. steering
B.1 paying of kickbacks
C. blockbusting
D. redlining

Answer: B. RESPA concerns itself only with educating consumers about the true costs of borrowing and standardizing lending practices. As such, referral fees are prohibited.

185. In most states, by paying the debt after a foreclosure sale, the mortgagor has the right to regain the property. What is this right called?

A. equitable right of redemption
B. owner's right of redemption
C. vendee's right of redemption
D. statutory right of redemption

Answer: D. This right of redemption is called statutory because it is legally mandated by law, as opposed to a custom lenders could follow or not at their option.

186. The lender is required, under RESPA, to provide a detailed GOOD FAITH ESTIMATE statement at the time of loan application or within three business days to:

A. the buyer.
B. the seller.
C. the buyer and seller.
D. neither the buyer nor the seller.

Answer: A. The good faith part of this requirement is the key element to consumers. By standardizing the forms and disclosures used by lenders, borrowers are no longer surprised by substantial and hidden costs at the time of closing.

187. In which of the following markets may a lender sell a loan that a mortgage banker has previously originated?

A. primary market
B. secondary market
C. mortgage market
D. consumer market

Answer: B. Many homeowners are surprised the first time they receive a letter from a lender they've never heard of informing them that they now hold the mortgage on their home and that future payments should be sent to them. This secondary market is where lenders buy and sell mortgages to balance their portfolios according to market conditions and their internal needs and objectives. It should be noted that the terms of mortgages bought and sold cannot be changed by the new note holders.

188. Which of the following is considered a conventional loan?

A. FHA insured
B. VA guaranteed
C. commercial bank's ARM loan
D. contract for deed

Answer: C. Once considered a form of creative financing, ARMs are now standard, conventional loans. Options A and B are part of various government programs to help low and moderate income families as well as veterans find affordable home financing.

189. Under an FHA graduated payment mortgage, which of the following fluctuates over the term of the loan?

A. interest rate
B. monthly payments
C. finance charge
D. annual rate

Answer: B. Graduated payment mortgages are aimed particularly at young families who expect to see their earnings rise over the next five to ten years. As such, payments for interest and principal are less than the actual costs in the early years and gradually rise to make up the difference.

190. The maximum permissible loan to value ratios are:

A. based on sale price or appraised value, whichever is lower.
B. not determined by federal statute in the case of FHA loans.
C. based on the banker's competitive market analysis.
D. fixed by law for conventional loans.

Answer: A. Although various banks, mortgage companies and programs have different LTVs, the lower, more conservative number is used.

191. All of the following are true of conventional loans except what?

A. They are made to the buyer without governmental insurance or guarantee.

B. The policy requirements of the lenders are not uniform.
C. The requirements to qualify are uniformly fixed by state law.
D. They require a higher down payment than non-conventional loans.

Answer: C. Not only are guidelines not uniform, qualification standards can vary enormously from lender to lender. There are no state-mandated qualifying requirements for conventional loans.

192. A buyer wants to take out an FHA loan. The broker should refer the buyer directly to:

A. any approved lending institution such as a bank or savings and loan association.
B. an FHA appraiser in the area.
C. the Federal Housing Administration Office.
D. the Federal National Mortgage Association.

Answer: A. Lenders must be approved by the Federal Housing Authority before they can offer FHA loans. Part of the approval process includes waiving fees customarily charged on conventional mortgages.

193. An owner advertised Beautiful acreage; only $5,000 down; owner will personally finance down payment. Would this be in violation of the Truth in Lending Act?

A. Yes. Acreage is not exempt from Reg Z.
B. Yes--since a down payment was stated.

C. No. Owners are not covered by Reg. Z.
D. No. Brokers can advertise the down payment.

Answer: C. Regulation Z requires disclosure of all financing terms and conditions if a low interest rate, downpayment or other enticement is featured in an ad. This does not apply in this case, however, because Regulation Z applies only to institutions, not individuals selling their own property.

194. A mortgage company makes a number of loans to be assembled into one package and sold to permanent investors. This process is an example of interim financing to the mortgage company and is called:

A. blanket financing.
B. package financing.
C. warehousing.
D. discounting.

Answer: C. Warehousing refers to the process whereby banks and other lenders make mortgage loans to consumers for the purpose of quickly selling those loans on the secondary market. The warehousing occurs when individual loans are bundled, often with a common element such as the size of the mortgage or credit worthiness of the borrowers, and sold as a single unit.

195. The primary purpose of Truth in Lending is to:

A. Control interest rates on behalf of the consumer.
B. Control the true costs to close a transaction.

C. Disclose the true costs of only an FHA loan.
D. Disclose the true costs of obtaining credit.

Answer: D. Truth in Lending, otherwise known as Regulation Z, is intended to do away with deceptive financing tactics, especially those involving hidden costs--for example, advertising a $250 car lease as zero-down and then tacking a $1,200 upfront payment at the time of contract disguised as an incidental acquisition fee.

196. Why is the RESPA closing statement allowed to be examined on or before closing?

A. to allow the buyer to see costs at or before closing to see if he/she can get the loan at a cheaper price
B. to make sure the title insurance came from the right company
C. to check for mathematical errors
D. to provide for special fees to specific parties for business related to the real estate transaction

Answer: C. This is not a step that should be dismissed. With the increased volume in home mortgages, the fact is a significant amount of closing statements do contain errors and it's easer and better to correct them before closing than after.

197. If a single parent is applying for a real estate loan, when would the fact have to be revealed that part of the parent's income is from child support?

A. when applying for a VA or FHA loan if the parent's income is less than $25,000

B. If more than 50% of the parent's income is from non-wage sources

C. If the parent was relying on the income for repayment of the loan

D. This type of income never needs to be disclosed. It would be a violation of ECOA.

Answer: C. Income of any type--whether alimony, child support, freelance work or a second job--only needs to be disclosed if the applicant is relying on it to qualify for the loan.

198. When the lender under a deed of trust requires title insurance, who would be the most likely person to pay for it?

A. the mortgagee
B. the trustee
C. the trustor
D. the beneficiary

Answer: C. Trustor is another name for the borrower and trustee is a supposedly neutral third party who holds naked legal title, the right to foreclose at the instructions of the beneficiary for non-payment of a promissory note. The beneficiary is the lender in a Deed of Trust. Even though it's the lender who requires the insurance to protect his/her position, it's the borrower who pays for it.

199. The Pickets are purchasing a home for $78,000 and the lender is giving them a 90% loan at 10% interest, plus a 2% loan origination fee. How much is the loan origination fee?

A. $1,404
B. $1,560
C. $1,650
D. $7,020

Answer: A. A loan for 90% of the $78,000 purchase price results in a $70,200 mortgage. Since the origination fee is based on the amount of the mortgage, not the price of the home, the fee is 2% of $70,200 or $1,404.

200. Discrimination is prohibited in lending practices under:

A. ECOA
B. RESPA
C. Truth in Lending Act
D. FNMA

Answer: A. Passed in 1992, the Equal Credit Opportunity Act prohibits a broad spectrum of discriminatory lending practices, including the granting or denial of credit or the costs associated with borrowing based on race, gender, marital status, source of income (e.g., public assistance) and other factors.

201. A buyer assumes the mortgage. How is the owner relieved of the liability?

A. subject to mortgage
B. novation
C. substitution
D. graduation

Answer: B. Essentially, novation means to substitute a new contract for an old one; thus the holder of the original is relieved of his or her responsibilities.

202. Which type of loan will result in the largest reduction of the principal balance most quickly?

A. 10% over 30 years
B. 11% over 20 years
C. 13% over 15 years
D. 14% over 20 years

Answer: C. The shorter the term of a loan, the more quickly principal is paid down and the faster equity builds. A 15-year loan at 13% interest rate would provide the LARGEST and FASTEST reduction in the principal. Interestingly, the payments on a 15-year loan are often not that much higher than the same loan with a 30-year payback. However, there are other considerations and options borrowers should understand.

203. Who is the largest purchaser in the secondary market?

A. Ginnie Mae
B. Fannie Mae
C. FHA

D. Freddie Mac

Answer: B. Fannie Mae stands for the Federal National Mortgage Association (FNMA). It was established by the National Housing Act specifically to start the secondary mortgage market, thus attracting more investors and funds to help support home ownership.

204. Which transaction requires a securities license?

A. leasing a commercial building
B. selling a commercial warehouse
C. selling shares in Fannie Mae
D. arranging a sale-leaseback on a commercial property

Answer: C. Even though Fannie Mae is a mortgage-based business, its shares sell just like any other stock and only people with a securities license may offer them for sale.

205. Who is NOT an originator of primary loans?

A. savings and loans
B. credit unions
C. commercial banks
D. FHA

Answer: D. The FHA encourages lenders to make these low-interest, low-down payment loans by insuring them against default. It does not actually lend money itself.

206. A buyer wanted to use a promissory note for consideration on the purchase of a property. Can he do this?

A. Yes. The buyer can do as he wishes since he is making the contract.
B. Yes. This is acceptable as long as the seller agrees.
C. No. Only money can be used for consideration.
D. No. Only the seller can write a promissory note.

Answer: B. This is a form of owner financing and is perfectly acceptable, so long as both parties agree to the terms and conditions.

207. If advertised alone, which would be in violation of TRUTH IN LENDING?

A. FHA financing available
B. Assumable loan
C. No down payment required.
D. easy financing terms

Answer: C. No down payment required triggers the Truth in Lending disclosures because it is a specific statement about only one aspect of the financing. Easy terms does not trigger the regulation because it's non-specific.

208. Why would a mortgagee (beneficiary) have an appraisal on the property?

A. to make sure the buyer did not pay too much
B. to determine the value of the property
C. to protect the buyer from fraud
D. to assure the property value is sufficient to cover the loan

Answer: D. Appraisals are third-party valuations of a property based on a wide range of variables. Lenders generally insist on this independent assessment to make sure the value of the property is at least sufficient to pay off the loan amount in case of default.

209. In a repayment of a mortgage loan, which type of interest is used?

A. simple
B. discount
C. compound
D. floating

Answer: A. Compound interest is associated with savings accounts and reflects the fact that money left on deposit earns interest on the interest it has already earned. Floating and Discount are terms associated with the bank-to-bank transactions and financial markets.

210. An owner was selling his own home. Can he advertise the down payment?

A. No, because it violates RESPA.
B. No, because it violates Regulation Z.

C. Yes--as long as it was listed with a broker.
D. Yes, because it was his own home.

Answer: D. Broadly speaking, an individual homeowner is free to sell his/her own home as he/she chooses and is not subject to Truth in Lending or real estate practice restrictions.

211. Which is true about restrictive covenants?

A. They are placed by private parties in a deed.
B. They are placed by government agencies in a deed.
C. They are voidable by successive owners.
D. They are placed by government agencies in the public record.

Answer: A. Restrictive covenants are most commonly associated with subdivisions and community management associations and are intended to maintain consistency within the neighborhood. While viewed as a benefit by most, they do limit the owner's use of the property and are binding on future owners.

212. Looking at shopping centers in the appraisal process, the social fiber of the community and distances from schools is called:

A. neighborhood analysis
B. market data approach
C. site analysis
D. social analysis

Answer: A. This involves more than just driving around. It is a formal process of identifying, measuring and analyzing the influences that help determine a neighborhood's vitality and desirability.

213. Which best describes why a buyer purchases a home using the market data approach?

A. Buyers buy on impulse.
B. Buyers buy based on how much income can be derived from other property.
C. Buyers buy after they compare the house with others.
D. Buyers buy based on current construction costs.

Answer: C. While emotion and impulse are certainly strong motivators, a home is also a considered purchase. What most people seek, within their affordability range, is value more than price. The only way to determine which home combines the elements of price, features, quality, condition, location and other factors that give a particular buyer the best value for his or her needs is to compare as many properties as possible.

214. A scale drawing shows a room to be 3 inches by 4 ½ inches. Carpet, which is $15 per square yard, is to be installed in the room. If the scale is 1 inch to 4 feet, how much would it cost to install the carpet?

A. $120
B. $202
C. $360

D. $3,240

Answer: C. At a scale of 4' to the inch, the room measures 12' x 18' or 216 square feet. Since there are nine square feet to one square yard, the room will require twenty-four square yards of carpet at $15 per yard.

215. A tenant leased 3000 square feet at $10 per square foot and 8% of gross income. The total annual rent she paid was $60,000. What was the gross income on which she paid percentage rent?

A. $120,000
B. $160,000
C. $300,000
D. $375,000

Answer: D. At $10 per square foot, the tenant's base rent is $30,000. Since the total rent was $60,000, that means the remaining $30,000 was due to the gross sales percentage. Since that figure is 8%, simply divide $30,000 by .08 to arrive at $375,000.

216. The Rose family owns a home in a semi-rural area, which is about five years old. Recently announced plans for a new regional airport will place their home directly in line with a main runway ending 1 mile before their home. If the airport is constructed, will this diminish the value of the Rose Home?

A. Yes, because of functional obsolescence.
B. Yes, because of economic obsolescence
C. No, because value would increase due to the location close to the airport.
D. No, because noise from aircraft passing overhead is not recognized as affecting property values.

Answer: B. Economic obsolescence occurs when factors unrelated to the property itself and outside of the owner's control diminish its value. A quick way to judge whether or not a property has become economically obsolete is to analyze whether, under the new circumstances, the location would still be chosen as a home site and, if yes, at what value compared with the current property.

217. Mrs. Jones, an appraiser, is appraising a single family residence for which she has located six closely comparable properties, all sold within the past six months. The subject property is rented for $500 per month. It is a custom-built home, approximately three years old. Mrs. Jones would probably give the most weight in her final estimate of value to which of the following appraisal methods?

A. cost approach
B. market data approach
C. income approach
D. gross rent multiplier

Answer: B. Market data would be used because it is the most reliable indicator of a home's true value. Since it is a single family residence rather than a multi-unit investment property, the fact that it is rented, as well as the amount of rent, is irrelevant to the calculations.

218. Which is the best example of functional obsolescence?

A. residential home built next to a factory
B. peeling paint
C. steep, narrow stairway in a 1 3/4 story home
D. residential home with central air conditioning

Answer: C. Functional obsolescence typically shows itself in one of two forms: first, in poor initial design, as in this case; second, when the features and design of the home have become outdated compared with competing properties.

219. A real estate agent should tell the buyer, his customer, which of the following?

A. how long a property has been on the market
B. the seller's motivation for marketing his property
C. a pending or recent zoning change
D. The seller is getting a divorce.

Answer: C. A zoning change is a material fact--something that can have a direct impact on the property's value or desirability. For example, if the zoning in a middle class neighborhood on the edge of a growing city was changed from residential to mixed use, it means that a number of homes could be turned into businesses, which will make the property less desirable to people seeking a quiet place to raise a family.

220. A square is 1/8 of a mile by 1/8 of a mile. How many acres is this?

A. 10 acres.
B. 20 acres.
C. 40 acres.
D. 160 acres.

Answer: A. One-eighth of a mile square is the same as 10 acres. Multiply 1/8 X 1/8 = 1/64 divided into 640 acres = 10 acres

221. The first step in an appraisal is:

A. a market data comparison.
B. to define the problem.
C. a neighborhood analysis.
D. to gather information.

Answer: B. Appraisers can legitimately come up with different values for the same property depending on the purpose of the appraisal. For example, an appraisal for a second mortgage generally would be more conservative than one for a competitive market analysis for the purpose of selling the home. Additionally, an appraisal for insurance purposes focuses more on the costs of replacing the structure rather than what the house, land and intangibles, such as curb appeal, would be worth on the open market.

222. A recorded subdivision plat is used in the:

A. geodetic survey system.
B. rectangular survey system.
C. lot and block system.
D. metes and bounds system.

Answer: C. Lot and block is the final survey of property being readied for development and identifies each individual parcel in a subdivision.

223. An appraiser is usually paid:

A. a fee based on a percentage of the appraised value.
B. a fee based on the amount of time and effort.
C. a fee agreed upon after the appraisal is completed.
D. a standard fee agreed upon by the National Appraisal Association.

Answer: B. There are two fundamental reasons for the time and effort rather than valuation method. First is the fact that the differences between any two properties make it impossible to relate the complexity of the task to the value of the property. A high-end property could be a relative no brainer while a particular mid-market home could have dozens of variables to be analyzed. The second reason is that basing fees on value places an obvious incentive on appraisers to estimate high, thus distorting reality.

224. The primary survey line running north and south in the rectangular survey system is the:

A. township line.
B. base line.
C. range line.
D. principal meridian.

Answer: D. Crossing a base line, the PM is the primary reference point for locating and describing land falling within its boundaries.

225. The zoning commission of Jefferson County requires that all new construction in a specific area adhere to a specific type of architecture. What type of zoning is this?

A. bulk
B. incentive
C. directive
D. aesthetic

Answer: D. Aesthetic zoning helps ensure consistency within a neighborhood or area, thus raising its visual appeal and, very often, its desirability and value as a place to live.

226. The appraisal approach most likely to be used in valuing a public library building would be:

A. market.
B. cost.

C. income.
D. residual.

Answer: B. The cost method is most often used for buildings where actual income or comparative commercial value are unavailable--such as schools and libraries.

227. Physical deterioration is considered curable whenever:

A. It is caused by lack of maintenance.
B. It does not result in loss of economic utility.
C. It costs less to correct than the resulting value increase.
D. It can be repaired regardless of the cost.

Answer: C. For example, let's say an older office building needs to update electric and add bathrooms, repartition offices and fire safety features to meet code for resale. The cost to complete the work is estimated at $2.2 million. However, the building is fully paid for and can easily be sold for $4 million. In this case, curing the defects makes sense. However, if those numbers were reversed, as is often the case, demolishing the building and starting over with a new structure or different use (e.g., retail space, a parking garage, etc.) would be the wiser choice.

228. The economic life of an investment can be described as:

A. the remaining chronological life of the improvements.
B. the time over which value generated exceeds cost of operation.
C. the time when yield is attributable to the land itself.

D. the actual age of the property.

Answer: B. Just like cars, buildings and their systems deteriorate over time and require repairs. Additionally, code changes can trigger expensive upgrades. At some point, those repairs begin to exceed the income generated and the building has reached the end of its economic life.

229. When an appraiser correlates the three approaches into a final estimate, he:

A. averages the estimate.
B. accords the greatest weight to the median value.
C. selects the estimate nearest that desired by the employer.
D. reconciles the differences according to the type of property being appraised and the quantity and quality of data available.

Answer: D. In order to maintain accuracy and transparency of his calculations, an appraiser reconciles differences and does not average comparable sales to arrive at a final value.

230. Apartment houses in an area were selling for $100,000 and a buyer offered $100,000 for an apartment building. The buyer is operating on the principle of:

A. highest and best use.
B. conformity.
C. substitution.
D. increasing returns.

Answer: C. An appraisal principle, substitution holds that the maximum value of a property is that price for which a comparable, equally desirable property can be purchased in a timely manner. For example,if two 4-bedroom homes with equal features, age, condition, lot size and desirability are on the market at the same time, buyers would not pay $250,000 for one when the other is available for $240,000. However, if the $240,000 is on the market now, but the owner wants to delay closing for six months while the other is available for immediate occupancy, there may well be buyers willing to pay the premium.

231. A feature found in a comparable property that is not present in the subject property will result in a:

A. a reduction adjustment to the comparable's selling price.
B. an increase adjustment to the subject property's selling price.
C. the reduction adjustment to the subject property's selling price.
D. an increase adjustment to the comparable's selling price.

Answer: A. It's important to remember that adjustments are made to the comparable, not the subject property. For example, let's assume two homes are identical in every respect, except the comparable property has a swimming pool the subject home lacks. If the subject property is on the market for $175,000 and a swimming pool typically adds $8,000 to the selling price of homes in that area, the appraiser would deduct $8,000 from the sale price of the comparable rather than adding it to the subject property to make his comparison.

232. Economic obsolescence in a property is generally:

A. a result of poor maintenance.
B. due to architectural faults.
C. a type of depreciation that is incurable.
D. caused by the aging process.

Answer: C. Implicit in the term economic obsolescence is the conclusion that repairs and upgrades have already been considered and would not present a cost-effective option. At this point, next to abandonment, demolition for re-use of the land is the only viable alternative.

233. When an appraiser uses the phrase effective age, he is referring to:

A. the number of years since the improvements were made.
B. the age of the property based upon its condition.
C. the estimated total life of an improvement.
D. the number of years during which the property will yield a worthwhile return on the investment made.

Answer: B. Effective age is a combination of many factors, including location, quality of construction and maintenance, architectural style, actual age, climate and so forth. A well-built building in a desirable location will have a much longer effective life than a cheaply constructed space in a poorly maintained office park setting.

234. The Adams family purchased the largest and most expensive house in a new subdivision. Five years later, when they were ready to move, they discovered the monetary value of the home had gone up proportionately less than the other houses in the neighborhood. This phenomenon is an example of the principle of:

A. diminishing return.
B. change.
C. regression.
D. substitution.

Answer: C. The regression principle is the reason people are cautioned against owning the most expensive house in the neighborhood. It's an observation of the fact that lower priced homes (and commercial buildings) have a much greater downward pull on the value of higher end properties than the other way around.

235. In valuing a single family residence by the comparison approach, an appraiser would make adjustments to:

A. the comparable properties.
B. the subject property.
C. both the comparable and the subject property.
D. current properties being offered for sale.

Answer: A. The objective of an appraisal is to arrive at a fair estimate of the subject property's value based on what comparable properties have actually sold for. The most reliable way of achieving this is to make additions and subtractions from the comparables rather than the other way around. In the example of a 3-bredroom ranch, property A might have sold for $225,000, but features a two-car garage instead of the subject property's 3-car garage. If the value of the extra garage space is $5,500, the first comparable is raised to $230,500. If the next property is identical to the subject, except it had a brand-new, high-end kitchen that added approximately $25,000 to the selling price and the home sold for $257,000, that comparable's price would be reduced to $232,000.

236. An owner was building a house for himself. Due to personal preference, he decided not to put in a bathtub. This would result in:

A. physical deterioration.
B. external obsolescence.
C. functional obsolescence.
D. social obsolescence.

Answer: C. Functional obsolescence can result from both outdated features as well as poor design. For example, while an older home with five bedrooms and only one bath is obsolete by today's standards, so too is a new home with no bathtubs or with bedrooms that can be accessed only by going through another bedroom.

237. How does one determine the gross rent multiplier?

A. Property value divided by the capitalization rate.
B. Property value divided by the monthly rent.

C. Property value divided by the net income.
D. Property value divided by the gross income.

Answer: B. This is used as a quick, short-hand guesstimate for a property's approximate value. Sometimes this calculation produces a positive cash flow; other times a negative one--and one is not necessarily better than the other. Far more detailed calculations are necessary to determine a property's real market value and attractiveness as an investment.

238. Restrictive covenants that run with the land:

A. are no longer effective when the title is transferred.
B. apply only until the developer has conveyed the title.
C. can be removed by a court of competent jurisdiction.
D. apply to and bind all successive owners of the property.

Answer: D. Often put in place to maintain the consistency and desirability of a neighborhood, restrictive covenants have withstood court tests and prohibit all future owners from certain actions or modifications of their property, such as adding outbuildings or creating additions above a certain height, putting up lights to illuminate a sports court, changing the architectural style of a home and so forth.

239. In doing a market analysis, an appraiser found a recently sold property where the owners had just gone through a divorce. The property had been listed for $60,000 for 3 months but was purchased for $40,000 by one of the spouses. Should the appraiser use this as a comparable?

A. Yes. You would use the actual sale price of $40,000.
B. Yes--because it was a comparable type property.
C. No--because it had only been listed for 3 months.
D. No--because of the divorce it was not an At arms' length transaction

Answer: D. At arm's length means, of course, transactions involving independent and objective parties with no unrelated motivations to distort the true value.

240. For the past 30 years, the Ls have operated a neighborhood grocery store. Last week the city council passed a zoning ordinance that prohibits packaged food sales in the area where the Ls' grocery store is located. The store is now an example of a/an:

A. illegal enterprise.
B. nonconforming use.
C. violation of eminent domain.
D. variance of the zoning laws.

Answer: B. This is an example of grandfathering that's common when new zoning rules are put into place. Basically it means that businesses and buildings that were in compliance before the new code was established may continue to operate or exist under their present owners. However, if the Ls want to sell their business, it must be to an enterprise that meets the new requirement.

241. Marian Kent, a real estate salesperson, is developing a web site to promote her services. What, if anything, must she specifically include in the content of her web site?

A. Name and location of her employing broker's office and a list of states in which she is licensed
B. Name of her employing broker's firm and a list of states in which she is licensed
C. Name and location of her employing broker's office and the specific period for which her real estate license is valid
D. No specific disclosures are required.

Answer: A. Each screen of the web site must list Marian's employing broker's office name and address as well as a list of all the states in which Marian is licensed.

242. What is the official view of listings based on net price?

A. They are lucrative and preferable to other types of listings that limit commissions.
B. They are allowable only with the permission of the Kentucky Board of Real Estate Brokers and Salespersons.
C. They are only legal in Kentucky if the seller gives written consent after receiving information clearly delineating the advantages and disadvantages of such a listing.
D. They are illegal in Kentucky.

Answer: D. Net listings are illegal at any time because they introduce potential conflict of interest for the broker.

243. How are commissions regulated in Kentucky?

A. Commissions are regulated by the Kentucky Board of Real Estate Brokers and Salespersons.
B. Commission guidelines are established by local groups of brokers.
C. Commissions are set by law.
D. Commissions are fully negotiable between brokers and clients.

Answer: D. Commissions are always fully negotiable between the broker and the buyer or seller.

244. When must funds received on behalf of a buyer be deposited in an escrow or trust account?

A. Within 3 days of the tendering the offer
B. Within 2 banking days of receiving all signatures on the contract
C. Within 5 business days of tendering the offer
D. Within 3 business days of finalizing all signatures for the contract

Answer: B. Other people's money must be deposited into an escrow account within two banking days after the final signature on a contract is obtained.

245. Lewis Oakley, a broker, receives an earnest money deposit from Rich Munroe for an offer on a house. What must Lewis do with the money?

A. Open an escrow account designated specifically for the Munroe transaction.
B. Deposit the money into the brokerage's existing non-interest-bearing escrow account for all such transactions.
C. Hold the deposit in a safe place at the brokerage office until the offer is finalized.
D. Deliver the money to the seller's attorney for safekeeping until the closing.

Answer: B. Earnest money must be deposited into an account for escrow funds; although the account need not separate one client's funds from another client's funds, in no circumstances may the money be commingled with the broker's personal funds.

246. What is accepted practice for managing an escrow account?

A. Escrow accounts are reserved solely for the brokerage's operating expenses.
B. The brokerage must keep a journal detailing all account activity and a ledger detailing each transaction.
C. Escrow accounts must be opened at an institution other than the broker's personal bank.
D. The name of the account must be specified as Escrow Account on all account materials to specify its purpose.

Answer: B. A detailed accounting must be kept for escrow funds, including a journal detailing all activity and a ledger detailing all transactions.

247. Which of the following activities may be performed by brokers and salespeople who are not lawyers?

A. Explaining the legalities specific preprinted contract clauses to a buyer or seller
B. Adding additional language to a preprinted contract that more specifically reflects the nature of the individual transaction
C. Completing blanks on preprinted form contracts
D. Completing a bill of sale after finalization of the contract

Answer: C. Brokers and salespeople who are not licensed as lawyers in Kentucky may fill in blanks on preprinted contracts at the direction of the clients who will sign the contract but should avoid the appearance of any unauthorized practice of law.

248. Which of the following is NOT a required element for a written listing agreement?

A. A provision requiring the party signing the listing agreement to cancel the agreement in writing on or after the date set for expiration
B. Legal description of the property
C. Fair housing statement that prohibits discrimination on the basis of religion, race, color, national origin, age, sex, disability, familial status, or marital status
D. Definite expiration date of the listing

Answer: A. While a legal description of the property, a fair housing statement, and a specific termination date for the listing are all required elements, there is no need for a provision requiring the person signing the agreement to cancel the listing in writing on or after the date of expiration.

249. In Kentucky, which of the following need NOT be included in a listing contract?

A. Fair housing language
B. Signatures of title holders
C. Disclosure of all sources of compensation
D. Disclosure of any known material defects

Answer: D. Known material defects are disclosed in a separate document that is not part of the listing contract.

250. What obligation does a licensed broker or salesperson have upon obtaining a listing?

A. Aggressively market the listing as widely as possible.
B. Establish a listing file with a unique number.
C. Communicate and cooperate with other brokerages wishing to participate in the marketing of the listing.
D. Provide the signers of the listing with a legible, signed, true, and correct copy of the listing.

Answer: D. The listing broker must provide the seller with a legible, signed, true, and correct copy of the listing upon obtaining the listing but need not follow any particular practices in marketing the property, communicating with other brokerages that wish to market the property, or setting up numbered files.

251. Within what period of time must a housing discrimination charge be filed with the Kentucky Civil Rights Commission?

A. 30 days
B. 180 days
C. 1 year
D. 2 years

Answer: B. A person must file a housing discrimination charge within 180 days.

252. With which agency or individual may a person file a complaint regarding fair housing practices?

A. With HUD or the Kentucky Civil Rights Commission
B. With the board of REALTORS®
C. With the named licensee's office
D. With the Kentucky Board of Real Estate Brokers and Salespersons

Answer: A. Complaints of unfair housing practices generally start with HUD, the Kentucky Department of Civil Rights, or the Kentucky Civil Rights Commission but may also start at the attorney general's office. REALTOR® organizations do not have jurisdiction in matters of alleged discrimination.

253. What is the legal view of a clause added to preprinted contracts in Kentucky?

A. As long as the language does not directly involve the conveyance of title to real property, the real estate broker may add a requested clause.
B. Only a licensed attorney may write the language for inclusion of a clause in a real estate sales contract in Kentucky.
C. As long as the clause is a substantive clause and not frivolous, it may be added to the contract.
D. Preprinted contracts must be used only as provided because they have been approved by the state board for general usage.

Answer: A. A broker may include additional clauses in the preprinted contract as long as they do not relate directly to conveyance of real property.

254. From whom may a Kentucky real estate salesperson collect compensation?

A. From either a buyer or seller
B. Only from the employing broker
C. From any party to a transaction or their designated representative
D. From any licensed real estate broker with whom the salesperson worked

Answer: B. All compensation must come from a salesperson's employing broker.

255. When may a salesperson be licensed under more than one broker simultaneously?

A. Never
B. Only with the written permission of the board
C. Only with the written consent of the brokers for whom the licensee is working
D. Only for supervision purposes when the licensee has offices in brokerage firms located in separate, non-adjacent counties

Answer: A. A salesperson may never be licensed with more than one broker at a time.

256. Gail has decided to leave her employing broker and work for a new employing broker in a larger brokerage. Which of the following steps must Gail take to notify the board?

A. When she renews her license, she may petition the board to transfer her license to a new employing broker.
B. She should prepare an official letter of termination that her current broker can forward to the board.
C. She must return her license to the board, along with a letter of termination.
D. Nothing; it is the current broker's responsibility.

Answer: D. When a salesperson terminates her affiliation with a broker, it is the broker's responsibility to notify the board within 5 days.

257. Mikhail Rubynov is a sole proprietor whose license has been suspended for two years due to mismanagement of client records. How will Mikhail's associated brokers and affiliated salespeople be impacted by his suspension?

A. Their licenses will be suspended for the same period of time.
B. Their licenses are revoked pending review.
C. Their licenses are suspended until they find new employing brokers.
D. Their licenses are not affected by the broker's suspension.

Answer: C. When a broker's license is suspended, his salespeople's and affiliate's licenses are suspended pending their affiliation with a new qualified broker or until the broker's license is reinstated.

258. When a broker's license is suspended, his salespeople's and affiliate's licenses are suspended pending their affiliation with a new qualified broker or until the broker's license is reinstated.

A. Yes, she may accept the money if more than 30 days have passed since the closing.
B. Yes, she may accept the money because she is licensed as an associate broker.
C. No, she may not accept the money if it comes from any party other than her employing broker.
D. No, she may not accept the money because she has already collected a fee for the transaction and this would be considered double billing.

Answer: C. A salesperson may only collect a fee from her employing broker or she will be violating state regulations.

259. What information must a broker supply to be eligible for a license for a branch office in a town 40 miles away from the home office?

A. Nothing; a branch office is not allowed to exist more than 25 miles from the main office city limits.
B. A letter from the board giving consent for the branch office.
C. A unique name for the branch office that does not imply a relationship with the home office
D. The name of a broker associate who will act as branch manager.

Answer: D. In cases where a branch office is more than 25 miles from the city limits of the main office, a broker associate must be designated as branch manager

260. To ensure entitlement to a commission, a broker must have all of the following essential components EXCEPT:

A. A binding contract
B. A ready, willing, and able buyer
C. A signed listing agreement
D. A closing

Answer: C. To receive a commission, a broker should produce a ready, willing, and able buyer who signs a binding contract and closes on the property. A signed listing agreement is not sufficient to collect a commission.

261. Joe Crouch, a Canton Broker, has three different trust accounts. Hans Hergesheimer, another Broker in town, tells Joe that he thinks he can only have one according to Kentucky law. Joe says he needs them, and that it is not illegal for a Broker to have more than one. Which of the following is true of this situation?

A. Joe can only maintain a single trust account in Kentucky.
B. Joe can only maintain two trust accounts as long as the Department approves it.
C. Brokers in Kentucky may maintain more than one trust account if they want to, as long as all trust fund provisions are followed.
D. Both A and B.

Answer: C. Hans was mistaken. The Kentucky regulations allow that a broker may maintain more than one trust account, as long as all trust fund provisions are followed.

262. What stipulation governs the inspection of records and escrow accounts in real estate offices?

A. The records need to be made available only to a CPA who makes an appointment for inspection.
B. The records will be opened to a state designee during the office's normal business hours.

C. The records should be available for inspection upon 48 hours' notice from the proper authority.

D. The records must be shown to a designee of the state at the designee's convenience.

Answer: B. The records and escrow accounts of a real estate office need to be available for inspection by a representative of the state during normal business hours, with or without prior notification.

263. An investment specialist introduced a broker to a young couple looking to relocate to Kentucky and purchase a starter home. This meeting eventually turned into a sale for the broker. How soon may the broker reward the investment specialist for the lead?

A. The broker may not pay the investment specialist for the lead.

B. The broker may pay the investment specialist only after completion of the transaction.

C. The broker may pay for the lead only after the offer has been signed by both parties.

D. The broker may pay for the lead as soon as funds are disbursed from the escrow account.

Answer: A. A broker may not pay a referral fee to an unlicensed party.

264. The laws and regulations set forth in Article 6 do not pertain to which of the following circumstances?

A. False advertising
B. Failure to pay a commission to a cooperating broker
C. Demonstration of incompetence
D. License fraud

Answer: B. Article 6 stipulates penalties for license fraud, false advertising, and commission of an act that demonstrates incompetence but does not govern commission disputes between brokers.

265. Floyd Hoopeston has lived in his condominium from May through November in each of the six years since he bought the new construction. He has recently decided to make his southern migration permanent and has just signed a contract with a buyer, Tracy Li. Under which circumstances does Tracy have the right to cancel the signed contract?

A. Within 5 days of execution of the contract
B. Within 5 days of receipt of resale documents
C. Within 10 days of receipt of resale documents
D. The contract may not be canceled in this situation

Answer: D. A condominium buyer would only have the right to cancel a signed contract if she were purchasing directly from the developer (and not as resale) and then only within 5 days of receipt of contract.

266. Of the following scenarios, which would NOT result in licensing proceedings against a salesperson?

A. A licensee accumulates offers on a house and presents them to the seller in a single bundle.
B. A licensee accumulates offers on a house and presents the best offer to the seller.
C. A licensee fails to submit an offer to a seller who is already under contract.
D. A licensee presents accumulated offers to a seller on a weekly basis.

Answer: C. Unless the listing agreement stipulates that subsequent offers must be shared, a licensee does not need to present offers to a seller who has already accepted an offer and signed a contract. In all other circumstances, though, offers must be presented immediately.

267. What heading should a preprinted offer to purchase display if it is intended to become a binding contract?

A. Offer to Purchase
B. Standard Purchase Offer and Contract
C. Real Estate Sale Contract
D. No particular heading is required.

Answer: D. Kentucky state law does not require a particular heading on a preprinted offer to purchase that is intended to become a binding contract.

268. Which of the following is true of a broker's commission in a real estate sales transaction?

A. The commission, which is negotiable between broker and seller, must be stipulated in the listing agreement.
B. The commission will be decided through mediation by the department if any dispute exists.
C. Commission funds are due at closing, payable by cash or cashier's check only.
D. Published rates set by the agreement of local brokers delineate standard commission rates by which all brokers must abide.

Answer: A. Commissions are fully negotiable and must be stated in the listing agreement. Typically, funds are disbursed at closing from the proceeds of the sale, so a separate cashier's check or cash payment is not necessary.

269. Jesse Waters, a top-rated broker, wants to earn the listing for the Millers' house but is competing with a number of other brokers for the listing. After considering the situation, Jesse entices the Millers to list their house with him based on the following guarantee: If the property does not sell within 90 days, Jesse promises to buy it. Given this advertising, Jesse must take all of the following steps EXCEPT which one?

A. Market the property as he would in any other circumstances, special agreement notwithstanding
B. Demonstrate financial capability to purchase the property if not sold after 90 days

C. Review the written details of the plan with the Waters before they sign the contract

D. Purchase the Waters' property at the established price before the 90-day period concludes

Answer: D. In this case, Jesse must indicate all terms of the offer, demonstrate the financial ability to abide by the terms of the agreement, and market the property as though no special agreement exists. Jesse is not bound, however, to purchase the house before the end of the 90-day period.

270. What is the age of legal competence in Kentucky?

A. 16
B. 18
C. 21
D. 18, unless emancipated or married at a younger age

Answer: B. The age of legal competence in Kentucky is 18.

271. Which of the following legal agreements need NOT be set forth in writing?

A. Exclusive-right-to-sell agreement
B. Multiple listing
C. Exclusive-agency listing
D. Open listing

Answer: B. The law does not address multiple listings but stipulates that open listings, exclusive-agency listings, and exclusive-right-to-sell listings must be in writing to be enforceable.

272. All of the following are protected classes under Kentucky fair housing law EXCEPT:

A. Disability
B. Race
C. Sexual preference
D. Ancestry

Answer: C. Sexual preference is not protected by fair housing law in Kentucky.

273. What ceiling is specified for interest rates on properties financed by sellers?

A. 8 percent
B. 11 percent
C. 15 percent
D. None exists

Answer: B. The statutory usury ceiling on purchase-money mortgages in Kentucky is set at 11 percent.

274. Does Kentucky Law require a landlord to allow a visually impaired girl with a guide dog to reside in an apartment complex with a no pets policy?

A. Yes, Kentucky law prohibits a landlord from refusing to rent the apartment to a visually impaired person on the basis of a no pets policy.
B. Yes, but the visually impaired tenant may be required to pay a special damage deposit upfront.
C. No, since a no pets policy can be enforced if applied to all circumstances equally, the visually impaired person will not be allowed to rent a unit in the complex.
D. Kentucky law does not provide guidance on the issue of working dogs to support people with disabilities.

Answer: A. According to the law, the landlord is specifically prohibited from refusing to rent the girl a unit based on the no pets policy.

275. The person ultimately responsible for preparing documents for a closing would be which of the following individuals?

A. The attorney for the seller
B. The listing broker
C. The lender
D. The salesperson facilitating the transaction

Answer: B. Responsibility for preparing closing documents ultimately resides with the listing broker.

276. Whose responsibility is it to file a 1099 for real property transactions?

A. The closing agent
B. The title company
C. The lender
D. The listing broker

Answer: A. The party that performed the closing for the seller is responsible for filing the 1099 for real property transactions.

277. Which of the following actions does not lie within the realm of responsibility of a broker preparing for a closing?

A. Oversight of the inspections
B. Delivery of documents and escrow monies to the appropriate attorney
C. Review of closing procedures with both parties to a transaction
D. Completion of required title searches

Answer: D. A broker who is not licensed as an attorney may not perform a title search because it could lead to the appearance of practicing law without a license.

278. What constitutes a tract per the Land Division Act?

A. The land an individual owned prior to March 31, 1997
B. The sum total of contiguous property purchased after March 31, 1997
C. Two or more parcels with a common property line, if in existence prior to March 31, 1997 and still under the same ownership

D. Four parcels of land fronting on a major road

Answer: C. A tract is defined as two or more parcels of land that share a common property line as long as the property was in existence prior to March 31, 1997 and is still under the same ownership.

279. What is the allowable depth-to-width ratio for a created parcel of land smaller than ten acres?

A. The depth may not exceed 3 times the width, with certain exceptions.
B. The depth may not exceed 4 times the width, with certain exceptions.
C. The depth may not exceed 4 times the width, with no exceptions.
D. Depth-to-width ratios only apply to parcels of land that exceed 10 acres.

Answer: B. A created parcel of land that is 10 acres or less in area may be no deeper than 4 times the width, with certain exceptions.

280. Russ Hayworth owns 15 acres of undeveloped land which he has decided to sell. Gene Lowes, a buyer, agrees to purchase 100% of the land at an agreed-upon price. If this land is transferred in a single action, what must the mandatory clause on the deed specify?

A. No clause is required.

B. The clause must give Gene Lowes the right to make All divisions under section 108 of the Land Division Act.
C. The clause must stipulate the exact number of division rights being conveyed to Gene Lowes.
D. The clause must specify general right to divide without inserting the number of division rights passed to Gene Lowes.

Answer: A. The deed for a parcel of land conveyed in its entirety need not specify division rights.

281. Blaise Wilkes owned a ranch on which valuable minerals were discovered in 1976. Subsequently, he has sold the property but retains ownership of the mineral rights. Which of the following is true?

A. Blaise must record his ownership of mineral rights every 20 years
B. Blaise need only record the mineral rights when first acquired in 1976; they are granted in perpetuity.
C. Blaise must have recorded the rights when he sold his property and wished to retain ownership of the mineral rights.
D. Once property has been transferred to a new owner, Blaise may not retain ownership of mineral rights to the property.

Answer: A. In order for mineral rights to be retained by anyone other than the owner of a property, they must be recorded every 20 years or they revert to the actual property owner, per the Kentucky Dormant Mineral Rights Act.

282. By when must all condominium documents be delivered to the purchaser in a new construction condominium sale?

A. Prior to the contract becoming binding
B. Within 5 business days of the seller's acceptance of the purchaser's offer
C. Prior to accepting the purchaser's offer
D. At least 48 hours prior to the closing

Answer: A. The contract to purchase a new condominium does not become binding on the purchaser until nine business days after receipt of the requisite documents from the developer.

283. Which of the following is NOT required of a Kentucky broker who promotes the sale of land located in another state?

A. Adherence to all restrictions and conditions stipulated by the real estate department
B. Reimbursement of any travel expenses the real estate department incurs while investigating the promotion
C. Disclosure of all details about the property to the real estate department
D. Licensure in both Kentucky and the state in which the property is located

Answer: B. Although a broker promoting property in another state need not be dually licensed, he or she does need to abide by the other terms of the Kentucky Out of State Land Sales Act.

284. What is the principal method of describing property in Kentucky?

A. Rectangular survey system
B. System of metes and bounds
C. Grid of meridians
D. Colonial block grant system

Answer: B. Kentucky property is typically described in terms of metes and bounds.

285. In which circumstances are subdivision developers regulated by the Interstate Land Sales Full Disclosure Act?

A. If 25 or fewer lots are sold outside Kentucky's limits
B. If 25 or fewer lots are sold within Kentucky's limits
C. If 25 or more lots are sold outside Kentucky's limits
D. If 25 or more lots are sold within Kentucky's limits

Answer: C. When 25 or more lots are sold across state lines, subdivision developers are subject to the regulations of the Interstate Land Sales Full Disclosure Act.

286. What type of activity performed without a permit in a designated wetlands area would violate Kentucky's Wetland Protection Act?

A. Constructing a boardwalk along a riverfront
B. Planting a vegetable garden on a half acre of land
C. Installing an in-ground swimming pool

D. Relandscaping an area previously overgrown with vegetation

Answer: C. installing an in-ground swimming pool requires excavation, so doing so without a permit violates the provision that calls for approval from the state before changing the contour of the earth in a designated wetland area.

287. Which of the following legal descriptions of property is not valid in Kentucky?

A. Torrens registration
B. Metes and bounds
C. Recorded plats
D. Rectangular survey system

Answer: A. Although metes and bounds is the principal method of describing property in Kentucky, recorded plats and rectangular survey system descriptions are also acceptable.

288. Where would a property be located in relationship to the intersection of the base line and the principal meridian if its location is described as the southeast quadrant of Section 5, Township 5 South, and Range 2 East?

A. Northwest of the initial point
B. Northeast of the initial point
C. Southwest of the initial point
D. Southeast of the initial point

Answer: D. The property would be located southeast of the intersection of the base line and the principal meridian.

289. Of the following descriptions of property, which is NOT considered legal in Kentucky?

A. Lot 5, Block 7 of Whitehall Subdivision, Alcona County, Kentucky
B. 2340 Oak St., Grand Rapids, Kentucky
C. A parcel beginning at the northwest corner of Section 4, T2N, R2W bounded on the east by Wild Rd, on the south by Worthington Court, and on the west by Jack Rabbit Crossing.
D. Section 3 of T2N, R4S

Answer: V. Mailing address is not considered an adequate legal property description in Kentucky.

290. How does one acquire land by adverse possession?

A. Use the land with owner's permission
B. Use the land for a period of 30 years
C. Use the land furtively to avoid detection
D. Use the land without permission

Answer: D. To acquire land by adverse possession requires one to use the land without the owner's permission.

291. The Simsons hope to acquire an easement on their neighbor's property. Their neighbor's property has a woods

that borders a public lake on which they frequently sail in warm weather. The Simsons have been hauling their speedboat through their neighbor's woods for 5 years; how much longer must they continue this pattern of use in order to obtain an easement?

A. 5 more years
B. 10 more years
C. 15 more years
D. 25 more years

Answer: B. To obtain an easement in Kentucky, continuous, open, and notorious use must be established for a period of 15 years.

292. What must a property owner do to prevent someone from acquiring an easement to cross his or her land?

A. Post a No Trespassing sign
B. Write a letter denying permission to cross the land
C. Follow procedures outlined in the Kentucky statutes
D. Write a letter granting permission to cross the land

Answer: C. A property owner must follow statutory procedures to prevent someone from acquiring an easement to their property; measures such as posting a sign or sending a letter may be insufficient.

293. What is the minimum age at which an individual may enter a legally enforceable contract?

A. 16, if married or emancipated; otherwise 18
B. 17, if married or emancipated; otherwise 18
C. 18, with no exceptions
D. 21, with no exceptions

Answer: C. To enter a legally enforceable contract, an individual must be at least 18, the legal age with no exceptions.

294. Alyssa, a college student, found the perfect apartment just at the edge of campus. She has two years until graduation and asked the landlord to give her a lease for the full two-year period in exchange for a small discount on rent. What type of lease may the landlord record for Alyssa's extended lease term?

A. A notice of lease
B. A lis pendens
C. A rent supplement notice
D. A notice of constructive occupancy

Answer: A. For a lease period that exceeds a year, a notice of lease may be recorded instead of an actual lease.

295. Sherry and Bill Vaughn signed a lease with a provision to waive their rights to the security deposit. Which of the following is true of the provision?

A. The provision is unenforceable, but the lease is still valid.
B. The provision is unenforceable, so the lease is invalid.

C. The provision is enforceable because the contract is signed.
D. The provision is enforceable only for the initial term of the lease.

Answer: A. Although the provision to waive the tenants' right to the security deposit is unenforceable, the lease is still valid.

296. Michael Laughlin skipped out before paying July's rent on a lease that expired at the end of July. Which of the following actions may the landlord take?

A. The landlord may confiscate the tenant's belongings.
B. The landlord may extend the lease automatically because the tenant left without notice.
C. The landlord may keep a portion of the security deposit to cover the rent owed.
D. The landlord may do nothing because the lease is terminated as of the date the tenant vacated the premises.

Answer: C. The landlord may use the security deposit to cover back rent if a tenant skips out on the last scheduled payment of the lease period.

297. Rachel Carson has been evicted from her apartment for continual violations of the apartment's no pets rule. If she does not remove her belongings, under summary process, what course of action is available to the landlord?

A. The landlord may sell the belongings and keep the proceeds.

B. The landlord may summon the sheriff to place the belongings on the street.
C. The landlord may keep the belongings for personal use.
D. The landlord may deliver the belongings to the town dump.

Answer: B. If an evicted tenant does not remove his or her belongings, under summary process, the sheriff may place the belongings on the street.

298. Which of the following rules applies to security deposits?

A. Landlords may only collect security deposits for residential units.
B. A landlord may apply a security deposit at the end of a lease period to cover rent owed by a tenant.
C. A landlord must return the security deposit to the tenant within 30 days of the end of the lease unless property has been damaged.
D. Security deposits must be placed in an interest-bearing account, and tenants must be paid accumulated interest when their security deposit is returned at the end of the lease period.

Answer: B. Security deposits, which apply to any type of rental property, can be used to cover damages, unpaid utilities, or back rent. If the security deposit is not returned to a tenant within 45 days of the end of the lease, a written explanation must be sent.

299. Jacob Frost has established a year-to-year tenancy with his landlord over the past 5 years. Now, the landlord wishes

to terminate the year-to-year tenancy and convert the apartments into a new form. What notice is the landlord required to provide Jacob?

A. 1 week
B. 30 days
C. 3 months
D. The number of days equivalent to the basis on which rent is paid

Answer: D. Depending on how often Jacob remits his rental payments, the landlord must give notice equivalent to how rent is paid (i.e. monthly, quarterly).

300. Maxim Apartments charges $450 monthly rent for each of their studio units. What is the maximum amount that the landlord may require for a security deposit according to the Kentucky Security Deposit Act?

A. $450.00
B. $675.00
C. $900.00
D. $1,350.00

Answer: B. The landlord may require a security deposit up to one and a half times the monthly rent.

REAL ESTATE MATH EXAM

1. The fastest way to calculate one month's interest on a real estate loan with an interest rate of 7.2% interest per annum is to multiply the principal balance by:

A.   0.006
B.   0.6
C.   7.2% and divide by 12
D.   12 and divide by 7.2%

Answer: A. By dividing the 7.2% rate by 12 first, you can find one month's interest by multiplying the loan amount by .006; 7.2% divided by 12 = .006, rate for one month.

2. A duplex with a fair market value of $20,000 and an outstanding loan balance of $12,000 was exchanged for a four-plex with a market value of $35,000 and an outstanding $18,000 loan balance. The owner of the duplex would pay in cash or secondary financing

A. $6,100
B. $8,100
C. $9,100
D. $15,100

Answer: C. Market Value - Loan = Equity Duplex $20,000 - $12,000 = $8,000 Four-plex $35,000 - $18,000 = $17,000 Difference in equities amounts to $9,000.

3. Mr. Brown, licensed broker, took an offer from Mr. Green on land for $6,000 with the following terms: $2,000

down and purchase money trust deed and note for the balance, payable $70 per month including interest at 7.2%. If the offer was accepted by the seller, what is the balance of the loan after the first 3 months payment?

A. $3,186
B. $3,467
C. $3,861
D. $3,790

Answer: C. $6,000 price - $2,000 down = $4,000 first trust deed. $4,000 x .006 = $24.00 interest first month. $70 - $24 = $46.00 applied to principal. $4,000 - $46 = $3,954 balance after first month. $3,954 x .006 = $23.72 interest second month. $70 - $23.72 = $46.28 applied to principal. $3954 - $46.28 = $3907.72 balance after second month $3,907.72 x .006 = $23.45. $70 - $23.45 = $46.55 applied to principal. $3,907.72 - $46.55 = $3,861.17.

4. After subtracting $140.00 escrow fees and 6% commission on gross sales price, a seller receives $13,584.00. What is the selling price?

A. $12,770
B. $14,440
C. $14,540
D. $14,600

Answer: D. Selling price (100%) = $13,584 + $140 + 6% 94% = $13,584 + $140 = $13,724 $13,724 divided by 94% = $14,600.

5. Keith Johnson purchased a property at 20% less than the listed price and later sold the property for the original listed price. What was the percentage of profit?

A.   10%
B.   20%
C.   25%
D.   40%

Answer: C. Assume that the property was listed at $10,000. Listed price less 20% = $8,000 purchase price. If it was sold at the listed price of $10,000, the owner made $2,000 profit. $2,000 profit divided by $8,000 cost = 25%.

6. Lots "A", "B" and "C" sold for a total price of $39,000. If lot "B" was priced at $6,400 more than lot "A", and lot "C" was priced at $7,100 more than lot "B", the price of lot "A" was:

A. $13,000.00
B. $6,366.67
C. $5,433.33
D. $4,633.00

Answer: B. $39,000 = A + B + C = A + $6,400 + A + $7,100 + $6,400 + A; 39,000 = 19,900 + (3 x A); 39,000 - 19,900 = 3 x A; 19,100 = 3 x A; 19,100 divided by 3 = A; $ 6,366.67 = A

7. Assume a real estate salesman sold a residence for $31,000. If the broker's commission was 6% and the salesman was to receive 45% of the total commission for selling the property, the salesman would receive:

A. $837.70
B. $959.95
C. $1,860.00
D.   None of the above

Answer: D. $31,000 x 6% = $1,860 Total commission $1,860 x 45% = $837.00 Choice "A" is close, but not exactly $837.00

8. Smith and Allen wish to exchange real property. Smith owns a property valued at $150,000 against which there is a $35,000 trust deed. Allen owns property worth $105,000 on which there is an existing first trust deed of $25,000 and a second trust deed of $20,000. Allen has $15,000 in cash which he is willing to pay towards the exchange. If Smith is willing to accept a second trust deed and note from Allen in order to effect the exchange, the amount of the note would be:

A. $20,000
B. $40,000
C. $50,000
D. $70,000

Answer: B. Market Value - Loan = Equity Smith $150,000 - $35,000 = $115,000 Allen $105,000 - $25,000 = $60,000 Differences in Equity $115,000 - $60,000 = $55,000; $55,000 - $15,000 Cash = $40,000 Second

9. An apartment house property costs $240,000 and this price has been verified to be an accurate estimate of the property value. In comparable circumstances it is also

verified that the owner may use a 10% capitalization rate to the purchase price in determining his net income. Should there be a 10% increase in rental income with no increase in the owner's expense and should the capitalization rate of the property be increased to 12%, what would be the estimated value of the property be?

A. $220,000
B. $240,000
C. $264,000
D. None of the above

Answer: A. Value x Cap Rate = Income $240,000 x 10% = $24,000 Income; 10% income increase = $2,400; New income = $26,400; new Cap Rate = 12%; Value = $26,400 divided by 12% = $220,000

10. Able purchased a $15,000 home. His down payment amounted to 6 2/3% of the purchase price; the balance was carried as a first trust deed bearing interest at 8.4% per annum. The principal is to be repaid at $50.00 per month. A three-year insurance policy costs $72.00; the property taxes are $360.00 per year. Able is required to make a proportionate monthly payment to a loan trust fund for these items. The total amount of the first monthly payment most nearly would be:

A. $267
B. $182
C. $186
D. $188

Answer: B. 6 2/3% = Fraction 1/15; $15,000 x 6 2/3% (or 0.07) = $1,000; $15,000-$1,000=$14,000 Loan; $14,000 x 0.084 = $1,176 Interest per year; $1,176 divided by 12 = $98 Interest per month Principal = 50.00 Principal 3-Year $72.00 divided by 36 months = 2.00 Insurance; $360 Taxes divided by 12 = $30.00 Taxes; 98 + 50 + 2 + 30 = $180.00 most nearly.

11. A husband and wife own a vacation home in the mountains. The annual taxes on the property are $400.00. Since the total taxes cannot exceed 1% of the full cash value of the property, the "full cash value" of the property would be:

A. $10,000
B. $20,000
C. $40,000
D. $80,000

Answer: C. $400 divided by 1% = $40,000

12. A house sold for $16,350, which amount was 9% more than the cost of the house. The cost of the house was:

A. $14,878.50
B. $15,000.00
C. $16,000.00
D. $17,821.50

Answer: B. Cost (100%) + Profit (9%) = $16,350 109% = $16,350 $16,350 divided by 109% = $15,000

13. The Southern Pacific Railroad Company sold ABS Developers three sections of land that had been divided into 20 acre parcels. 16 sold at $4,000 each and the remainder sold at $5,000 each. Which of the following was most nearly the total amount realized by the seller?

A. $350,000
B. $358,000
C. $475,000
D. $500,000

Answer: C. Three sections = 3 x 640 acres = 1920 acres; 1920 divided by 20 acres per parcel = 96 parcels; 16 parcels x $4,000 each = $ 64,000; 80 parcels x $5,000 each = $400,000; 96 parcels = $464,000; Closest answer is $475,000

14. An acre is to be divided into four equal lots. If the lots are parallel to each other, rectangular, and 200 feet deep, the width of each lot would most nearly be:

A.   15 feet
B.   55 feet
C.   200 feet
D.   218 feet

Answer: B. One acre = 43,560 square feet; 43,560 divided by 200 = 217.80; 217.80 divided by 4 = 54.45 feet; 55 is nearest

15. A prospect is considering the purchase of an income property which has an operating statement showing $94,500.00 deducted from gross income to arrive at the net income. The deductions amount to 60% of the gross income.

If the prospect wants a 12% return on the purchase price of any investments he makes, what should he pay for the property?

A. $81,000
B. $196,000
C. $504,000
D. $720,000

Answer: C. Expenses = $94,500 = 60% of Gross Income or $94,500 = 0.6 x Gross Income $94,500 divided by 0.6 = Gross Income = $157,500 Gross Income - Expenses = Net Income $157,500 Gross income - $94,500 Expenses = $63,000 Net Income Value = Net Income divided by Rate of Return; Value = $63,000 divided by 12% = $36,000 divided by 0.12 = $525,000

16. Richard Rock sold his residence which was unencumbered. Total deductions in escrow amounted to $215.30 in addition to a broker's commission of 6% of the selling price. The selling price was the only credit item. Richard Rock received a check for escrow amounting to $15,290. The selling price was most nearly:

A. $16,200
B. $16,266
C. $16,430
D. $16,495

Answer: D. Selling price (100%) = $15,290 + $215.30 + 6%; $15,290 + $215.30 = $15,505.30 or 94%; $15,505.30 divided by 94% = $16,495

17. Mr. and Mrs. Smith acquired a home in 1977 for $48,000. In 1987 they sold it for $60,500 and moved into an apartment unit. During the ten year period of ownership, permanent improvements totaling $12,750 were made to their house. If Mr. Smith's income consists entirely of wages, how would the sale affect his 1987 federal income return?

A.   No affect
B. $125.00 loss
C. $250.00 loss
D. $12,500 gain

Answer: A. Cost $48,000 + Additions $12,750 = $60,750; Book value = $60,500; Selling price = $ 250 loss Losses are not deductible on the sale of a residence.

18. Eddie Ronquillo sold his house and took back a note for $4,200 secure a second deed of trust. He promptly sold the note for $2,730. This represents a discount of:

A.   28%
B.   35%
C.   55%
D.   65%

Answer: B. Face amount: $4,200; Net amount: $2,730; $4,200 - $2,730 = $1,470 % discount = $1,470 divided by $4,200 = 35%

19. An owner depreciated the improvements based on a cost basis of $160,000 using the straight line method. Improvements are depreciated 37.5% to date and the

remaining economic life is estimated to be 15 years. Which of the following is correct? The:

A. Rate of depreciation exceeds 4% per annum
B. Time of depreciation to date is over ten years
C. Value of the building is $120,000
D. Rate of depreciation cannot be determined from the data given

Answer: A. 100% - 37.5% = 62.5% remaining to depreciate; 62.5% divided by 15 years = 4.17% per year

20. What is the monthly return on an income property with a 6 1/2% return on its value of $46,500?

A. $251.88
B. $302.50
C. $151.25
D. $3,630.00

Answer: A. $46,500 x .065 = $3,022.50 Income; $3,022.50 divided by 12 = $251.88 per month.

21. Andrew Blacker was the owner of a straight note with an annual interest rate of 8.4%. In 5 years, he had received $5,460 in interest. What was the principal amount of the note?

A. $1,092
B. $13,000
C. $6,500
D. $3,250

Answer: B. $5,460 divided by 5 years = $1,092 annual interest; $1,092 divided by .084 = $13,000 principal amount

22. The Phillips sold their home for $36,850, which represents a 17% profit over the original price. What was the original price?

A. $31,495
B. $35,000
C. $53,540
D. $19,850

Answer: A. Cost Rule: Selling Price divided by (100% + %) 100 + 17 = 1.17 $36,850 divided by 1.17 = $31,495

23. If a building's costs increased 20 percent, the value of the investor's dollar has decreased by:

A.   16 and 2/3%
B.   20%
C.   25%
D.   33 and 1/3%

Answer: A. The material I bought yesterday for $100 now costs 20% more or $120. If I only have $100, I can only buy 100/120 or 5/6ths of what I could yesterday. My dollar has decreased 1/6 or 16 2/3%.

24. One month's interest on a 5 year straight note amounted to $225.00. At a 7 1/2% per year interest rate, what was the face amount of the note?

A. $2,700
B. $1,688
C. $36,000
D. $44,000

Answer: C. 12 x $225 = $2,700; $2,700 divided by .075 = $36,000

25. Escrow closed May 1 with interest on a $4,415 second trust deed paid to June 1. The interest rate is 7 2/10%. What is the debt to the buyer, if the buyer assumes the loan?

A. $22.09
B. $26.49
C. $4,415.00
D. None of the above

Answer: B. Since the sellers paid one month's interest in advance, this must be returned to them by the buyer. This will be a debit on the buyer's statement. $4,415 x .006 (7.2% divided by 12) = $26.49

26. A man owns an apartment building with 20,000 square feet of living space and wants to carpet 60% of the area. If the carpet costs $6.00 a square yard, what is the total cost of the carpeting?

A. $3,996
B. $4,000
C. $7,998
D. $24,000

Answer: C. 20,000 x .60 = 12,000 square feet; 12,000 divided by 9 (9 square feet = 1 square yard) = 1,333 square yards; 1,333 x $6.00 = $7,998

27. One month's interest on a straight note amounted to $45. At 4 1/2% per year, what was the face amount of the note?

A. $2,025
B. $1,200
C. $12,000
D. $24,000

Answer: C. $45 x 12 = $540 interest/year; $540 divided by .045 = $12,000

28. If the interest is paid at a rate of $60 per month and the rate of interest is 8% per year, what is the principal amount of the loan?

A. $5,760
B. $8,560
C. $9,000
D. $90,000

Answer: C. 12 months x $60 = $720 interest/year; $720 divided by .08 = $9,000

29. Mr. Morton paid $945 interest on a straight note loan of $7,000, at a rate of 9%. What was the term of the loan?

A.   18 months

B.   36 months
C.   48 months
D.   60 months

Answer: A. $7,000 x .09 = $630 interest for 1 year; $630 divided by 12 = $52.50 interest/month; $945 (interest) / $52.50 = 18 months

30. A man paid $140 in interest for a 90 day period on a $7,000 loan. What was the interest rate on the loan?

A.   6%
B.   8%
C.   10%
D.   11%

Answer: B. $140 x 4 (12 months divided by 3 months) = $560; $560 divided by $7,000 = 8%

31. A rectangular parcel containing 540 square yards which has a frontage of 45' would be how many feet deep?

A.   54' deep
B.   108' deep
C.   270' deep
D.   540' deep

Answer: B. 1 sq. yard = 9 sq. ft. 540 x 9 = 4,860 sq. ft. Area = L x W W = 45, so 4,860 divided by 45 = 108 ft.

32. How many acres are contained in a parcel of land 1,320' by 2,640'?

A. 40 acres
B. 60 acres
C. 80 acres
D. 120 acres

Answer: C. 1,320' x 2,640' = 3,484,800'; 3.484,800' divided by 43,560' = 80 acres

33. If $150 interest is paid in 8 months on a straight note loan of $2,500, what is the annual rate of interest?

A. 9%
B. 10%
C. 11.50%
D. 12%

Answer: A.8 months = 2/3 year = $150 interest; $150 divided by 0.67 = $227.27 interest for 8 months; $2257.27 divided by $2,500 = .09 = 9%

34. A parcel of land 1/4 mile by 1/4 mile is how many acres?

A. Ten acres
B. Twenty acres
C. Forty acres
D. Eighty acres

Answer: C. 5280 divided by 4 = 1320; 1320 x 1320 = 1,742,400; 1,742,400 divided by 43,560 = 40 acres

35. A man bought a home for $31,680 and now wishes to sell. He is informed that the cost of selling will amount to 12% of the selling price. He wishes to sell at a price so as not to have a loss. How much would the home have had to appreciate in order to offset the selling costs?

A. $1,080
B. $2,160
C. $4,320
D. $5,400

Answer: C. Selling Price Rule: 100% - (Net divided by %) = Gross Selling Price; 100% - 12% = 88%; $31,680 divided by .88 = $36,000; $36,000 (gross selling price) - $31,680 (purchase price) = $4,320 (appreciation)

36. A building that has interior dimensions of 26' x 30' and has 6" walls would cover how much square footage of land?

A. 58
B. 428
C. 837
D. 3,680

Answer: C. L = 26' + 6" + 6" = 27'; W = 30' + 6" + 6" = 31'; 27' x 31' = 837 square feet

37. A rectangular parcel of land measures 1,780' x 1,780' and contains how many acres?

A. 73
B. 316

C.   632
D.   1,780

Answer: A. 1,780 x 1,780 = 3,168,400 square feet; 3,168,400 divided by 43,560 = 73 acres

38. A borrower paid $120 interest on a 90-day straight note. The principal was $6,000. What was the interest rate?

A.   6%
B.   7%
C.   8%
D.   9%

Answer: C. $120 x 4 = $480; $480 divided by $6,000 = .08 = 8%

39. A man borrowed $750 on a straight note at an interest rate of 7.2%. If his total interest payment was $67.50, the length of the loan was?

A.   Twelve months
B.   Fifteen months
C.   Twenty four months
D.   Thirty months

Answer: B. $750 x 7.2% = $54; $54 divided by 12 months = $4.50 interest/month; $67.50 divided by $4.50 = 15 months

40. A house sold for $16,350 which was 9% more than its original cost. What was the original cost?

A. $15,000
B. $20,000
C. $25,000
D. $30,000

Answer: A. 100% + 9% = $16,350; $16,350 divided by 1.09 = $15,000

41. A homeowner sold his house for $23,000. This selling price represented a 15% profit over what he had originally paid for the house. What was the original price of the home?

A. $15,000
B. $20,000
C. $25,000
D. $30,000

Answer: B. 100% + 15% = $23,000; $23,000 divided by 1.15 = $20,000

42. Assume that a second trust deed of $1,000 was to be paid in annual installments of $300 plus 6% interest, with a balloon payment of the balance at the end of the third year. The remaining balance of the principal after the second annual installment was paid would be:

A. $400.00
B. $424.00
C. $505.60
D. $520.00

Answer: A. Since the payments on the principal are $300 per year and the borrower has made two payments plus whatever interest was due, the balance would be $400. $1,000 - $600 = $400

43. Mr. John listed his home with Broker Bob for $35,000. The broker was to receive a commission rate of 6%. The broker brought an offer at 10% less than the listed price. The owner agreed to accept the offer if the broker reduced his commission by 20%. If they all agree to these terms, what amount of commission would the broker receive?

A. $812
B. $1,012
C. $1,312
D. $1,512

Answer: D. $35,000 x .10 = $3,500; $35,000 - $3,500 = $31,500; $31,500 x .06 = 1,890; $1,890 x .20 = $378; $1,890 - $378 = $1,512

44. A man had an income property which suffered a $300 monthly loss of net income when a freeway was built nearby. At a capitalization rate of 12%, how much did his property lose in value?

A. $20,000
B. $30,000
C. $40,000
D. $50,000

Answer: B. $300 x 12 = $3,600; $3,600 divided by .12 =

$30,000

45. Kent was the owner of a straight note with an annual interest rate of 8.4%. In five years he had received $5,460 in interest. The principal amount of the note was most nearly?

A. $12,000
B. $13,000
C. $14,000
D. $15,000

Answer: B. $5,460 divided by 5 = $1,092; $1,092 divided by 8.4% = $13,000

46. An investor owns a 20-unit apartment house. When compared to comparable apartment properties he loses $200 net income a month because his property is located next to a busy freeway. Appraisers are using a 12% capitalization rate for this neighborhood of income properties. The subject property has suffered a loss in value in the amount of:

A. $20,000
B. $25,000
C. $30,000
D. $35,000

Answer: A. $200 x 12 = $2,400; $2,400 divided by 12% = $20,000

47. In order to earn $208 per month from an investment that yields a 6% return you would have to invest approximately:

A. 12480
B. $20,800
C. $24,960
D. $41,600

Answer: D. $208 x 12 = $2,496; $2,496 divided by 6% = $41,600

48. A man bought two 60 foot lots for $18,000 each and divided them into three lots which he sold for $15,000 each. What was his percentage of profit?

A. 15.00%
B. 25.00%
C. 28.00%
D. 30.00%

Answer: B. $18,000 x 2 = $36,000; $15,000 x 3 = $45,000; $45,000 - $36,000 = $9,000; $9,000 divided by $36,000 = .25 = 25%

49. If a man paid $50,000 for a business which gave him a 6% return on his money, how much did he make during the first year that he owned it?

A. $1,500
B. $3,000
C. $4,500
D. $6,000

Answer: B. $50,000 x 6% = $3,000

50. An investor was going to have a building constructed which was to cost $150,000 and could, when completed, be leased for $2,500 per month. The annual operating expenses for the property would be $6,000. The amount he could invest in the land to realize a 12% return would be:

A. $50,000
B. $75,000
C. $100,000
D. $150,000

Answer: A. $2,500 x 12 = $30,000; $30,000 - $6,000 = $24,000; $24,000 divided by .12 = $200,000; $200,000 - $150,000 = $50,000

51. An investor purchased property for a total price of $72,000, paying $20,000 down and financing the balance of $52,000 using a straight note. If the investor eventually sold the property after it had doubled in value and had made no principal payments on the loan, each dollar invested would show a return of:

A. $2.00
B. $4.60
C. $5.60
D. $8.70

Answer: B. New selling price is $72,000 x 2 = $144,000; $144,000 less $52,000 loan = $92,000 return; $92,000 divided by $20,000 = $4.60

52. Which of the following contains the largest area?

A. 4 square miles
B. 5,280' X 10,560'
C. 2 sections
D. 1/10 of a township

Answer: A. A parcel that is 4 square miles is the largest. 1/10 of a town- ship is 3.6 square miles. 5,280' X 10,560' is a parcel that is 1 mile X 2 miles or 2 square miles. 2 sections contain 2 square miles.

53. Harris obtained a loan in the amount of $20,000 and paid the mortgage lender four discount points and an origination fee of 2%. If the payments on the loan were $163.00 per month, including 8% interest and the average balance over a five year period was $18,500, the gross amount earned by the lender is the 5 years was most nearly:

A. $5,100
B. $6,000
C. $7,400
D. $8,600

Answer: D. The lender earned the discount points, origination fee and interest. $20,000 x 4% = $800 in points; $20,000 X 2% = $400 in origination fee; $18,500 X 8% = $1480 annual interest x 5 years = $7400 Total of these three amounts is $8600

54. An individual who receives $225 per month on a money market savings account that pays 7 1/2% per year, has

invested which of the following amounts?

A. $12,500
B. $27,000
C. $36,000
D. $48,000

Answer: C. $225 x 12 = $2700 per year; $2700 divided by 7.5% = $36,000

55. A seller took back a second trust deed and note in the amount of $11,400 payable $240 per month, including interest at 7% per annum. If interest on the note begins July 15 and the first payment is made on August 15, the amount of the first payment that is applied to the principal is:

A. $66.50
B. $79.80
C. $173.50
D. $240.00

Answer: C. $11,400 x 7% = $798 per year; $798 divided by 12 = $66.50 per month; $140 - $66.50 = $173.50

56. Humphreys sold his residence which was unencumbered. Total de- ductions in escrow amounted to $215.30 in addition to a broker's commission of 6% of the selling price. The selling price was the only credit item. Humphreys received a check from escrow amounting to $15,290. The selling price was most nearly:

A. $16,200
B. $16,266
C. $16,430
D. $16,495

Answer: D. Selling price (100%) = $15,290 + $215.30 + 6%;
$15,290 + $215.30 = $15,505.30 or 94%; $15,505.30 divided by
94% = $16,495

**57. Ms. Rodgers sold her house and took back a note for
$4200 secured by a second deed of trust. She promptly sold
the note for $2730. This represents a discount of:**

A.   28%
B.   35%
C.   51%
D.   73%

Answer: B. Face amount = $4200; Net amount = $2730; $4200
- $2730 = $1470; Discount = $1470 divided by $4200 = 35%

**58. After subtracting $140 escrow fees and 6% commission
on gross sales price, a seller receives $13,584. What is the
selling price?**

A. $12,770
B. $14,440
C. $14,540
D. $14,600

Answer: D. Selling price (100%) = $13,584 + $140 + 6%;

$13,584 + $140 = 94% or $13,724; $13,724 divided by 94% = $14,600

59. A man purchased a property at 20% less than the listed price and later sold the property for the original listed price. What was the percentage of profit?

A.   10%
B.   20%
C.   25%
D.   40%

Answer: C. Assume the property was listed at $10,000. Listed price less 20% is $8000 purchase price. If it was sold at the listed price of $10,000, the owner made $2000 profit. $2000 profit divided by $8000 cost = 25%

60. Escrow closed May 1st with interest on a $4415 second trust deed paid to June 1st. If the interest rate is 7.2%, the debit to the buyer, if the buyer assumed the loan, would be:

A. $22.09
B. $26.49
C. $4,415.00
D.   None of the above

Answer: B. Since the sellers paid one month's interest in advance, this must be returned to them by the buyer. This will be a debit on the buyer's statement. $4415 X .006 (7.2% divided by 12) = $26.49

61. A board foot of lumber could be obtained from a piece of lumber that is:

A.   6" X 6" X 1"
B.   6" X 12" X 1"
C.   12" X 1" X 1"
D.   6" X 12" X 12"

Answer: D. A board foot of lumber contains 144 cubic inches of lumber. Choice "D" is the only one that exceeds 144 cubic inches.

62. Assume that a second trust deed of $1000 was to be paid in annual installments of $300 plus 6% interest, with a balloon payment of the balance at the end of the third year. The remaining balance of the principal after the annual installment had been paid was:

A. $400
B. $424
C. $506
D. $520

Answer: A. Since the payments on the principal are $300 per year and the borrower has made two payments plus whatever interest was due, the balance is $400. $1000 - $600 = $400

63. Assume a real estate salesman sold a residence for $31,000. If the broker's commission was 6% and the salesman was to receive 45% of the total commission for selling the property, the salesman would receive:

A. $837.70
B. $959.95
C. $1,860.00
D. None of the above

Answer: D. $31,000 X 6% =$1860 total commission; 45% of $1860 = $837.00 Choice "A" is close, but not exactly $837.00

64. If Broker Christianson brought in an offer of 10% less than the listing price of $15,300 and the seller would agree to the price if the broker would accept a 20% reduction of his commission, the broker's commission would amount to:

A. $660.96
B. $689.85
C. $735.84
D. $827.82

Answer: A. $15,300 - $1530 (10%) = $13,770; $13,770 x 6% = $826.20; 80% of $826.20 (less 20%) = $660.96

65. A man enters into a lease agreement on a grocery store with the following terms: $350 minimum monthly rent or 5% grocery sales, 7% of meat sales, 6% of deli sales, and 8% of produce sales, whichever is greater. The grocery sales were $27,000 annually, meat sales $500 per month, deli sales $300 per month and produce sales $3,000 annually. What was the annual rent on the store?

A. $3,180
B. $4,200

C. $4,386
D. $5,120

Answer: B. Grocery Sales: $27,000 x 5% = $1350; Meat Sales: ($500 x 12) x 7% = $420; Deli Sales: ($300 x 12) x 6% = $216; Produce Sales: $3,000 x 8% = $240; Total of above = $2226 (or) the minimum rent would be $350 x 12 = $4,200, since $4,200 is greater, then the annual rent would be $4,200.

66. A building was insured for $19,500 at a rate of .18 per hundred. If the three year policy was 2 1/2 times the one year rate, what amount per month should be added to the monthly payments to properly cover the insurance cost?

A. $7.31
B. $2.92
C. $2.44
D. $1.46

Answer: C. $0.18 x 2.5 = $0.45 per $100; ($19,500 x $0.45) divided by 100 = $87.75; $87.75 divided by 36 = $2.44

67. What is the annual interest rate on a $16,000 loan when the interest payments are $160.00 per quarter on the full amount? At least:

A.   3%, but less than 4%
B.   4%, but less than 5%
C.   5%, but less than 6%
D.   6%, but less than 7%

Answer: B. $160.00 x 4 = $640.00; $640.00 divided by $16,000 = 4%

68. A homeowner sold his house for $23,000. If the selling price represented a 15% profit over what he had originally paid for the house, the original price of the home was:

A. $19,550
B. $20,000
C. $27,000
D.   None of the above

Answer: B. Selling price = cost (100%) + profit (15%) = 115% = $23,000; $23,000 divided by 1.15 = $20,000

69. An owner of a section of land dedicates an easement for a road along the south side of his section. The easement contained 3 acres. The width of the road was approximately:

A.   Twenty feet
B.   Thirty feet
C.   Forty feet
D.   Fifty feet

Answer: A. The length of the road is one mile, or 5280 feet. The total area is three acres, or 130,680 square feet (43,560 x 3 = 130,680 square feet) 130,680 divided by 5280 feet = 24.75 feet

70. There are five units in a condo. Smith paid $12,600, Jones paid $13,500, Kahn paid $13,750, Poe paid $14,400 and Clark paid $15,250. If there was an $1800 annual

maintenance fee and each owner was to pay his proportionate share based upon the ratio of his unit purchase price to the total purchase price of all units, the monthly share of Smith's unit would be:

A. $8.00
B. $27.00
C. $32.40
D. $36.00

Answer: B. Total purchase price was $69,500 $12,600 divided by $69,500 = 18%; $1800 divided by 12 months = $150 per month; $150 x 18% = $27.00

71. A property in probate was offered for sale and an offer of $12,000 was received. If anyone else wishes to bid on the property at the time of the confirmation, the initial minimum overbid must be:

A. $12,000
B. $13,000
C. $13,100
D. $13,500

Answer: C. The first additional bid (overbid) must be at least the original bid plus 10% of the first $10,000 of the original bid and 5% of any excess. Original bid = $12,000 $10,000 x 10% = $1,000 $2,000 excess at 5% = $100 Total of above = $13,100

72. The total number of lineal feet on one side of a Section is:

A.   1,000

B.   2,640
C.   5,280
D.   43,560

Answer: C. One side of a section is one mile long, or 5280 feet

73. Arnold held a straight note which carried an annual interest rate of 8.4%. If in five years he had received $5,460 in interest, the principal amount of the note was:

A. $10,000
B. $11,500
C. $13,000
D. $15,000

Answer: C. $5460 divided by 5 = $1092 interest per year; $1092 divided by 8.4% = $13,000.

74. Escrow companies normally base their prorations on an escrow year of:

A.   350 days
B.   355 days
C.   360 days
D.   365 days

Answer: C. 12 months at 30 days each = 360 days per year.

75. Eddie Ronquillo sold his home for $17,200. If this represents 9% more than what he paid for it, the cost of the home was most nearly:

A. $15,424
B. $15,500
C. $15,800
D. $16,000

Answer: C. $17,200 divided by 1.09 = $15,779.82 Closest answer is $15,800.

76. An individual borrowed $750 on a straight note at an interest rate of 7.2%. If the total interest payment on the loan was $81.00, the term of the loan was:

A. 15 months
B. 18 months
C. 21 months
D. 24 months

Answer: B. Calculate the amount of interest expense for one month and then find how many months worth of interest was paid. $750 x 7.2% = $54.00 per year; $54.00 divided by 12 = $4.50 per month; $81.00 divided by $4.50 = 18 months.

77. The Richard Rock sold his home and had to carry back a second trust deed and note of $5310. If he sold the note for $3823.20 before any payments had been made on the note, the rate of discount amounted to:

A. 25%
B. 28%
C. 54%
D. 72%

Answer: B. $5310 (original amount of note) $3823.20 (net received from sale) 5310 - 3823.20 = $1486.80 (amount of discount) $1486.20 divided by $5310 = 28% discount.

78. A real estate syndicate paid $193,600 for a lot on which they planned to build a high rise apartment. If the lot was 200 feet deep and they paid $4.40 per square foot, the cost per front foot was:

A. $220
B. $440
C. $880
D. $960

Answer: C. $193,600 divided by $4.40 = 44,000 square feet of lot; 44,000 divided by 200 feet = 220 feet frontage; $193,600 divided by 220 feet = $880 per front foot.

79. A rectangular parcel of land that measures 220' X 330' contains most nearly:

A. 1 1/4 acres
B. 1 3/5 acres
C. 1 2/3 acres
D. 2 acres

Answer: C. 220' x 33' = 72,600 square feet; 72,600 divided by 43,560 square feet per acre = 1.67 acres; 1.67 = 1 2/3 acres.

80. A borrower signed a straight note for a term of eight months in the amount of $2500. If she paid $150 in interest on the loan, the interest rate was:

A. 8%
B. 9%
C. 9%
D. 10%

Answer: C. $150 divided by 8 months = $18.75 per month; $18.75 x 12 = $225 per year; $225 divided by $2500 = 9%.

81. An income property was appraised for $100,000 based on a 6% capitalization rate. If an investor used an 8% cap rate, the value of the property would be:

A. $60,000
B. $75,000
C. $80,000
D. $90,000

Answer: B. $100,000 x 6% = $6000 net income; $6000 divided by 8% = $75,000 value

82. If a note in the amount of $22,250 specifies monthly payments over a period of 30 years at 6.6% interest per annum, what is the first month's interest payment?

A. $111.25
B. $122.38
C. $130.71
D. $140.50

Answer: B. $22,250 x 6.6% = $1468.50 $1468.50 divided by 12 = $122.38

83. If Haeli McDonald paid a commission of 6% of the selling price of a property valued at $54,375, the selling broker would receive:

A. $4,275.00
B. $3,375.00
C. $3,262.50
D. $3,191.50

Answer: C. $54,375 x 6% = $3262.50

84. A bank agreed to lend the owner of a piece of property a sum equal to 66 2/3% of its appraised valuation. The interest rate charged on the amount borrowed is 5% per annum. The first year's interest amounted to $200.00. What was the valuation placed upon the property by the bank?

A. $3,000.00
B. $4,000.00
C. $5,333.33
D. $6,000.00

Answer: D. $200.00 divided by 5% = $4000 loan $4000 divided by 66.66% = $6000

85. A married couple purchased a property for a total price of $18,000, paying $5000 down and having the seller take back a first trust deed in the amount of $13,000. The terms of the $13,000 trust deed called for no payments in the first year. If at the end of the first year, they were to sell the

property at twice its original cost, their original dollar is now worth:

A. $2.00
B. $4.60
C. $7.20
D. $8.00

Answer: B. The owners had an equity or investment of $5000. If the property doubles in value to $36,000 and you deduct the $13,000 loan, their equity increased to $23,000. $5000 divided into $23,000 equals $4.60.

86. If a borrower pays $1650 interest per quarter on a straight note of $60,000, the interest rate would be:

A.   8.50%
B.   9.00%
C.   10.50%
D.   11.00%

Answer: D. $1650 = interest for 3 months; $1650 x 4 = $6600 interest for one year; $6600 divided by $60,000 = .11 or 11%.

87. Maria Watson sold a residence that was free and clear of all liens and received a check for $30,580. If closing costs of $430.60 had been deducted as well as the broker's 6& commission, the actual selling price would have been most nearly:

A. $31,590
B. $31,825

C. $32,885
D. $32,990

Answer: D. $30,580.00 (net) + 430.00 (closing costs) + 6% commission = selling price ; $31,010.60 divided by 94% = $32,990.00.

88. The number of townships in a tract of land that is 28 miles square is most nearly:

A. Eleven
B. Seventeen
C. Twenty two
D. Fifteen

Answer: C. A township is 6 miles square and contains 36 square miles 28 miles x 28 miles = 784 square miles; 784 divided by 36 = 21.77 townships.

89. Clever executed a promissory note in the amount of $7000. If the note called for the payment of interest only and Clever paid off the entire sum in 90 days together with interest of $210, the interest rate on the note was most nearly:

A. 9%
B. 10%
C. 11%
D. 12%

Answer: D. 90 = approximately 1/4 of a year $210 interest for 90 days x 4 = $840 interest for one year $840 divided by $7000

= 12%.

90. Broker Thomas is listing a property owned by Gibson. Gibson has advised Thomas that he wished to realize $37,000 cash from the sale after paying Thomas a 4% commission and paying $600 in closing costs. To accomplish this and assuming that the property is free and clear, the selling price must be at least:

A. $37,856
B. $38,480
C. $39,110
D. $39,167

Answer: D. $37,000 + $600 + 4% = selling price; $37,600 divided by 96% = $39,167

91. The interest rate on a straight note in the amount of $27,000 that calls for interest payments of $573.75 each quarter would most nearly be:

A.   6.6%
B.   7.2%
C.   8.6%
D.   9.2%

Answer: C. $573.75 x 4 = $2295 interest for one year $2295 divided by $27,000 = 0.85 or 8.5% 8.6% is closest.

92. A commercial office building yields an annual net income of $174,000. If an appraiser applied a capitalization rate of 8% to the property, the market value of the property would most nearly be:

A. $1,392,000
B. $1,666,000
C. $1,932,000
D. $2,175,000

Answer: D. $174,000 income divided by 8% = $2,175,000.

93. An individual who receives $225.00 per month on a money market savings account that pays 7.5% per year, has invested which of the following amounts?

A. $125,000
B. $27,000
C. $36,000
D. $48,000

Answer: C. $225 x 12 = $2700 per year $2700 divided by 7.5% = $36,000   .

94. A holder of a second trust deed and straight note with a face amount of $3740 sold it for $2431. This amounted to a discount of:

A. 26%
B. 35%
C. 45%
D. 55%

Answer: B. $3740 - $2431 = $1309 discount $1309 divided by $3740 = 35%

95. A seller took back a second trust deed and note in the amount of $11,400, payable $240 per month, including interest at 7% per annum. If interest on the note begins July 15 and the first payment is made on August 15, the amount of the first payment that is applied to the principal is:

A. $66.50
B. $79.80
C. $173.50
D. $240.00

Answer: C. $11,400 x 7% = $798 per year $798 divided by 12 = $66.50 per month $240 - $66.50 = $173.50.

96. A homeowner made a regular monthly payment of $550 on her home loan. Out of the total payment, the lender deducted the interest that was due for the month and applied the remaining balance of $43.85 to the principal. If the outstanding balance of the loan was $56,500, the interest rate on the load was most nearly:

A. 8.50%
B. 9.25%
C. 10.75%
D. 12.50%

Answer: C. $550 - $43.85 = $506.15 interest for 1st month $506.15 x 12 = $6073.80 per year $6073.80 divided by $56,500 = 11%.

97. A square parcel of land that is 1780' X 1780' contains most nearly:

A. 27 acres
B. 54 acres
C. 65 acres
D. 73 acres

Answer: D. 1780' X 1780' = 3,168,400 square feet 3,168,400 divided by 43,560 = 72.736 acres.

98. An investor purchased two lots and paid $18,000 for each one. Since each lot had a 60' frontage he was able to subdivide the combined parcels in 3 lots with equal front footage. If the 3 lots sold for $15,000 each, his rate of profit on his investment was:

A. 20%
B. 25%
C. 33%
D. 40%

Answer: B. 3 lots x $15,000 each = $45,000 selling price $45,000 less cost of $36,000 (2 x $18,000) = $9000 profit; $9000 divided by $36,000 = 25%.

99. A one acre parcel of land that is square is divided into four lots of equal size. If the lots are rectangular, parallel to each other and are 240' deep, the width of each lot is most nearly:

A. 45.4'
B. 90.8'
C. 181'

D.   240'

Answer: A. 43,560 square feet divided by 240' = 181.5' wide 181.5 divided by 4 = 43.375' 45.4' is closest.

100. Natalie Johnson owns a $100,000 property based on a 6% capitalization rate. If due to changes in economic conditions investors now require a higher capitalization rate or 8%, what would the value of the property be using the same dollar income?

A. $90,000
B. $75,000
C. $80,000
D. $60,000

Answer: B. $100,000 if capitalized at 6% would give a net income projection of $6,000. $6,000 net income capitalized at 8% would give $75,000 in value. $6,000 divided by 0.08 (8%) = $75,000.

TEST SECTION

In this section there will be no answers to the questions. You will be able to test yourself here by answering the questions on a separate sheet of paper. Number your papers 1 through 232 (Vocabulary) 1 through 200 (State Exam) 1 through 100 (Math Exam) and write down the letter of the answer you think is correct. Score yourself at the end by using the correct answers in the Study Section to see how you did. If you did not score at least 90%, go back to the Study Section and read through the exam again and continue to study and memorize the answers until you are scoring 90% or better. This will insure you pass your actual exam on the 1st try.

REAL ESTATE VOCABULARY EXAM

1. Which of the following describes the term "appreciation"?

A.   Kind words expressed to someone about something they did
B.   An increase in the value of property
C.   An item of value owned by an individual
D.   None of the above

2. When ownership of a mortgage is transferred from one company or individual to another, it is called

A.   an assumption
B.   an assignment
C.   an assessment
D.   all of the above

3. A mortgage loan which requires the remaining balance be paid at a specific point in time is called a/an

A.   balloon mortgage
B.   early due mortgage
C.   mortgage of convenience
D.   promissory note

4. The following reason accounts for why bridge loans are not used much anymore:

A.   More second mortgage lenders now will lend at a high loan to value

B.　　Sellers would rather accept offers from Buyers who have already sold their property

C.　　Neither A or B

D.　　Both A and B

5. A title which is free of liens or legal questions as to ownership of the property is called a _____ title.

A.　　good

B.　　cloudy

C.　　clear

D.　　free

6. What is the collateral in a home loan?

A.　　The property itself

B.　　A person's good name

C.　　The amount of savings a person has

D.　　The current automobile the person owns

7. The adjustment date on an adjustable-rate mortgage is

A.　　the date the interest rate changes

B.　　the date the stock market goes up

C.　　30 days from the date the mortgage was taken out

D.　　all of the above

8. What is the deposit made by a potential buyer to show he is serious about buying a house called?

A.　　Serious money deposit

B.　　Earnest money deposit

C.   "Nothing ventured, nothing gained" deposit

D.   Down payment

9. A right-of-way which gives persons other than the owner access to or over a property is known as an

A.   easement

B.   ingress

C.   egress

D.   none of the above

10. Which best describes a "subdivision"?

A.   Houses in the same neighborhood similar in style and size

B.   A housing development created by dividing a tract of land into individual lots

C.   A development which is "substandard"

D.   None of the above

11. When someone contributes to the construction or rehabilitation of a property with labor or services rather than cash, that contribution is called

A.   a personal contribution

B.   sweat equity

C.   a big help to the contractors

D.   toil and labor

12. A two-step mortgage is defined as

A.   an adjustable rate mortgage with one interest rate for the first five or seven years and a different rate for the remainder of the term.

B.   a mortgage which is both adjustable and fixed

C.   a mortgage which is named after a dance step

D.   all of the above

13. A legal document evidencing a person's right to or ownership of a property is called a

A.   quitclaim deed

B.   title

C.   yearly lease

D.   accurate appraisal

14. If you were buying a house that included furnishings, you would receive a written document transferring title to the personal property. This document is called a/an

A.   title

B.   deed

C.   bill of sale

D.   evidence of payment

15. An oral or written agreement that is binding in a court of law is called a

A.   gentlemen's agreement

B.   contract

C.   business deal

D.   promissory note

16. The part of the purchase price of a property that the

buyer pays in cash and does not finance with the mortgage is called the

A.   deposit
B.   second mortgage
C.   down payment
D.   deed of trust

17. A female named in a will to administer an estate is called an

A.   executor
B.   executrix
C.   individual representative
D.   able inheritor

18. The greatest possible interest a person can have in real estate is called

A.   fee complex
B.   fee simple
C.   no additional fees
D.   ownership

19. Required for properties located in federally designated flood areas, this type of insurance compensates for physical property damage resulting from flooding. It is called

A.   water damage insurance
B.   hurricane insurance
C.   there's no such thing
D.   flood insurance

20. The following is true of a government loan:

A.   It is guaranteed by the Department of Veterans Affairs (VA)

B.   It is guaranteed by the Rural Housing Service (RHS)

C.   It is insured by the Federal Housing Administration (FHA)

D.   All of the above

21. The person conveying an interest in real property is called

A.   the buyer

B.   the grantee

C.   the grantor

D.   the mortgagor

22. Insurance that covers in the event of physical damage to a property from fire, wind, vandalism, or other hazards is called

A.   act of God insurance

B.   hazardous insurance

C.   hazard insurance

D.   there is no such insurance

23. A liquid asset is

A.   an asset which is not in solid form

B.   an asset which cannot be frozen

C.   a cash asset or an asset easily turned into cash

D.   an asset that is hard to get to

24. Another term for the lender in a mortgage agreement is the

A.   banker
B.   mortgagee
C.   mortgagor
D.   private mortgage company

25. If you are buying a house and asking the Seller to provide all or part of the financing, you are asking for _____financing.

A.   special
B.   owner
C.   personal
D.   non-bank

26. A point is

A.   the part of the pen you sign a contract with
B.   a score in a basketball game
C.   the reason for telling the story
D.   1% of the amount of the mortgage

27. What does a power of attorney grant someone?

A.   The ability to attend law school
B.   Complete or limited authority on behalf of someone else
C.   Complete control over which medical facility someone

uses

D.   The right to inherit an estate

28. The principal is

A.   the amount borrowed or remaining unpaid
B.   part of the monthly payment that reduces the remaining balance of a mortgage
C.   an ethic or value
D.   both A and B

29. A promissory note is

A.   a written promise to repay a specified amount over a specified period of time
B.   an oral promise to repay a specified amount over a specified period of time
C.   a note passed back and forth in class
D.   a note you deliver to another telling them of your intentions

30. Which of the following best describes a real estate agent?

A.   A licensed person who negotiates and transacts the sale of real estate
B.   The owner of a real estate firm
C.   A person who negotiates and transacts the sale of real estate but is not licensed
D.   A person who sells both property and insurance

31. When does an assumption take place?

A.   When someone believes something and it turns out to be true
B.   When the buyer assumes the seller's mortgage
C.   When the seller assumes the buyer's mortgage
D.   All of the above

32. A legal document conveying title to a property is called a/an

A.   sales contract
B.   option to purchase
C.   deed
D.   contract for deed

33. If you have a loan and transfer the title to another individual without informing the lender, it is likely that the lender will demand payment of the outstanding loan balance. He is able to do this because of a clause in your mortgage called the

A.   due on demand clause
B.   acceleration clause
C.   amortization schedule
D.   both A and B

34. The most common type of bankruptcy is called

A.   Chapter 11 bankruptcy
B.   Chapter 11 no asset bankruptcy
C.   Chapter 7 no asset bankruptcy
D.   Chapter 7 bankruptcy

35. Which of the following best describes a "broker"?

A.   Someone who owns a real estate firm
B.   Some real estate agents working for brokers
C.   Someone who acts as an agent and brings two parties together for a transaction and earns a fee for this
D.   All of the above

36. A normal contingency in a real estate contract would be that the

A.   purchaser is able to obtain a satisfactory home inspection from a qualified inspector.
B.   seller is allowed to come back and spend 2 weeks in the house each year
C.   purchaser is able to have occupancy as soon as the sales contract is signed
D.   seller is allowed to dig up some of the landscaping and take it with him

37. If you go to a bank or mortgage company to apply for a home, what type of mortgage would you be applying for?

A.   Government
B.   Conventional
C.   American
D.   Adjustable rate

38. A report of someone's credit history which is prepared by a credit bureau and used by a lender in the loan qualification process is called a

A.   personal affidavit
B.   credit card history
C.   savings account history
D.   credit report

39. If you have not made your mortgage payment within 30 days of the due date, the mortgage is considered to be in

A.   arrears
B.   default
C.   trouble
D.   bankruptcy

40. A term used by appraisers to estimate the physical condition of a building. It may be different from the building's actual age.

A.   Estimated age
B.   Longevity
C.   Preferred age
D.   Effective age

41. The difference between the fair market value of a property and the amount still owed on the mortgage and other liens is the owner's financial interest in the property and is called his

A.   equity
B.   balance due
C.   indebtedness
D.   none of the above

42. You put in a new driveway to your property, but in the process the paving goes across your property line onto your neighbor's property a few inches. This is called an

A.   illegal driveway
B.   extra benefit for your neighbor
C.   encroachment
D.   easement

43. A government loan that is not a VA loan would be a/an

A.   FHA mortgage
B.   FDA mortgage
C.   This type loan does not exist
D.   ARM mortgage

44. If you convey an interest in real property to a relative, that person is known as the

A.   receiver
B.   mortgagor
C.   grantee
D.   lucky relative

45. You decide you want to buy a boat and you want to borrow against the equity in your home. You would get a mortgage loan up to a specified amount which is in second position to your first mortgage. This arrangement is called a

A.   perfectly acceptable way to buy a boat
B.   leverage against your house

C.   home equity line of credit
D.   line of credit for personal purposes

46. You are your sister are joint tenants in a home your mother left you. Your sister has three children in her will and you have one. If she dies first, who does the property go to?

A.   It is divided equally between her three children
B.   It goes entirely to you
C.   It is divided equally between her three children and your one
D.   It goes into her estate

47. What is the best description of a lien?

A.   Something that doesn't stand up straight in a house
B.   Something that's illegal
C.   A legal claim against property that must be paid off when it's sold
D.   None of the above

48. What is a lock-in?

A.   A gated community which locks the gate at midnight
B.   An agreement from a lender guaranteeing a specific interest rate for a specific time at a certain cost
C.   What parents do with wayward children
D.   A type of key available at most hardware stores

49. The right of a government to take private property for public use upon payment of its fair market value. It is the

basis for condemnation proceedings.

A.   Eminent domain
B.   Governmental domain
C.   Encroachment
D.   Both A and B

50. A mortgage with a lien position subordinate to the first mortgage on a piece of property is called a

A.   second mortgage
B.   first subordinate mortgage
C.   mortgage which isn't legal
D.   lien position mortgage.

51. An adjustable-rate mortgage, also known as an ARM is

A.   one in which the interest rate is fixed over time
B.   one in which the interest rate changes periodically, depending on index changes
C.   one in which the interest rate changes periodically, depending on the stock market
D.   a type of mortgage that the mortgagor can adjust himself

52. A schedule that shows how much of each payment will be applied to principal and how much toward interest over the life of the loan is called a/n

A.   amortization schedule
B.   annual percentage rate
C.   assumption
D.   both A and C

53. The term applied to a mortgage in which you make the payments every two weeks, thereby making thirteen payments a year rather than twelve. This mortgage is paid off faster than a normal mortgage.

A. Twice-monthly mortgage
B. Accelerated mortgage
C. Bi-weekly mortgage
D. None of the above

54. The limitation of how much an adjustable rate mortgage may adjust over a six-month period, annual period, and over the life of the loan is called a

A. buy-down
B. high point
C. top stop
D. cap

55. When is a real estate transaction considered to be "closed"?

A. When the buyer has signed all the sales contracts
B. When the closing documents have been recorded at the local recorder's office
C. When all the documents are signed and money changes hands
D. Both B and C.

56. A record of an individual's repayment of debt, reviewed by mortgage lenders in determining credit risk is called a

A.   credit affidavit
B.   credit history
C.   there is no such record
D.   credit worthiness

57. If you sell your property to a neighbor and the lender demands repayment in full, this means you have a _____ in your mortgage.

A.   seller pays all provision
B.   buyer pays all provision
C.   due-on-sale provision
D.   none of the above

58. The sum total of all the real and personal property owned by an individual at time of death is called their

A.   estate
B.   probate
C.   will
D.   all of the above.

59. If you list your property with a real estate agent and sign a written agreement that they are the only ones entitled to a listing for a specific time you have given them an

A.   exclusive listing
B.   exclusive right to advertise
C.   exclusive right to show
D.   inclusive listing

60. Fair market value could be defined as

A.   how much a property is worth, determined by a realtor's market analysis
B.   the most a buyer, willing, but not compelled to buy, would pay
C.   the least a seller, willing, but not compelled to sell, would take
D.   both B and C

61. If a lender agrees to make a loan to a specific borrower on a specific property, he has made a

A.   decision to make the loan
B.   statement that both the buyer and the property pass inspection
C.   firm commitment
D.   both B and C

62. If you buy a house and build cabinets into the wall, then sell that house, the cabinets stay because they have become a

A.   type of attachment
B.   fixture
C.   part of the house
D.   none of the above

63. A home inspection is

A.   a thorough inspection by a professional which evaluates the structural and mechanical condition of a property
B.   not required by law

C.   often a contingency in a contract that it turns out satisfactorily
D.   both A and C.

64. An insurance policy which combines personal liability insurance and hazard insurance coverage for a dwelling and its contents is called

A.   homeowner's insurance
B.   buyer's insurance
C.   errors and omissions insurance
D.   all of the above

65. Which of the following is true of a lease-option?

A.   It is an alternative financing option
B.   Each month's rent may also consist of an additional amount applied toward the
purchase
C.   The price is already set in the beginning
D.   All of the above

66. In simple terms, a sum of borrowed money (principal) usually repaid with interest is called a

A.   mortgage
B.   loan
C.   conventional loan
D.   alternative mortgage

67. A property description which is recognized by law and is sufficient to locate and identify the property without oral

testimony is known as the property's

A.   address
B.   911 address
C.   legal description
D.   identifying information

68. The date on which the principal balance of a loan, bond, or other financial instrument becomes due and payable is called

A.   its due date
B.   maturity
C.   end of the paper trail
D.   delivery

69. The person borrowing money in a mortgage agreement is called the

A.   mortgagor
B.   mortgagee
C.   borrower
D.   lessee

70. Which of the following is true about an origination fee?

A.   It applies to both government and conventional loans
B.   It is usually 1% on a government loan
C.   It is usually 2% on a conventional loan
D.   Both A and B

71. Which of the following falls under the term "personal

property"?

A. A garage attached to a house
B. A sofa
C. The front porch of a home
D. The windows in a home

72. In some cases if a borrower pays off a loan before it is due he may encounter a penalty called a

A. penalty for early withdrawal
B. loan to value penalty
C. prepayment penalty
D. there is never a penalty for paying a loan off early

73. Which of the following statements is true regarding the term "pre-approval"?

A. It applies only to the property
B. It is done before the loan application is complete
C. It s a loosely used term
D. None of the above

74. PITI reserves applies to

A. a cash amount the borrower must have on hand after down payment and closing Costs.
B. an amount which is financed with the mortgage
C. both A and B
D. none of the above

75. Why would a public auction take place?

A.   It's a good way to buy property
B.   To inform the public about property for sale
C.   To help auctioneers get employment
D.   To sell property to repay a mortgage in default

76. The term "realtor" applies to

A.   any real estate agent who has passed the state exam
B.   any real estate agent whose license is active
C.   any real estate agent who is a member of a local real estate board affiliated with
       the National Association of Realtors.
D.   any real estate agent who belongs to his local board

77. "Remaining term" refers to

A.   the remaining school term for a real estate class
B.   the original amortization term minus the number of payments that have been applied
C.   the months left in a pregnancy
D.   all of the above

78. Which of the following is not true of a "revolving debt"?

A.   It is a type of credit arrangement, like a credit card
B.   It revolves around no interest for the first six months
C.   A customer borrows against a pre-approved line of credit
D.   The customer is billed for the amount borrowed plus any interest due

79. Which of the following does a survey not show?

A.   Precise legal boundaries of a property
B.   Location of improvements, easements, rights of way
C.   Encroachments
D.   Location of furnishings within the dwelling

80. What is meant by "seller carry-back"?

A.   The seller physically carries his furnishings out of the house on the day of closing
B.   The seller agrees to be on the mortgage with the buyer
C.   the seller provides financing, often in combination with an assumable mortgage
D.   The seller carries the principal, but not the interest on a loan

81. A title company is one which

A.   is usually not needed in a real estate transaction
B.   is not called upon until one year after the sale is closed
C.   specializes in examining and insuring titles to real estate
D.   specializes in preparing deeds and deeds of trust

82. A state or local tax which is payable when title passes from one owner to another is called a

A.   title tax
B.   transfer tax
C.   revenue stamps
D.   real estate tariff

83. What is Truth-in-Lending?

A.   A state law requiring lenders to fully disclose in writing all terms and conditions
of a mortgage

B.   A federal law requiring lenders to fully disclose in writing all terms and
        conditions of a mortgage

C.   A local law requiring lenders to fully disclose in writing all terms and conditions of a mortgage

D.   None of the above

84. A VA mortgage

A.   is a conventional mortgage for the state of Virginia

B.   is guaranteed by the Department of Veterans Affairs

C.   originates in Texas but ends up in Virginia

D.   in available to anyone applying for a mortgage

85. Which of the following is not true of "amortization"?

A.   Over time the interest portion increases as the loan balance decreases

B.   Over time the interest portion decreases as the loan balance decreases

C.   Over time the amount applied to principal increases so the loan is paid off in the
specified time

D.   None of the above

86. The valuation placed on property by a public tax assessor for taxation purposes is called

A. real value
B. fair market value
C. assessed value
D. predicted value

87. If a veteran is eligible for a VA loan, he or she would receive a document from the VA called

A. Certificate of Authenticity
B. Certificate of Approval
C. Certificate of Met Requirements
D. Certificate of Eligibility

88. Which of the following usually earns the largest commissions in a real estate transaction?

A. Attorneys
B. Realtors
C. Loan officers
D. Home warranty companies

89. An unwritten body of law based on general custom in England and used to an extent in some states is called

A. common law
B. uncommon law
C. casual law
D. it isn't law if it's not written down

90. If a real estate agent is trying to determine the market value of a property, one thing they would use is recent sales

of similar properties or

A. neighbors' estimates of the value of the property
B. records from several years back in the same neighborhood
C. comparable sales
D. sales they estimate to happen in the future

91. A person to whom money is owed is known as a

A. debtor
B. creditor
C. mortgagee
D. lender

92. Discount points refer to

A. a system of figuring out how much the property will be discounted
B. points paid in addition to the one percent loan origination fee
C. usually only FHA and VA loans
D. both B and C

93. Which of the following can the Equal Credit Opportunity Act (ECOA) not discriminate against?

A. Race, color or religion
B. National origin
C. Age, sex, or marital status
D. All of the above

94. An exclusive listing is one which gives a licensed real estate agent the exclusive right to sell a property

A.   until it sells
B.   until the owner takes it off the market
C.   for a specified period of time
D.   none of the above

95. Which of the following is true about Fannie Mae's Community Home Buyer's Program?

A.   It is an income-based community lending model
B.   It has flexible underwriting guidelines to increase low to moderate income
         family's buying power
C.   Borrows who participate must attend pre-purchase home-buyer education sessions
D.   All of the above

96. The mortgage that is in first place among any loans recorded against a property and usually refers to the date in which loans are recorded, but not always, is called a

A.   primary mortgage
B.   first in line mortgage
C.   first mortgage
D.   both A and B

97. The legal process by which a borrower in default under a mortgage is deprived of his or her interest in the mortgaged property is called a

A.   takeover by the mortgage company
B.   public auction
C.   foreclosure
D.   proceeds sale

98. Loans against 401K plans are

A.   not allowed for down payments on property
B.   an acceptable source of down payment for most types of loans
C.   too great a risk for most people to take
D.   only allowed if you're accumulated $50,000 in the plan

99. A late charge is

A.   the penalty a borrower pays when a payment is late a stated number of days
B.   usually put into play when the payment is fifteen days late on a first mortgage
C.   usually not applicable to most people
D.   both A and B

100. A person's financial obligations are known as his

A.   payments
B.   assets
C.   liabilities
D.   credit risks

101. Which of the following is not true of annual percentage rate (APR)?

A. It is the note rate on your loan
B. It is not the note rate on your loan
C. It is a value created according to a government formula intended to reflect the true
cost of borrowing and expressed as a percentage
D. It is always higher than the actual note rate on your loan

102. An individual qualified by education, training, and experience to estimate the value of real property and personal property and who usually works independently is called an

A. estimator of value
B. appraiser
C. on-site inspector
D. underwriter

103. Which of the following best describes a "balloon payment"?

A. Payment delivered with a "bang"
B. First of many payments on a mortgage
C. The final lump sum payment due at the termination of a balloon mortgage
D. Payments which go higher and higher each year

104. When a borrower refinances his mortgage at a higher amount than the current loan balance with the intention of pulling out money for personal use, it is referred to as a

A. refinance extra
B. cash-out refinance

C. home equity refinance
D. adjustable lump sum refinance

105. A certificate of deposit is

A. the same as a down payment
B. a liquid asset
C. a deposit held in a bank paying a certain amount of interest to the depositor over a
certain time
D. a deposit held in a bank which pays double the amount of normal interest over
time

106. Common area assessments are

A. sometimes called Homeowners Association Fees
B. paid by individual owners of condominiums or planned unit developments
C. used to maintain the property and common areas
D. all of the above

107. A short-term interim loan for financing the cost of construction is called a

A. flexible loan
B. convertible loan
C. construction loan
D. not a loan, but a promissory note

108. In simple terms, debt is

A.   credit extended to someone
B.   an amount owed to another
C.   an amount owed to another with interest
D.   repayable

109. Which of the following is not true of the term "depreciation"?

A.   It is a decline in the value of property
B.   It is an accounting term showing the declining monetary value of an asset
C.   It is a true expense where money is actually paid
D.   Lenders add back depreciation expense for self-employed borrowers and count it
       as income

110. Which of the following would not be paid by escrow disbursements?

A.   Real estate taxes
B.   Hazard insurance
C.   Mortgage insurance
D.   Personal property taxes

111. The lawful expulsion of an occupant from real property is called

A.   conviction
B.   divorce from bed and board
C.   eviction
D.   there is no way to lawfully remove an occupant from real property

112. If you have a loan in which the interest rate does not change during the term of the loan you have a _____ mortgage.

A. fixed-rate
B. conventional fixed-rate
C. owner financing
D. all of the above

113. The following is true of a Home Equity Conversion Mortgage (HECM).

A. It is also known as reverse annuity mortgage
B. You don't make payments to the lender, the lender makes payments to you
C. It enables older homeowners to convert their equity into cash
D. All of the above

114. A written agreement between property owner and tenant stipulating the conditions under which the tenant may possess the property for a specified period of time and the payment due is called a/an

A. contract
B. option
C. lease
D. lease-option

115.   A lender is

A. the firm making the loan
B. the individual representing the firm making the loan
C. the individual offering owner financing
D. both A and B

116. A margin is

A. a measurement of error
B. an artificial line not to write in on a loan document
C. both A and B
D. the difference between the interest rate and the index on an adjustable rate mortgage

117. Which of the following is the best definition of a mortgage broker?

A. A mortgage company which originates loans, then places with other lending institutions
B. A mortgage company which originates loans, then keeps them in house
C. An individual which originates loans, then sells on the secondary market
D. Much like a real estate broker, receives a commission on loans

118. The term "note rate" refers to

A. the speed at which a musician plays scales
B. the interest rate stated on a mortgage note
C. the interest rate stated on a personal loan
D. the rate at which a note is amortized

119. If you have not made your mortgage payment, you are likely to receive which of the following?

A.   Notice of non-payment
B.   A written eviction notice
C.   Notice of default
D.   A letter from an attorney

120. A payment that is not sufficient to cover the scheduled monthly payment on a mortgage loan is called a

A.   late payment
B.   partial payment
C.   "too little, too late" payment
D.   a drop in the bucket

121. PITI stands for

A.   principal, interest, taxes and insurance
B.   principle, interest, taxes and insurance
C.   prepayment, interest, tariff and insurance
D.   none of the above

122. Which of the following describes "prepayment"?

A.   An amount paid to reduce the interest on a loan before the due date
B.   An amount paid to reduce the principal on a loan before the due date
C.   Can result from a sale, owner's decision to pay off the loan, or foreclosure

D.   Both B and C

123. What is private mortgage insurance?

A.   Mortgage insurance that is arranged for by the buyer privately
B.   Mortgage insurance provided by a private mortgage insurance company
C.   Insurance required for loans with a loan-to-value percentage in excess of 80%
D.   Both B and C

124. If you were trying to buy a home you and the seller would need to sign a written contract called a/an

A.   purchase agreement
B.   down payment agreement
C.   option to purchase
D.   all of the above

125. What is a recorder?

A.   A public official who keeps records of real property transactions
B.   The county clerk
C.   The registrar of deeds
D.   All of the above.

126. The principal balance on a mortgage is

A.   the outstanding balance of principal and interest
B.   the outstanding balance of principal only

C. the amount the mortgage has been paid down
D. none of the above

127. Which of the following is not true about qualifying ratios?

A. There are two types of ratios—"top" or "front" and "back" or "bottom"
B. The "top" ratio is a calculation of the borrower's monthly housing costs (principal, taxes, insurance, mortgage insurance, homeowners' association fees) as a percentage of monthly income
C. the "back" ratio includes all monthly costs as well as "back" taxes
D. Both calculations are used in determining whether a borrower can qualify for a mortgage

128. The definition of "real" property is

A. property that has nothing artificial on it, only natural materials
B. land and appurtenances, including anything of a permanent nature such as structures, trees and minerals
C. things located within houses such as furniture, accessories, appliances, and clothing
D. all of the above

129. In joint tenancy, if one person dies and the other inherits the property, this is called

A. tenants in common
B. whatever is stated in the will

C.   following the wishes of the deceased
D.   right of survivorship

130. A secured loan is

A.   backed by collateral
B.   when the borrower promises something of value to the lender
C.   when the bank is not in danger of failing
D.   when the bank has been bailed out

131. A mortgage or other type of lien that has a priority lower than that of the first mortgage is called

A.   a second mortgage
B.   subordinate financing
C.   first subordinate financing
D.   all of the above

132. If you were buying a house and wanted to protect yourself against any loss arising from disputes over ownership of your property, you would purchase

A.   hazard insurance
B.   errors and omissions insurance
C.   title insurance
D.   deed insurance

133   Which of the following is true of the Veteran's Administration (VA)?

A.   It encourages lenders to make mortgages to veterans

B.   It is an agency of the federal government which guarantees residential mortgages made to eligible veterans
C.   The guarantee protects the lender against loss
D.   All of the above

134. The form used to apply for a mortgage loan, which contains information about a borrower's income, savings, assets, debts, and more is called a/an

A.   application for funds
B.   income documentary
C.   both A and B
D.   application

135. An assessment does which of the following?

A.   Places a value on property for the purpose of real estate sales
B.   Is the same as a competitive market analysis
C.   Places a value on property for the purpose of taxation
D.   Is usually carried out by the mayor of a town

136. Which of the following is not true about the "bond market"?

A.   It refers to the daily buy and selling of thirty-year treasury bonds
B.   Lenders do not usually follow this market closely
C.   The same factors that affect the bond market affect mortgage rates at the same time
D.   Fluctuations in this market cause mortgage rates to change daily

137. What does the term "buydown" mean?

A.   Usually refers to a fixed rate mortgage where the interest rate is "bought down" for a temporary period, usually one to three years.

B.   A lump sum is paid and held in an account used to supplement the borrower's monthly payment

C.   These funds can sometimes come from the seller to induce someone to buy their property

D.   All of the above

138. Certificate of Reasonable Value (CRV) applies to

A.   an FHA loan
B.   a conventional loan
C.   a VA loan
D.   a car loan

139. If you are buying a piece of property and have someone else who is obligated on the loan and is on the title to the property, that person is called a

A.   spouse
B.   family member or friend who shares the property and payments with you
C.   co-borrower
D.   none of the above

140. How would you define "collection"?

A.   A plate, usually at church, where money is donated

B.   It goes into effect when a borrower falls behind
C.   It applies to several or many things in the same category on a loan application
D.   It only applies to trash

141. Which of the following is true of "condominium"?

A.   It applies to ownership, not to construction or development
B.   It is a type of ownership where all of the owners own each other's interior units
C.   It is an ownership where owners own the property, common areas, and buildings together
D.   both A and C

142. An organization which gathers, records, updates, and stores financial and public records information about the payment records of individuals being considered for credit is called a

A.   credit repository
B.   credit reporting agency
C.   mortgage company
D.   bank

143. In some states a recorded mortgage is replaced by a

A.   contract for deed
B.   promissory note
C.   deed of trust
D.   deed

144. If you have failed to pay mortgage payments when they are due, it is called

A. delinquency
B. foreclosure
C. collections
D. no big deal

145. Which of the following would not be considered an "encumbrance", limiting the fee simple title, on a piece of property?

A. Leases
B. Mortgages
C. Easements or restrictions
D. Furniture not paid for

146. An earnest money deposit is put into this until delivered to the seller when the transaction is closed.

A. the realtor's bank account
B. the attorney's bank account
C. the buyer's bank account
D. an escrow account

147. Which of the following is true of the Federal National Mortgage Association (Fannie Mae)?

A. It is the nation's largest supplier of mortgages
B. It is congressionally chartered, shareholder owned
C. It is the same as Freddie Mac

D.   both A and B

148. An employer-sponsored investment plan allowing individuals to set aside tax-deferred income for retirement or emergency purposes is called a _____ plan.

A.   436(k)/401B
B.   339(k)/372B
C.   401(k)/403B
D.   both A and B

149. Which of the following is true of the Government National Mortgage Association, also known as Ginnie Mae?

A.   It is government owned
B.   It was created by Congress on September 1, 2002
C.   Provides funds to lenders for making home loans
D.   Both A and C

150. At what amount is a loan considered to be a "jumbo" loan, which exceeds Fannie Mae's and Freddie Mac's loan limits? It is also known as a non-conforming loan.

A. $417,000
B. $227,150
C. $300,000
D.   Jumbo refers to the percentage borrowed, not the amount

151. Usually part of a homeowner's insurance policy, this type insurance offers protection against claims alleging that a property owner's negligence or inappropriate action resulted in bodily injury or property damage to another

party.

A. Malpractice insurance
B. Liability insurance
C. Hazard insurance
D. Collision insurance

152. A lender refers to the process of getting new loans as

A. selling his product
B. loan origination
C. his bread and butter
D. more than just a job

153. The percentage relationship between the amount of the loan and the appraised value or sales price (whichever is lower) is called

A. value to loan
B. first-time homebuyer's loan
C. loan to value
D. both B and C

154. If you are applying for a loan, the lender gives and guarantees you a specific interest rate for a specific time. This period of time is called the

A. period of no return
B. rate-freeze period
C. lock-in period
D. period at which you cannot seek other financing

155. A credit report which reports the raw data pulled from two or more of the major credit repositories is called a

A.   multi-credit report
B.   merged credit report
C.   this is not legal
D.   none of the above

156. Sometimes called a first trust deed, this is a legal document pledging a property to the lender as security for payment of a debt.

A.   promissory note
B.   deed of trust
C.   owner financing document
D.   mortgage

157. Which of the following is not true of mortgage insurance?

A.   It covers the lender against some of the losses incurred resulting from default on a home loan
B.   It is sometimes is mistakenly referred to a PMI (private mortgage insurance)
C.   It is required on all loans having a loan to value of more than 90%
D.   No "MI" loans are usually made at higher rates

158   A no-point loan has an interest rate

A.   lower than if you pay one point
B.   the same as if you pay one point

C.   higher than if you pay one point
D.   a no-point loan does not exist

159. The total amount of principal owed on a mortgage before any payments are made is called the

A.   total amount due
B.   original principal balance
C.   a lot less than you'll actually pay
D.   your down payment times ten

160. A planned unit development (PUD) is different from a condominium because

A.   a condominium usually has more amenities
B.   there are fewer units in a condominium development
C.   in a condominium the individual owns the airspace of the unit
D.   all of the above

161. The term that means a limit on the amount that the interest rate can increase or decrease over the life of an adjustable rate mortgage is

A.   term cap
B.   life cap
C.   ARM cap
D.   none of the above

162. If a commercial bank or other financial institution extends you credit up to a certain amount for a certain time, you are receiving a

A.   line of credit
B.   personal loan
C.   unsecured loan
D.   both B and C

163. The term "modification" means

A.   a change in your mortgage without having to refinance
B.   a change in house plans before building begins
C.   the right of the bank to modify the interest rate without telling you
D.   both B and C

164. Which of the following is true of the term "mortgage banker"?

A.   They are generally assumed to originate and fund their own loans
B.   It is a loosely applied term to those who are mortgage brokers or correspondents
C.   They usually sell loans on the secondary market to Fannie Mae, Freddie Mac, or Ginnie Mae.
D.   All of the above.

165. Which of the following describes "prime rate"?

A.   It is the interest rate banks charge to their preferred customers
B.   The same factors that influence the prime rate also affect interest rates of mortgage loans
C.   Changes in the prime rate are usually not widely

publicized in the news media

D.   Both A and B

166. A no cash-out refinance is

A.   intended to put cash in the hands of the borrower
B.   calculated to cover the balance due on the current loan
and any costs associated with obtaining the new mortgage
C.   often referred to as a "rate and term refinance"
D.   both B and C

167. A legal document requiring a borrower to repay a mortgage loan at a stated interest rate during a specified period of time is called a

A.   note
B.   deed of trust
C.   mortgage
D.   both B and C

168. The date when a new monthly payment amount takes effect on an adjustable-rate mortgage or graduated-payment mortgage is called the

A.   new payment date
B.   payment change date
C.   new payment due date
D.   change payment date

169. A quitclaim deed does which of the following?

A.   Transfers with warranty whatever interest or title a grantor may have at the time the conveyance is made

B.   Transfers without warranty whatever interest or title a grantor may have at the time the conveyance is made

C.   Does not transfer interest at all

D.   Quitclaim deeds are no longer used

170. In a refinance transaction, what happens?

A.   One loan is paid off with the proceeds from a new loan using the same property as security

B.   An additional loan is added to the present loan

C.   The loan's interest rate changes

D.   The term of the loan is increased

171. The amount of principal that has not yet been repaid is called the

A.   amount owed

B.   balance of the loan

C.   remaining balance

D.   all of the above

172. If you made an arrangement to repay delinquent installments or advances, you would be setting up a

A.   good faith payment plan

B.   repayment plan

C.   another loan to pay off

D.   oral contract

173. Your neighbor has given you a right of first refusal on a piece of land he plans to sell. What does this mean?

A. He has given you the first opportunity to purchase it before he offers it for sale to others
B. He expects you to refuse to buy it
C. He expects you to pay more for it than anyone else
D. None of the above

174. You are selling the house you live in, but the house you're moving to is not completed. You need to stay on in the house a while after closing. You work out a deal with the new purchaser called a

A. no-rent lease agreement
B. delayed possession for the new purchaser
C. sale-leaseback
D. lease for one year past closing

175. In a tenancy in common

A. ownership passes to the survivors in the event of death
B. ownership does not pass to the survivors in the event of death
C. there are no provisions made for the death of the owners
D. when one person dies, the others have to move

176. The duties of a "servicer" include

A. collecting principal and interest payments from borrowers
B. managing borrowers' escrow accounts
C. usually a servicer services mortgages purchased by an investor in the secondary mortgage market

D.   all of the above

177. In "third-party origination"

A.   an independent political party originates a loan
B.   a lender uses another party to completely or partially originate, process, underwrite, close, fund, or package the mortgages it plans to deliver to the secondary mortgage market.
C.   three parties are involved in the loan process
D.   all of the above

178. A title search of a property would show the following to be true:

A.   the seller is the legal owner of the property
B.   there are no liens or other claims against the property
C.   the previous owners came over on the Mayflower
D.   both A and B

179. A trustee

A.   is known to be trustworthy
B.   is someone who has a great deal of trust in others
C.   is a fiduciary who holds or controls property for the benefit of another
D.   is usually a job for relatives

180. When a person is "vested" he can

A.   use a portion of a fund such as an individual retirement fund

B.   use a portion of a fund without paying taxes on it
C.   have access to a bulletproof vest when in dangerous situations
D.   both A and C

181. Which of the following is not true of the term "appraised value"?

A.   It usually comes out lower than the purchase price when using comparable sales
B.   It is an opinion of a property's fair market value
C.   It is based on comparable sales
D.   None of the above

182. If a buyer qualifies and is able to take over the seller's mortgage when buying his home, this type of mortgage is called

A.   "pass on down" mortgage
B.   assumable mortgage
C.   owner financing
D.   both B and C

183. A call option is most similar to

A.   a lifetime cap
B.   a buy-down
C.   an acceleration clause
D.   all of the above

184. A "chain of title" would show

A.   the transfers of title to a piece of property over the years
B.   members of the "chain gang" who had previously owned the property
C.   neither A nor B
D.   both A and B

185. Which of the following is true of a cloud on title?

A.   It usually cannot be removed except by deed, release, or court action
B.   It is the result of conditions revealed by a title search that adversely affect the title to real estate
C.   both A and B
D.   neither A nor B

186. Which of the following applies to "closing costs"?

A.   They are divided into two categories—"non-recurring closing costs" and "pre-paid items"
B.   Lenders try to estimate the amounts of non-recurring and pre-paids on a Good Faith Estimate shortly after receiving the loan application
C.   Pre-paids are items which recur over time, such as property taxes and homeowners insurance
D.   All of the above

187. What is "community property"?

A.   Property that is owned by an entire condominium development
B.   Property that is owned by an entire subdivision of single-family homes

C.   Property acquired by a married couple during the marriage and considered to be jointly owned
D.   Both A and B

188. If an apartment complex is converted to a condominium, this is called

A.   a condominium conversion
B.   an apartment conversion
C.   either an apartment or condominium conversion
D.   fewer options for people to rent

189. This is an adjustable rate mortgage that allows the borrower to change the ARM to a fixed rate mortgage within a specific time.

A.   due-to-change ARM
B.   convertible ARM
C.   fixed rate ARM
D.   two-fold mortgage

190. If someone gives you "credit," you are

A.   agreeing to receive something of value in exchange for a promise to repay the lender at a later date
B.   getting something you deserve for something you did
C.   very lucky, because this doesn't happen often
D.   both B and C

191. In an effort to avoid foreclosure (which may or may not happen), you might give the lender

A.   the payments he is due, all at one time
B.   your car and any other valuable personal property you have
C.   a "deed in lieu" (of foreclosure)
D.   a "deed in lieu" (of foreclosure), which then will not affect your credit badly

192. When a lender performs this calculation annually to make sure the correct amount of money for anticipated expenditures is being collected, the lender is performing

A.   checks and balances
B.   an escrow analysis
C.   a detailed loan analysis
D.   lenders don't do this

193. The report on the title of a property from the public records or an abstract of the title is called

A.   a title report
B.   an examination of title
C.   an examination of deed, survey and title
D.   title insurance

194. A consumer protection law that regulates the disclosure of consumer credit reports by consumer/credit reporting agencies and establishes procedures for correcting mistakes on one's credit record is called the

A.   Credit Reporting Act
B.   Fair Credit Reporting Act

C.	Consumer Protection Act
D.	Truth-in-Lending Act

195. If you inherit from someone, the best type of estate to inherit is called

A.	a fee simple estate
B.	general, all-encompassing estate
C.	life estate
D.	none of the above

196. A homeowner's association does which the following?

A.	It manages the common areas of a condominium project or planned unit development
B.	It owns title to the common elements in a condominium development
C.	It doesn't own title to the common elements in a planned unit development
D.	All of the above

197. In simple terms a judgment is

A.	a personal opinion about real estate
B.	an individual's way of making decisions about legal matters
C.	a decision made by a court of law
D.	an opinion of an attorney

198. This is a way of holding title to a property wherein the mortgagor does not actually own the property but rather has a recorded long-term lease on it.

A. contract for deed
B. rent-to-own contract
C. long-term lease
D. leasehold estate

199. Which of the following are duties of a loan officer?

A. The solicitation of loans
B. Representation of the lending institution
C. Representation of the borrower to the lending institution
D. All of the above

200. The amount paid by a mortgagor for mortgage insurance, either government or private is called

A. mortgage insurance premium
B. private mortgage insurance premium
C. FHA insurance premium
D. VA insurance premium

201. Which of the following statements is not true of mortgage life and disability insurance?

A. It begins immediately after someone becomes disabled
B. It pays off the entire debt if someone dies during the life of the mortgage
C. It is a type of term life insurance often bought by borrowers
D. In this type insurance, the amount of coverage decreases as the principal declines

202. Which is the best definition of "multi-dwelling units"?

A.   They are properties that provide separate housing units for more than one family with several different mortgages

B.   They are properties that provide separate housing units for more than one family, but with a single mortgage

C.   They are properties that provide separate housing units for more than one family, but are leased rather than owned

D.   They are properties that provide separate housing units for more than one family on a lease-option basis

203. Which of the following is true of "negative amortization"?

A.   It is also called "deferred interest"

B.   Because some ARM's allow the interest rate to fluctuate, the borrower's minimum payment may not cover all the interest

C.   The unpaid interest is added to the balance of the loan and the loan balance grows larger instead of smaller

D.   All of the above

204. For someone to be determined to be "pre-qualified" for a loan, what has taken place?

A.   The person has given a written statement saying he can afford the loan

B.   A loan officer has given a written opinion of the borrower's ability to qualify based on debt, income, or savings

C.   The loan officer has reviewed a credit report on the borrower

D.   The information given to the loan officer is in the form of written documentation

205. The four components of a monthly mortgage payment on impounded loans are

A.   principal, interest, taxes, maintenance
B.   principal, interest, insurance, bank fees
C.   principal, interest, taxes, miscellaneous charge
D.   principal, interest, taxes, insurance

206. The term "periodic rate cap" refers to

A.   an adjustable rate mortgage
B.   a limit on the amount the interest rate can increase or decrease during any one adjustment period
C.   conventional fixed-rate loans
D.   both A and B

207. The acquisition of property through the payment of money or its equivalent is called

A.   a purchase money transaction
B.   having a down payment and mortgage
C.   simply, buying property
D.   a sales transaction

208. What is a recording?

A.   A sound file of music to study real estate by
B.   Details of a properly executed legal document noted in the registrar's office
C.   A document, such as a deed or mortgage note which becomes public record

D.   Both B and C

209. If a landlord wants to protect himself against loss or rent or rental value due to fire or other casualty that would render the premises unusable for a time he would purchase

A.   hazard insurance
B.   fire insurance
C.   rent-loss insurance
D.   there is no such insurance

210. The right to enter or leave designated premises is called

A.   the right of ingress or egress
B.   the right to enter or leave
C.   the right of non-trespass
D.   an easement

211. "Secondary market" means

A.   a market which is not as important as the primary market
B.   the buying and selling of existing mortgages, usually as part of a "pool" of mortgages
C.   a market of lower real estate values
D.   none of the above

212. The property that will be pledged as collateral for a loan is called

A.   the back-up plan
B.   the credit
C.   security

D.   the borrower's former home

213. If you were purchasing a piece of property, either you or your bank would want to know if you were paying a fair price and would order

A.   a market analysis by a realtor
B.   an appraisal
C.   survey
D.   termite inspection

214. Which of the following is an example of "transfer of ownership"?

A.   The purchase of property "subject to" the mortgage
B.   Joint tenancy
C.   The assumption of the mortgage debt by the property purchaser
D.   Both A and C

215. Which of the following does not apply the Treasury index?

A.   An index used to determine interest rate changes for certain fixed-rate loans
B.   It is based on the results of auctions that the U. S. Treasury holds for its Treasury bills and securities
C.   derived from the U. S. Treasury's daily yield curve
D.   None of the above

216. What are assets?

A.   Items of value owned by an individual
B.   Items that can be quickly converted into cash are called "liquid assets"
C.   Real estate, personal property, and debts owed to someone by others
D.   All of the above.

217. One who establishes the value of a property for taxation purposes is called

A.   a government tax appraiser
B.   an assessor
C.   an appraiser
D.   all of the above

218. A certificate of deposit index is

A.   one of the indexes used for determining interest rate changes on some adjustable rate mortgages
B.   is an average of what banks are paying on certificates of deposit
C.   both A and B
D.   neither A nor B

219. Which of the following is true of "common areas"?

A.   They include swimming pools, tennis courts, and other recreational facilities
B.   They are portions of a building, land, and amenities owned or managed by a planned unit development or condominium project's homeowners' association
C.   They have shared expenses by the project owners for the

operation and maintenance

D.   all of the above

220. In a condominium hotel you would find the following:

A.   Rental or registrations desks
B.   Daily cleaning services
C.   No individual ownership
D.   Both A and B

221. A type of multiple ownership where the residents of a multi-unit housing complex own shares in the cooperative corporation that owns the property and gives each resident the right to occupy a specific apartment or unit is called

A.   an investment condominium
B.   an investment planned unit development
C.   a cooperative
D.   a government-run housing project

222. Which is true of the cost of funds index (COFI)?

A.   It represents the weighted-average cost of savings, borrowings, and advances of the financial institutions such as banks and savings & loans in the 11th District of the Federal Home Loan Bank
B.   It is one of the indexes used to determine interest rate changes for certain government fixed rate mortgages
C.   It is an index used to determine interest rate changes for certain adjustable-rate mortgages

D.   Both A and C

223. Once you buy a house, the amount you pay each month includes an extra amount above principal and interest. This extra money is held in a special account to pay your taxes and homeowners insurance when it comes due. This account is called

A.   an escrow account
B.   a savings account
C.   a regular checking account
D.   both B and C

224. Which of the following does the Federal Housing Administration do?

A.   Lends money and plans and constructs housing
B.   Insures residential mortgage loans made by government lenders
C.   Sets standards for construction and underwriting
D.   None of the above

225. If you purchase a type of insurance called homeowner's warranty, you would do so because

A.   It will cover repairs to certain items, such as heating or air conditioning if they break down within the coverage period
B.   The seller will sometimes pay for it
C.   Both A and B
D.   Neither A nor B

226. A type of foreclosure proceeding used in some states

that is handled as a civil lawsuit and conducted entirely under the auspices of a court is called

A.   a legal foreclosure
B.   a court-appointed foreclosure
C.   a judicial foreclosure
D.   a civil foreclosure

227. Which of the following is not part of loan servicing?

A.   Processing payments, sending statements
B.   Managing the escrow account
C.   Handling pay-offs and assumptions
D.   Sending a monthly statement to the owner

228. A period payment cap applies to

A.   any mortgage taken out in the U.S.
B.   adjustable rate mortgages
C.   fixed-rate loans
D.   government loans

229. The commitment issued by a lender to borrower or other mortgage originator guaranteeing a specified interest rate for a specified period of time at a specific cost is called

A.   a rate lock
B.   under lock and key
C.   a promissory note
D.   a deed of trust

230. A fund set aside for replacement of common property

in a condominium, PUD, or cooperative project, particularly that which has a short life expectancy, such as carpet or furniture is called

A. a capital improvements fund
B. a replacement reserve fund
C. a savings fund
D. a contingency fund

231   The term "servicing" describes

A. the collection of mortgage payments from borrowers
B. what the mechanic does to your car
C. duties of a loan servicer
D. both A and C

232. A two- to-four family property

A. consists of a structure that provides living space for two to four families and ownership is evidenced by two to four deeds
B. consists of a structure that provides living space for two to four families and ownership is evidenced by a single deed
C. is not a deeded property
D. is an illegal form of ownership

1. Many states determine the order of water rights according to which users of the water hold a recorded beneficial use permit. This allocation of water rights is determined by:

A. accretion.
B. riparian theory.
C. littoral theory.
D. the doctrine of prior appropriation.

2. The right to control one's property includes all of the following EXCEPT:

A. the right to invite people on the property for a political fund-raiser.
B. the right to exclude the utilities meter reader.
C. the right to erect "no trespassing" signs.
D. the right to enjoy pride of ownership.

3. Which of the following types of ownership CANNOT be created by operation of law, but must be created by the parties' expressed intent?

A. community property
B. tenancy in common
C. condominium ownership
D. tenancy by the entireties

4. Which of the following is/are considered to be personal property?

A. wood-burning fireplace
B. furnace
C. bathtubs
D. patio furniture

5. The word "improvement" would refer to all of the following EXCEPT:

A. streets.
B. a sanitary sewer system.
C. trade fixtures.
D. the foundation.

6. All of the following are physical characteristics of land EXCEPT:

A. indestructibility.
B. uniqueness.
C. immobility.
D. scarcity.

7. Certain items on the premises that are installed by the tenant and are related to the tenant's business are called:

A. fixtures.
B. emblements.

C. trade fixtures.
D. easements.

8. Personal property includes all of the following EXCEPT:

A. chattels.
B. fructus industriales.
C. emblements.
D. fixtures.

9. A person who has complete control over a parcel of real estate is said to own a:

A. leasehold estate.
B. fee simple estate.
C. life estate.
D. defeasible fee estate.

10. A portion of Wendell's building was inadvertently built on Ginny's land. This is called an:

A. accretion.
B. avulsion.
C. encroachment.
D. easement.

11. The purchase of a ticket for a professional sporting event gives the bearer what?

A. an easement right to park his car

B. a license to enter and claim a seat for the duration of the game

C. an easement in gross interest in the professional sporting team

D. a license to sell food and beverages at the sporting event

12. If the owner of the dominant tenement becomes the owner of the servient tenement and merges the two properties, what happens?

A. The easement becomes dormant.

B. The easement is unaffected.

C. The easement is terminated.

D. The properties retain their former status.

13. Homeowner Ginny acquired the ownership of land that was deposited by a river running through her property by:

A. reliction.

B. succession.

C. avulsion.

D. accretion.

14. The rights of the owner of property located along the banks of a river are called:

A. littoral rights.

B. prior appropriation rights.
C. riparian rights.
D. hereditament.

15. The local utility company dug up Frank's garden to install a natural gas line. The company claimed it had a valid easement and proved it through the county records. Frank claimed the easement was not valid because he did not know about it. The easement:

A. Was valid even though the owner did not know about it.
B. Was an appurtenant easement owned by the utility company.
C. Was not valid because it had not been used during the entire time that Frank owned the property.
D. Was not valid because Frank was not informed of its existence when he purchased the property.

16. Jim and Sandy are next-door neighbors. Sandy tells Jim that he can store his camper in her yard for a few weeks until she needs the space. Sandy did not charge Jim rent for the use of her yard. Sandy has given Jim a(n) what?

A. easement appurtenant
B. easement by necessity
C. estate in land license
D. License

17. Your neighbors use your driveway to reach their garage on their property. Your attorney explains that the

ownership of the neighbors' real estate includes an easement appurtenant giving them the driveway right. Your property is the:

A. leasehold interest.
B. dominant tenement.
C. servient tenement.
D. license property.

18. Quintin owned two acres of land. He sold one acre to Frank and reserved for himself an appurtenant easement over Frank's land for ingress and egress. Frank's land:

A. Is the dominant tenement.
B. Is the servient tenement.
C. Can be cleared of the easement when Quintin sells the withheld acre to a third party.
D. Is subject to an easement in gross.

19. Ginny owns 50 acres of land with 500 feet of frontage on a desirable recreational lake. She wishes to subdivide the parcel into salable lots, but she wants to retain control over the lake frontage while allowing lot owners to have access to the lake. Which of the following types of access rights would provide the greatest protection for a prospective purchaser?

A. an easement in gross
B. an appurtenant easement
C. an easement by necessity
D. a license

20. Sam and Nancy bought a store building and took title as joint tenants. Nancy died testate. Sam now owns the store:

A. as a joint tenant with rights of survivorship.
B. in severalty.
C. as a tenant in common with Nancy's heirs.
D. in trust.

21. When real estate under an estate for years is sold, what happens to the lease?

A. It expires with the conveyance.
B. It binds the new owner.
C. It is subject to termination with proper notice
D. It is valid but unenforceable.

22. Evan lives in an apartment building. The land and structures are owned by a corporation, with one mortgage loan covering the entire property. Like the other residents, Evan owns stock in the corporation and has a lease on his apartment. This type of ownership is called a(n):

A. condominium.
B. planned unit development.
C. time-share.
D. cooperative.

23. Tom leases store space to Kim for a restaurant, and Kim installs her ovens, booths, counters, and other equipment. When do these items become real property?

A. when they are installed
B. when Kim defaults on her rental payments
C. when the lease takes effect
D. when the lease expires, if the items are not taken by the tenant

24. Jim, Manny and Harry are joint tenants owning a parcel of land. Harry conveys his interest to his long-time friend Wendell. After the conveyance, Jim and Manny:

A. become tenants in common.
B. continue to be joint tenants with Harry.
C. become joint tenants with Wendell.
D. remain joint tenants owning a two-thirds interest

**25. In a gift of a parcel of real estate, one of the two owners was given an undivided
60 percent interest and the other received an undivided 40 percent interest. The two owners hold their interests as what?**

A. cooperative owners
B. joint tenants
C. community property owners
D. tenants in common

26. To create a joint tenancy relationship in the ownership of real estate, there must be unities of:

A. grantees, ownership, claim of right, and possession.
B. title, interest, encumbrance, and survivorship.
C. possession, time, interest, and title.
D. ownership, possession, heirs, and title.

27. What is a Schedule of Exceptions on a title policy?

A. encumbrances
B. tax liens
C. list of things not insured in the policy
D. defects

28. When a company furnishes materials for the construction of a house and is subsequently not paid, it may file a(n):

A. deficiency judgment.
B. lis pendens.
C. estoppel certificate.
D. mechanic's lien.

29. Which of the following liens does not need to be recorded to be valid?

A. materialman's lien
B. real estate tax lien
C. judgment lien
D. mechanic's lien

30. The system of ownership of real property in the United States is what?

A. incorporeal
B. allodial
C. inchoate
D. feudal

31. A mechanic's lien would be properly classified as a(n):

A. equitable lien.
B. voluntary lien.
C. general lien.
D. statutory lien.

32. Under which of the following types of liens can both the real property and the personal property of the debtor be sold to pay the debt?

A. real estate tax lien
B. mechanic's lien
C. judgment lien
D. assessment lien

33. A homeowner owned a house on a lot. The front ten feet of the lot were taken by eminent domain for a sidewalk. Would the homeowner be entitled to compensation?

A. Yes. The land was taken for public use by eminent domain.
B. Yes. He must be paid for the use of the sidewalk.
C. No. He still had use of the house and lot.
D. No. Compensation is not given on land taken for public use.

34. The covenant in a deed which states that the grantor is the owner and has the right to convey the title is called:

A. covenant of further assurance.
B. covenant of warranty forever.
C. covenant of seisin.
D. covenant against encumbrances.

35. The recording of a deed:

A. Is all that is required to transfer the title to real estate.
B. Gives constructive notice of the ownership of real property.
C. Insures the interest in a parcel of real estate.
D. Warrants the title to real property.

36. Which of the following provides a buyer with the best assurance of clear, marketable title?

A. certificate of title

B. title insurance
C. abstract of title
D. general warranty deed

37. What do liens and easements have in common?

A. Both are encumbrances.
B. Both must be on public record to be valid.
C. Neither can be done without the consent of the owner.
D. Both are money claims against the property.

38. The title to real estate passes when a valid deed is:

A. signed and recorded.
B. delivered and accepted.
C. filed and microfilmed.
D. executed and mailed.

39. The primary purpose of a deed is to:

A. Prove ownership.
B. Transfer title rights.
C. Give constructive notice.
D. Prevent adverse possession.

40. A special warranty deed differs from a general warranty deed in that the grantor's covenant in the special warranty deed:

A. Applies only to a definite limited time.
B. Covers the time back to the original title.
C. Is implied and is not written in full.
D. Protects all subsequent owners of the property.

41. Which of the following deeds contains no expressed or implied warranties?

A. a bargain and sale deed
B. a quitclaim deed
C. a warranty deed
D. a grant deed

42. When the grantor does not wish to convey certain property rights, he or she:

A. must note the exceptions in a separate document.
B. may not do so, since the deed conveys the entire premises.
C. may note the exceptions in the deed of conveyance.
D. must convey the entire premises and have the grantee reconvey the rights to be retained by the grantor

43. A partition suit is used for which of the following?

A. determination of party fences
B. to allow construction of party walls
C. to force a division of property without all the owners' consents

D. to change a tenancy by entireties to some other form of ownership

44. The condemnation of private property for public use is exercised under which government right?

A. taxation
B. escheat
C. manifest destiny
D. eminent domain

45. When a claim is settled by a title insurance company, the company acquires all rights and claims of the insured against any other person who is responsible for the loss. This is known as what?

A. caveat emptor
B. surety bonding
C. subordination
D. subrogation

46. Which of the following would be used to clear a defect from the title records?

A. a lis pendens
B. an estoppel certificate
C. a suit to quiet title
D. a writ of attachment

47. A bill of sale is used to transfer the ownership of what?

A. real property
B. fixtures
C. personal property
D. appurtenances

48. A written summary of the history of all conveyances and legal proceedings affecting a specific parcel of real estate is called a(n):

A. affidavit of title.
B. certificate of title.
C. abstract of title.
D. title insurance policy.

49. When the preliminary title report reveals the existence of an easement on the property, it indicates that the easement is a(n):

A. lien.
B. encumbrance.
C. encroachment.
D. tenement.

50. The list of previous owners of conveyance from whom the present real estate owner derives his or her title is known as the:

A. chain of title.
B. certificate of title.
C. title insurance policy.
D. abstract of title.

51. A person agrees to sell a property for $500,000. The buyer gives the seller $150 as valuable consideration for a six-month option. Which of the following statements is true?

A. The $150 is valuable consideration if the seller accepted it.
B. The buyer must have at least 5% down as valuable consideration.
C. The buyer must have at least 20% down.
D. The seller cannot accept money for the option.

52. Which of the following activities is a violation of the Federal Fair Housing Act?

A. a nonprofit church that denies access to its retirement home to any person because of race
B. a nonprofit private club that gives preference in renting units to its members at lower rates
C. the owner of a single-family residence selling his/her own home who gives preference to a buyer based on his/her sex
D. discrimination in the sale of a warehouse based on the prospective purchaser's gender

53. A Savings & Loan institution would be violating the Federal Fair Housing Act by denying a loan to Mr. and Mrs. Happy Borrower for which of the following reasons?

A. low earnings
B. too old
C. too many loans
D. minority background

54. The Civil Rights Act of 1866 prohibits discrimination in housing based on which of the following reasons?

A. race
B. religion
C. sex
D. marital status

55. An agent working as a subagent of the seller would suggest that the buyer hire an inspector from an outside service in all of the following cases EXCEPT:

A. when they smell gas in the basement.
B. when there is a slow drain in the toilet.
C. when a hinge is off the door.
D. when there is sawdust in the kitchen cabinets.

56. The federal anti-discriminatory laws apply to which of the following?

A. a broker selling a single-family home
B. a private club not open to the general public
C. office building sales
D. the rental of industrial property

57. A tenant complained to HUD about his landlord's discriminatory practices in his/her building. A week later the landlord gave the tenant an eviction notice. Under which of the following situations would the Federal Fair Housing Act be violated?

A. when the tenant is two months behind in his/her rent
B. when the landlord evicts the tenant for reporting him to HUD
C. when the tenant has damaged the premises
D. when the tenant is conducting an illegal use on the premises

58. The Federal Fair Housing Act states that a prima facie (at first view) case against a broker for discrimination be established after a complaint has been received because the broker has failed to do which of the following?

A. The broker has failed to display a HUD Equal Opportunity poster.
B. The broker has failed to join an affirmative marketing program.
C. The broker has failed to join the HUD anti-discriminatory task force.

D. The broker has failed to attend mandatory classes on fair housing.

59. A broker is discussing a new listing with a prospective Mexican American buyer. The buyer wants to inspect the property immediately, but the owner of said property has instructed the broker, in writing, not to show the house during the owner's three-week absence. The buyer insists on viewing the property. The broker should:

A. Show the property to avoid a violation of the Federal Fair Housing Act.
B. Request the Real Estate Commission arbitrate the problem.
C. Inform the buyer of the seller's instructions.
D. Notify the nearest HUD office.

60. A three-story apartment complex built in 1965 does not meet with the handicapped access provisions for the 1988 Fair Housing Act. The owner must:

A. Make the ground floor handicapped accessible.
B. Make the 1st and 2nd floors accessible.
C. Make the entire building accessible.
D. The owner doesn't have to comply since it's less than 4 stories.

61. What type of a listing agreement allows the owner to appoint an exclusive agent to sell his property, but retains the right to sell the property himself?

A. open
B. exclusive right to sell
C. multiple listing
D. exclusive agency

62. Under an Exclusive Right to Sell Listing agreement, if the seller produces a ready, willing and able buyer he:

A. will not have to pay a commission since he produced the buyer.
B. will only have to pay the broker half the commission since he produced the buyer.
C. owes the listing broker a full commission.
D. will not be able to turn the buyer over to the listing agent since the agent has the exclusive right to sell the property.

63. Which of the following would not terminate an agency relationship?

A. abandonment by the agent
B. revocation by the principal
C. submission by the agent of two offers at the same time
D. fulfillment of the agency purpose

64. The buyer of an apartment complex is told that the refrigerator in one of the apartments goes with the sale. After taking title, he discovered that the refrigerator belonged to the tenant. Which is true about this situation?

A. Since the refrigerator was in the apartment, it automatically belongs to the new owner.
B. The refrigerator is the personal property of the tenant. The seller had no right to offer it to the buyer.
C. The refrigerator was plugged into the wall and that makes it real property.
D. The tenant will have to get permission from the new owner to remove the refrigerator.

65. The illegal process of a banker refusing to approve loans for a neighborhood based on the racial composition of the area is:

A. blockbusting.
B. steering.
C. redlining.
D. panic peddling.

66. The illegal practice of directing minorities to areas populated by the same race or religion is called:

A. steering.
B. blockbusting.
C. redlining.
D. panic peddling.

67. Carl Chauvinist, the owner of an apartment complex, lives in one unit of a triplex and routinely refuses to rent either of the other two units to a female. Can he do this?

A. Yes. He may do this if he does not use a broker or discriminate in advertising.
B. Yes. He may do this if he doesn't ask the tenant's age.
C. No. Carl can never discriminate on sex.
D. No. Carl must live in a single family home to discriminate.

68. An aggrieved party with a Fair Housing violation claim has how long to file a complaint with the Department of Housing and Urban Development?

A. 1 month
B. 1 week
C. 1 year
D. 7 years

69. Jim Jones, the landlord, rents a property to Tom Smith, a handicapped person. Mr. Smith, with Mr. Jones' permission, modifies the house to suit his needs. When the lease expires, which of the following requirements would not have to be met by Mr. Smith?

A. Mr. Smith must remove the "grab rails" in the bathroom that were installed for his use.
B. Mr. Smith must raise the kitchen cabinets that were lowered for his use.
C. Mr. Smith must repair the walls where the "grab rails" in the bathroom were removed.

D. Mr. Smith must restore the wide doorways, that were installed for him, to the original size.

70. All of the following are duties of the property manager EXCEPT:

A. reporting to the owner all notices of building violations.
B. providing upkeep and maintenance on the property.
C. maintaining financial records and accounts.
D. securing tenants of a particular ethnic origin in accordance with the owner's wishes.

71. A mobility impaired person was renting a unit in an apartment complex. Half the units had been assigned parking spaces near the door; the other half had not. The owner:

A. may charge extra money to the handicapped person for providing the parking space near the door.
B. must take a vote of all tenants to see if they want to allow the handicapped person a parking space.
C. must give a parking space near the door to the handicapped person, if one is available and a need is demonstrated.
D. must allow the handicapped person to live there for a month and if a space becomes available during that time, give the parking space to the handicapped person.

72. A salesperson is involved in a transaction where an individual wishes a six month lease with an option to buy. What is true about this situation?

A. The individual must go to an attorney since it is too complicated a transaction for a salesperson.
B. This transaction is too complicated for a salesperson. Only a person with a broker's license should handle this transaction.
C. A salesperson could use two standard forms, fill in the blanks and request that his or her broker review the forms before signing.
D. The salesperson should write the purchase offer. A lease for 6 months does not need to be in writing.

73. A void contract is one that is:

A. not in writing.
B. not legally enforceable.
C. rescindable by agreement.
D. voidable by only one of the parties.

74. The essential elements of a contract include all of the following EXCEPT:

A. offer and acceptance.
B. notarized signatures.
C. competent parties.
D. consideration.

75. If, upon the receipt of an offer to purchase his property under certain conditions, the seller makes a counteroffer, the prospective buyer is:

A. bound by his original offer.

B. bound to accept the counteroffer.

C. bound by whichever offer is lower.

D. relieved of his original offer.

76. The amount of earnest money deposit is determined by:

A. the real estate licensing statutes.

B. an agreement between the parties.

C. the broker's office policy on such matters.

D. the acceptable minimum of 5 percent of the purchase price.

77. If the buyer defaulted some time ago on a written contract to purchase a seller's real estate, the seller can still sue for damages, if he is not prohibited from doing so by the:

A. statute of frauds.

B. law of agency.

C. statute of limitations.

D. broker-attorney accord.

78. A competent and disinterested person who is authorized by another person to act in his or her place and sign a contract of sale is called:

A. an attorney in fact.

B. a substitute grantor.

C. a vendor.

D. an agent.

79. An option:

A. requires the optionor to complete the transaction.
B. gives the optionee an easement on the property.
C. does not keep the offer open for a specified time.
D. makes the seller liable for a commission.

80. When a prospective buyer makes a written purchase offer that the seller accepts, then the:

A. Buyer may take possession of the real estate.
B. Seller grants the buyer ownership rights.
C. Buyer receives legal title to the property.
D. Buyer receives equitable title to the property.

81. H agrees to purchase V's real estate for $230,000 and deposits $6,900 earnest money with Broker L. However, V is unable to clear the title to the property, and H demands the return of his earnest money as provided in the purchase contract. Broker L should:

A. Deduct his commission and return the balance to H.
B. Deduct his commission and give the balance to V.
C. Return the entire amount to H.
D. Give the entire amount to V to dispose of as he decides.

82. A buyer makes an earnest money deposit of $1,500 on a $15,000 property and then withdraws her offer before the seller can accept it. The broker is responsible for disposing of the earnest money by:

A. turning it over to the seller.
B. deducting the commission and giving the balance to the seller.
C. returning it to the buyer.
D. returning it to the buyer.

83. Broker K arrives to present a purchase offer to Mrs. D, an 80 year old invalid who is not always of sound mind, and finds her son and her daughter-in-law present. In the presence of Broker K, both individuals persistently urge D to accept the offer, even though it is much lower than the price she has been asking for her home. If D accepts the offer, she may later claim that:

A. Broker K should not have brought her such a low offer for her property.
B. She was under undue duress from her son and daughter-in-law, and, therefore, the contract is voidable.
C. Broker K defrauded her by allowing her son and daughter-in-law to see the purchase offer he brought to her.
D. Her consumer protection rights have been usurped by her son and daughter-in-law.

84. The law that requires real estate contracts to be in writing to be enforceable is the:

A. law of descent and distribution.
B. statute of frauds.
C. parole evidence rule.
D. statute of limitations.

85. A(n) _____ is when an owner takes his property off the market for a definite period of time in exchange for some consideration, but he grants the right to purchase the property within that period for a stated price.

A. option
B. contract of sale
C. right of first refusal
D. installment agreement

86. A breach of contract is a refusal or a failure to comply with the terms of the contract. If the seller breaches the purchase contract, the buyer may do all of the following EXCEPT:

A. Sue the seller for specific performance.
B. Rescind the contract and recover the earnest money.
C. Sue the seller for damages.
D. Sue the broker for non-performance.

87. To assign a contract for the sale of real estate means to:

A. Record the contract with the county recorder's office.

B. Permit another broker to act as agent for the principal.
C. Transfer one's rights under the contract.
D. Allow the seller and the buyer to exchange positions.

88. The property manager suspects that the tenants in a property are engaging in illegal drug trafficking. What should the property manager do?

A. Cancel the property management agreement.
B. Observe the property for 30 days and then tell the owner.
C. Notify the owner immediately of the suspicious activity.
D. Don't worry. It's the owner's problem.

89. A zoning change has been announced that will result in the loss of value of the property to a property owner. What should a property manager do?

A. Advise the owner immediately.
B. Terminate the property management agreement.
C. Follow the owner's instructions that were previously given.
D. Keep his/her mouth shut.

90. A broker and seller terminate the listing contract. An offer is received in the mail by the broker after the termination of the listing contract. The offer is for full price and includes all of the terms and conditions of the seller. Why is this NOT a valid contract?

A. There is no consideration involved.

B. No acceptance has been given.
C. No earnest money has been enclosed.
D. There is no current listing agreement.

91. Which of the following is true if, after accepting an offer in writing, a seller withdraws acceptance and cancels the transaction?

A. The broker, having facilitated a written acceptance of an offer, is entitled to a commission and may deduct it from the deposit.
B. The broker, having facilitated a written acceptance of an offer, is entitled to compensation and may sue the seller for the commission.
C. The broker, in failing to successfully facilitate the transaction, is not entitled to any compensation.
D. The seller, having accepted an offer in writing, is bound by the offer and must proceed with the transaction.

92. Grand Rapids Realty has entered agency agreements with both the McFaddens (sellers) and Jeanie Powers (a buyer). Jeanie Powers is interested in making an offer on the McFaddens' ranch house. Is this allowable?

A. Yes, as long as both the McFaddens and Ms. Powers agree, in writing, to the dual agency.
B. Yes, as long as the McFaddens agree to be responsible for the commission.
C. Yes, as long as Grand Rapids Realty has written agency agreements on file for both the McFaddens and Ms. Powers.

D. No, dual agency is not allowable.

93. After a seller's listing agreement with ABC Realty expires, what restrictions exist if the seller decides to list with a different agency and ABC Realty has an interested buyer?

A. ABC Realty is barred from working with the seller due to previous client-agency confidentiality agreements and must refer the buyer to another agency.
B. ABC Realty may represent the buyer but may not disclose any information about the physical condition of the property.
C. ABC Realty may represent the buyer but may not disclose any information about offers made on the property when it was listed with ABC Realty.
D. ABC Realty may only represent the buyer if at least 60 days have passed since the termination of the listing agreement with the seller.

94. Which of the following is true in the case where a real estate salesperson refers buyers to a particular lender knowing that the lender pays a fee for referrals?

A. The salesperson has acted injudiciously.
B. The salesperson is well within the bounds of good business practice if a written buyer agency agreement exists.
C. The salesperson has acted in the best interests of the buyers if the lender offers a competitive interest rate and reasonable terms.
D. The salesperson may do so only upon informing the buyers of the referral fee.

95. For which of the following actions must an agency agreement exist between buyer and real estate office?

A. To provide a buyer with specifications of available properties
B. To explain agency relationships
C. To negotiate a reasonable price on a property
D. To provide information about prospective lenders' mortgage interest rates

96. Which of the following is true of buyer-brokerage contracts in Kentucky?

A. The appropriate form must be used for the contract to be valid.
B. The contract must be in writing to be enforceable.
C. Such contracts are not regulated.
D. Such contracts are illegal.

97. A broker serving as a dual agent may collect a commission from both parties if which of the following criteria is met?

A. If both the buyer and seller are represented by attorneys who have explained the dual agency
B. If both the buyer and the seller given informed consent to the dual compensation
C. If the broker is licensed to serve as a dual agent
D. If the buyer and the seller are related by blood.

98. Which of the following type of agency relationships is recognized in Kentucky?

A. Designated agency
B. Disclosed dual agency
C. Subagency
D. All of the above

99. According to the Kentucky Board of Real Estate Brokers and Salespersons, which of the following is NOT a required element of a listing agreement?

A. Exact expiration date
B. Signatures of both broker and seller
C. Qualified expert's report of property condition
D. True copy forwarded to the seller after signing

100. In which of the following circumstances is a seller's disclosure statement NOT required?

A. If the property is a commercial property
B. If the seller is listing the property as "for sale by owner"
C. If the seller has not resided on premises for at least one year
D. If the buyer has resided on the property as a tenant

101. The seller's disclosure statement should be delivered to the buyer before which of the following events?

A. Before the buyer sees the property
B. Before the seller accepts an offer in writing
C. Before the home inspection
D. Before the closing

102. To whom may a real estate agent divulge confidential information about a client?

A. To no one; confidential information must be safeguarded in all cases
B. To the supervising broker for the purposes of obtaining advice or assistance for the client
C. To any associate working under the same supervising broker
D. To another client with whom a dual agency has been established and who has an established need for such information

103. Which of the following is true regarding disclosure of deaths in the state of Kentucky?

A. Violent deaths must be disclosed.
B. Suicides must be disclosed.
C. AIDS-related deaths may not be disclosed.
D. Deaths from natural causes may never be disclosed

104. Which of the following conditions applies to a salesperson who is interested in purchasing a property listed with his or her supervising broker?

A. The salesperson must receive permission, in writing, from the Kentucky Board of Real Estate Brokers and Salespersons in order to make an offer on a listing held by the supervising broker.
B. The salesperson must resign his or her affiliation with the sponsoring broker and obtain a new sponsoring broker before becoming eligible to make an offer on the property.
C. The salesperson must inform the property owner, in writing, that he or she is a licensee in order to make an offer on the property.
D. The salesperson may not make an offer on a property listed by the supervising broker because Kentucky law forbids an agent with special knowledge of a transaction (i.e. access to confidential information) from personally benefiting from a transaction within 2 years of affiliation with an office.

105. Cody Rand bought a house in January which was found to have a leaky basement during spring rainstorms five months later. Although the sellers had discussed the basement leaks with the listing agent, they had agreed not to divulge those details to prospective buyers. The broker claims that Cody did not specifically ask about the basement. As a result, which of the following options is open to Cody?

A. Since he did not specifically ask about the basement before buying the property, Cody has no legal redress in this situation.
B. Cody can sue the broker for nondisclosure of necessary information on the condition of a property.

C. Cody can sue the seller for nondisclosure of necessary information on the condition of the property.
D. Cody can sue the inspector for failure to detect a substantial flaw in the condition of the property.

106. At which point in proceedings would an agent be considered particularly remiss in their responsibilities if a written disclosure regarding agency relationships had not yet been distributed to a prospective buyer?

A. At an open house
B. At the time of showing properties
C. Upon first meeting
D. At the closing table

107. The Bormans (sellers) accept an offer from the Rodins (buyers) before providing the seller's disclosure statement. Which of the following actions may the Rodins take?

A. The Rodins may withdraw from proceedings any time prior to the closing.
B. The Rodins may sue the Bormans for not providing the mandatory disclosure statement.
C. The Rodins may sue the broker after closing for failure to provide the disclosure statement.
D. The Rodins must request a seller's disclosure statement within 72 hours of the seller's acceptance of their offer or the Rodins will have no legal grounds to terminate the agreement.

108. A buyer receives a seller's disclosure statement immediately after the seller accepts the offer. The statement discloses a crack in the foundation. Which of the following is true?

A. The buyer may require the seller to satisfactorily correct the crack in the foundation before the closing.
B. The buyer may void the offer on the property within 48 hours.
C. The buyer may void the offer on the property within 72 hours.
D. The buyer may make an addendum offer requesting reasonable compensation to cover the expense of correcting the foundation crack.

109. Which of the following pieces of information is NOT considered confidential in a dual agency relationship?

A. The buyer's financial situation
B. That the buyer's offer exceeds the seller's minimum price
C. That the buyer would actually be willing and able to pay more than they offered
D. Comparable market data for the seller after the buyer has requested and received such information

110. At which point must an agency relationship be formally established between the broker and a buyer or seller?

A. Prior to receiving any information that is considered confidential

B. Prior to showing any properties or making a substantial business contact

C. At least by the time that a written offer is tendered and accepted

D. At any time before the closing

111. Which of the following entities administers the real estate license law in Kentucky?

A. Kentucky Association of REALTORS®

B. Kentucky Board of Real Estate Brokers and Salespersons

C. Kentucky Department of Civil Rights

D. Department of Housing and Urban Development (HUD)

112. Who selects the members of the Kentucky Board of Real Estate Brokers?

A. Real estate licensees

B. State association of REALTORS®

C. The governor

D. The state house of representatives

113. Which of the following is required under Kentucky law?

A. Sellers must divulge all known material defects that might affect the sale.

B. Brokers must reveal any material defects that might affect the sale even if the seller has already done so in the seller's disclosure statement.
C. The broker must keep all information shared by the seller confidential.
D. The broker must share all relevant information provided by the seller.

114. Which of the following actions is under the authority of the Kentucky Board of Real Estate Brokers and Salespersons?

A. Writing rules and regulations for real estate licensees to follow
B. Administering licensing exams at the testing sites
C. Enacting the laws that real estate licensees must follow
D. Composing examination questions for the state licensing exam

115. In the following situations, which is NOT grounds for the Kentucky Board of Real Estate Brokers and Salespersons to initiate an investigation of a licensee?

A. The Board votes to investigate a random selection of licensees on an annual basis in an attempt to uncover illegal practices.
B. Mira Token has written a letter to the Board complaining about dissatisfaction with practices at Cartwright Brokerage, including their failure to appropriately advise her of agency relationships and to represent her interests adequately. Based on

the letter, the Board decides to investigate the supervising broker.

C. By its own initiative the Board decides to investigate a licensee rumored to be in violation of license laws requiring disclosure statements.

D. Based on rumors of unfair and illegal practices, a member of the Board makes a motion to investigate a licensee suspected of corrupt practice.

116. In Kentucky, which of the following individuals needs a real estate license?

A. Miller Reeve and his partner, Don Brock, are selling an apartment they own jointly.

B. Patty Lehmann is a leasing agent who employs 2 other leasing agents.

C. Hayley Jones is a tenant of Somerset Village Apartments who receives half off her monthly rent for the referral of prospective tenants.

D. Brent Hughes is a licensed attorney acting under a power of attorney to convey real estate to the nephew of a deceased client.

117. All of the following individuals are exempt from having a real estate license EXCEPT which one?

A. Home Hunters, a non-profit real estate referral service

B. Coast-2-Coast, a company that charges a flat fee to match business people from across the country who wish to exchange properties and assists them in doing so

C. Myles Lewis, executor of his uncle's will, who is selling his deceased uncle's house per terms of the will

D. Jewel Morton, a full-time student who refers prospective tenants in exchange for $100 off her monthly rent of $400

118. All of the following activities are considered to be "engaging in the real estate business" EXCEPT which one?

A. Collecting apartment rent

B. Building residential homes

C. Selling residential homes

D. Reselling manufactured houses

119. An applicant for the real estate licensing exam in Kentucky must submit which of the following along with an application?

A. A current photo

B. A sworn statement attesting to the applicant's character

C. An appropriate fee

D. A recommendation letter from a real estate education instructor

120. Is an office manager in violation of the license law if she performs the following activities without a salesperson's license: coordinating the flow of paperwork, preparing advertising copy, hiring and supervising clerical support staff.

A. Yes, the office manager is in violation of the license law because she is performing duties that require a real estate license.

B. Yes, all people working in a broker's office in direct contact with confidential information are required to hold a salesperson's license.

C. No, she is not in violation of the license law because she is performing non-real estate activities that do not require licensure.

D. No, she is not in violation of the license law because she is not showing properties to clients or interacting with them outside the agency office.

121. Which of the following is NOT a requirement for obtaining a broker's license in Kentucky?

A. Upstanding moral character
B. Active employment as a licensed salesperson for at least 3 years (or equivalent)
C. Completion of 90 hours of approved post-license real estate education coursework
D. Minimum age of 21

122. For what period of time will a passing score on a licensing examination be valid?

A. 90 days
B. 6 months
C. 1 year
D. 2 years

123. None of the following transactions requires a real estate license EXCEPT which one?

A. The daughter of a couple living abroad has written authorization to sell her parents' home.
B. An entrepreneur negotiates the sales of businesses, including equipment and buildings, for a fee.
C. An apartment superintendent shows units to prospective tenants as part of his general duties.
D. An individual owns and personally manages a six-unit apartment building including collecting rents, showing available units, and providing maintenance.

124. An applicant for a real estate license in Kentucky must meet which of the following requirements?

A. Demonstrate good moral character
B. Show proof of passing the license examination within a two-year period prior to date of application for licensure
C. Be at least 21 years old
D. Provide evidence of at least two years of college (or equivalent work experience)

125. What penalty may an unlicensed individual who engages in activities deemed to constitute real estate business face for a first-time offense?

A. A fine not to exceed $250

B. Imprisonment of not more than 30 days
C. A fine not to exceed $500
D. Community service of 90 hours

126. On what date do real estate salespersons' licenses expire in Kentucky?

A. January 31 of each year
B. October 31 of each year
C. January 31 of every odd-numbered year
D. October 31 of every even-numbered year

127. What is the renewal requirement for a salesperson's or broker's license in Kentucky?

A. The licensee must have completed six hours of continuing education during each year of the three year license cycle for a total of 18 hours of class time.
B. The licensee need only remit a fee of $250.
C. The licensee must show documentation of active status as a real estate agent.
D. The licensee must have completed a prescribed sequence of continuing education courses in fair housing, real estate law, and finance management in the past three years of licensure.

128. What is the deadline to renew an expired license without financial penalty?

A. There is no grace period without financial penalty after the expiration date.
B. 30 days
C. 60 days
D. 90 days

129. Which of the following is true of continuing education coursework required for license renewal?

A. There are no mandatory continuing education requirements.
B. A minimum of 6 hours of approved continuing education courses must be completed every renewal year.
C. Specified classes in listing, ethics, and fair housing must be completed on a biennial basis for license renewal.
D. Of the 6 hours of continuing education required during each license period, at least 3 hours must be from a list of core real estate classes specified by the Board.

130. Besides remitting the appropriate fee, a salesperson who has failed to renew her license for three full years must take all of the following steps EXCEPT:

A. Take a 40-hour salesperson prelicense class.
B. Take and pass the state salesperson's licensing exam.
C. Complete a new application for licensure.
D. Submit a written appeal to the Kentucky Board of Real Estate Brokers and Salespersons petitioning for reinstatement of the expired license.

131. Barbara Walker, a real estate salesperson, has let her license lapse for 27 months. What must she do to renew her license at this point?

A. Complete 6 hours of approved continuing education for the licensing year and submit a new application along with the appropriate fee.
B. Submit an application, the appropriate fee, and a letter explaining the licensee's reasons for allowing the license to lapse for a prolonged period of time.
C. Retake the state licensing exam and submit a new application with the appropriate fee.
D. Remit the required licensing fee along with a late renewal fee of $75 for each full or partial twelve-month period since license expiration.

132. Which of the following activities is an unlicensed real estate assistant unable to perform?

A. Assemble and collate legal documents for a closing
B. Prepare and distribute promotional flyers and materials
C. Compute commission checks for active agents
D. Clarify the details of simple contract documents for prospective buyers

133. According to Kentucky law, which of the following statements about personal real estate assistants applies?

A. A personal real estate assistant must hold a real estate license.

B. A personal real estate assistant may not be licensed.
C. An unlicensed personal real estate assistant may perform general secretarial duties such as inserting factual information into contracts under the supervision of the employing broker.
D. An unlicensed personal real estate assistant may host open houses and staff booths at home shows independently with the employing broker's knowledge and authorization.

134. Ron Sidwell is an Indiana resident who wishes to obtain a Kentucky real estate broker's license. What must he do?

A. Establish a principal place of business in Kentucky or be licensed under a resident
Kentucky broker
B. File an irrevocable consent agreement in Indiana
C. Be a licensed salesperson or broker in any state
D. Complete all education course requirements in Indiana

135. Cara, an unlicensed real estate assistant for a successful broker, has been indispensable in facilitating a recent transaction. She put in many extra hours working closely with the prospective buyers, explaining transaction details, and encouraging them to accept the seller's counteroffer. At the culmination of the sale, the broker wishes to compensate Cara for her efforts. Which of the following is true under Kentucky law?

A. The broker may not pay a commission to Cara because they are both in violation of the license law regarding unlicensed assistants.

B. The broker may reward Cara with a commission only if she is working as an independent contractor.

C. The broker may compensate Cara with a gift of tangible personal property but is not permitted to pay a commission for services provided as an unlicensed assistant.

D. The broker may compensate Cara for her services by paying her a percentage of the broker's commission for the sale.

136. An on-site apartment manager negotiates apartment leases in the normal course of business. Which of the following statements is true?

A. The apartment manager is violating apartment law.

B. The apartment manager must hold a real estate license.

C. The apartment manager must hold a property manager's license.

D. The apartment manager is exempt from real estate licensing requirements because he/she lives on site.

137. Which of the following individuals is NOT exempt from the provisions of the Kentucky Real Estate License Act?

A. An apartment tenant who receives half off her monthly rent for referring a new tenant to the owner.

B. A resident property manager responsible for maintenance

C. A property owner engaged in selling or leasing his own property

D. An individual who accepts fees to recruit prospective buyers or renters of real estate

138. Milton Wesley wants to list his single-family home for sale. Which of the following statements is applicable to him?

A. If he is a licensed attorney, he may list his property himself without engaging the services of a real estate licensee.
B. He does not need a real estate license to sell his house on his own.
C. He must first obtain a real estate license to be eligible to sell real estate, including his own home.
D. He must apply for and receive a temporary license from the Kentucky Board of Real Estate Brokers and Salespersons to legally sell his house.

139. Which of the following steps is required of an applicant for a real estate salesperson's license in Kentucky?

A. Demonstrate United States citizenship
B. Provide evidence of an associate degree or equivalent in real estate from an approved school
C. Complete a 40-hour course in the general principles of real estate
D. Complete an application for licensure and submit it, along with a statement of goals and a recommendation from a sponsoring broker

140. The annual continuing education requirement in Kentucky can be satisfied by which of the following?

A. 6 hours of coursework offered by an approved CE sponsor

B. A 4-hour course on real estate office management software offered through the local community college

C. An approved professional internship of at least 15 hours with a broker other than the sponsoring broker

D. Documentation of weekly supervision with the sponsoring broker over the course of 52 weeks to discuss professional issues related to the licensee's development

141. Which of the following is true of Kentucky real estate licenses?

A. They expire on October 31 after a three-year period of licensure.

B. They expire on October 31 after a two-year period of licensure.

C. They are renewed automatically unless a licensee is on probation or holds a license that has been previously suspended or revoked.

D. They expire annually on the anniversary date of the individual salesperson's license.

142. Barry Gordon holds a Kentucky broker's license but claims Illinois as his home state. Which of the following is true?

A. He is exempt from the requirement to maintain a place of business in Kentucky as long as he has an office in Illinois.

B. He must maintain a physical office in Kentucky regardless of whether or not he operates an office in Illinois.

C. He need not maintain a physical office in Kentucky as long as he employs at least one Kentucky licensee as a salesperson or associate broker.

D. As long as he concurrently maintains an active broker's license in Illinois, he is exempt from any requirement to maintain physical office space in Kentucky.

143. Which one of the following circumstances would NOT warrant revocation of a broker's license in Kentucky?

A. Acceptance of a commission rate above the average amount
B. Felony conviction
C. Intermingling escrow funds with personal accounts
D. Incomplete or misidentification of status as a real estate licensee in advertising materials

144. In which of the following circumstances must an individual be licensed as a real estate salesperson or broker?

A. To construct houses
B. To buy a house for personal use
C. To sell one's own property
D. To sell 30 newly constructed homes in a popular subdivision

145. A salesperson's license may be revoked in which of the following circumstances?

A. She establishes an exclusive-right-to-sell listing contract with sellers.

B. She sells her primary residence without engaging a broker's aid.

C. She represents a buyer in a transaction after providing information on agency relationships.

D. She deposits a buyer's earnest money into her personal savings account.

146. Which of the following actions performed by a licensee is NOT a violation of the license law?

A. Placing a For Sale sign before receiving the owner's consent

B. Assisting a co-worker with illegally passing the licensing examination

C. Placing a newspaper ad that identifies the licensee as such

D. Being declared mentally incompetent

147. All of the following are violations of the license law EXCEPT which one?

A. Shawn Birk, a broker, offers employment to successful new licensees on site at a testing center.

B. Amelia Lands, a licensed salesperson, publicizes an open house attendance prize drawing to entice attendees.

C. Wayne Janson discourages a seller from accepting an offer based on the fact that the prospective buyer is a practicing Catholic.

D. Myra Wells places a For Sale sign on the Lohmans' property after receiving written permission to do so.

148. What information must be included in a real estate salesperson's directory listing along with his name?

A. Roy Walters, Real Estate Salesperson, Residential Property Specialist. Sponsoring broker: Willie James.
B. Roy Walters, Real Estate Salesperson, Residential Property Specialist. 505 Waters St., Suite B.
C. Roy Walters, Real Estate Salesperson, Residential Property Specialist. Licensed since
January 1999.
D. Roy Walters, Real Estate Salesperson, Residential Property Specialist. License valid through October 31 of current year.

149. Real estate licensees must include which of the following pieces of information when advertising real estate?

A. The licensee's phone number and street address
B. The name of a licensed real estate broker
C. The property owner's name and address
D. Nothing more than a phone number to call for information

150. What specific content is required for a web site developed by a broker's office?

A. Nothing governs the content of web sites for brokerage offices.
B. Names of active licensees working for the broker must be listed.
C. Information about agency relationships must be prominently placed on the home page.

D. The name and addresses of the office and any states in which the brokerage holds licenses must be specified.

151. A real estate licensee has a buyer agency agreement. What is the seller in this situation?

A. a customer
B. a client
C. a fiduciary
D. an agent

152. An optionor and an optionee make a contract for an option on a commercial piece of property. If the optionee decides to exercise his option, when must he perform?

A. He must exercise his option within 6 months under state law.
B. He must exercise his option under the terms of the option contract.
C. He must exercise his option under the terms of the option contract.
D. He can exercise his option whenever he wants.

153. When can a landlord evict a disabled blind or disabled tenant from the premises?

A. If the tenant gets a dog and the apartment policy does not allow pets
B. If the tenant insists on a handicapped parking place
C. If the tenant makes modifications to his unit at his expense
D. If the tenant has loud parties and makes too much noise

154. Broker Carr, with ABC Real Estate Company, listed the property with a seller. Broker Smith, with XYZ Real Estate Company, called Broker Carr, and disclosed that he was a Buyer Agent. Broker Smith wrote a contract with a buyer for the sale of the property. What, if any, is the relationship between the buyer's broker, the seller and the listing broker?

A. There is not a relationship between the parties. Broker Carr represents the Seller and Broker Smith represents the Buyer.
B. customer
C. agency
D. dual agency

155. A buyer bought a property without telling the seller of his intended purpose for the property. The contract contains no contingency clauses and it is a properly executed contract. After the closing, the buyer is unable to obtain the zoning he needs for his commercial project. What is the contract at this stage?

A. void
B. voidable
C. breach
D. enforceable

156. The seller and the buyer finally agreed to a purchase price of $203,500 with the closing to occur on June 15, 2011. The taxes for the year 2011 in the amount of $2,500 have not

been paid by the seller. (Taxes are paid in arrears). How much would the tax proration amount to, and how would it appear on a full settlement statement? Base your answer on a 365 day year, and the buyer is responsible for the day of settlement.

A. $1,130.14 debit the seller and credit the buyer
B. $1,130.14 debit the buyer and credit the seller
C. $2,500 credit the seller and debit the buyer
D. Nothing. The seller does not owe since the buyer is buying

157. A seller listed his home for six months on February 26. On April 29, a buyer made an offer on the property. The listing broker presented the offer to the seller on April 30. The seller accepted the offer on May 1, with the closing to occur on June 15. Assuming the closing took place on June 15, when did the listing expire?

A. 26-May-04
B. 15-Jun-04
C. 26-Aug-04
D. 15-Dec-04

158. The sellers listed their property for six months on February 26 for $104,500. They agreed to pay the listing broker a 7% commission at closing on the agreed upon sale price. A buyer made an offer on the property on March 29 for $102,000. The seller countered the offer on April 1 at $103,500, and the buyer accepted the counter offer with the closing to occur on June 15. How much commission did the

seller owe the listing broker, and how would it appear on the settlement statement?

A. $3,622.50. Debit the seller.
B. $7,140. Credit the seller.
C. $7,315. Debit the seller.
D. $7,245. Debit the seller.

159. The seller and the buyer agreed to a purchase price of $103,500 with the closing to occur on June 15. The seller's loan balance after the June 1 payment was $39,440. with an interest rate of 10%.The monthly payment was $440 principal and interest. What was the loan balance the day of closing, and how much interest did the seller owe the bank?

A. loan balance $39,440; interest due $10,350
B. loan balance $39,000; interest due $3,944
C. loan balance $39,000; interest due $862.50
D. loan balance $39,440; interest due $164.33

160. The buyer and seller agreed to a purchase price of $103,500. The buyer received an 80% loan. How much was the buyer's loan and how did it appear on the settlement statement?

A. $103,500. Credit the buyer and debit the seller.
B. $100,000. Debit both the seller and the buyer.
C. $ 95,000. Credit both the seller and the buyer.
D. $ 82,800. Credit the buyer only.

161. A home improvement company was negotiating with a homeowner to add on two rooms to a home. The company agreed to take a second mortgage as long as the homeowner also included the rest of the property in the loan. The company and the homeowner agreed to a price and the company provided the necessary disclosure form on Monday and the homeowner signed the agreement at noon the following day. Assuming that the week had five business days, until what time could the homeowner rescind the loan?

A. Tuesday, midnight
B. Thursday, midnight
C. Friday, midnight
D. There is no rescission on a house.

162. The seller under a land contract is called:

A. the grantor.
B. the grantee.
C. the vendor.
D. the vendee.

163. On an 8% straight term loan of $6,071, the borrower paid total interest of $1,700. How long did he have the loan?

A. 30 months
B. 36 months
C. 42 months
D. 48 months

164. The finance charges recorded on the Truth in Lending statements would include all of the following EXCEPT:

A. loan fees charged by the lender.
B. insurance premiums for mortgage insurance payment.
C. discount points and service fees.
D. recording fees and title insurance premiums.

165. A mortgage broker:

A. arranges loans between borrowers and investors.
B. is a lender.
C. buys mortgages in the secondary mortgage market.
D. buys mortgages and resells them at a profit.

166. The Smiths' purchased a residence for $75,000. They made a down payment of $15,000 and agreed to assume the seller's existing mortgage, which had a current balance of $23,000. The Smiths' financed the remaining $37,000 of the purchase price by executing a second mortgage whereby the seller became a mortgagee. This type of loan is called a:

A. wraparound mortgage.
B. package mortgage.
C. balloon note.
D. part purchase mortgage.

167. On a $50,000 loan the borrower is required to pay two points. How much does the borrower have to pay the lender?

A. $49,000.00
B. $50,000.00
C. $51,000.00
D. $52,000.00

168. The discount points charged by a lender on a federal VA or FHA loan are a percentage of the:

A. sales price.
B. appraised price.
C. loan amount.
D. down payment.

169. An increase in the availability of money would lead to which effect?

A. Interest rates would go up.
B. Interest rates would go down.
C. Interest rates would NOT be affected due to RESPA guidelines.
D. Interest rates would NOT be affected due to TRUTH IN LENDING.

170. When the amortized payment of a mortgage remains constant over the period of the loan but leaves an

outstanding balance to be paid at the end, this payment is called:

A. an escalation payment.
B. a balloon payment.
C. a satisfaction payment
D. an acceleration payment.

171. In an installment land contract, what type of title did the seller retain?

A. joint
B. legal
C. equitable
D. record

172. Which of the following is true of a second mortgage?

A. It has priority over a first mortgage.
B. It cannot be used as a security instrument.
C. It is not negotiable.
D. It is usually issued at a higher rate of interest.

173. Usury MOST nearly means:

A. making loans without the benefit of co-signors.
B. lending money at fluctuating interest rates.
C. being capable of multiple usage.
D. illegal interest.

174. A borrower bought a $74,000 house with no down payment. The loan was probably:

A. a conventional insured loan.
B. a VA loan.
C. an FHA loan.
D. a conventional loan.

175. A house sold for $42,000. The buyer made a 20% down payment. Monthly interest on the loan was $252. What was the interest rate on the loan?

A. 5%
B. 7%
C. 9%
D. 11%

176. Which of the following describes a mortgage that requires principal and interest payments at regular intervals and is called the liquidation of debt by periodic installment until the debt is satisfied?

A. amortized loan
B. annuity loan
C. acceleration loan
D. assemblage loan

177. Under RESPA, a copy of REAL ESTATE SETTLEMENT COSTS AND YOU must be given:

A. within one day before closing.
B. at the time of loan application, or within 3 days of application.
C. within 5 days of application.
D. at closing.

178. The clause in a trust deed or mortgage which permits the mortgagee to declare the entire unpaid sum due upon a default by a mortgagor is called:

A. a judgment clause.
B. an acceleration clause.
C. an escalator clause.
D. a forfeiture clause.

179. An impound or reserve account MOST benefits whom?

A. the borrower
B.1 the lender
C. the trustee
D. the trustor

180. The lender is not insured or guaranteed against a loss, by reason of the borrower's default in repayment, under which type of loan?

A. FHA
B. Conventional
C. VA
D. GI

181. A VA loan may be granted for the purchase of a one-family to four-family property if:

A. The veteran certifies the rent collected will equal the mortgage payments.
B. The loan will be amortized for not more than 20 years.
C. The down payment will be at least 10%.
D. The veteran agrees to live there.

182. Which of the following would usually occur in a sale-and-leaseback transaction?

A. The seller gets a return on the purchase in the form of rental payments.
B. The property is sold on the condition that the new owner lease it back to the seller at the time title passes.
C. The buyer keeps capital in inventories rather than in realty.
D. The rent that the seller pays is not income-tax deductible.

183. A standardized yardstick expressing the true annual cost of borrowing is expressed as the what?

A. ECOA
B. Regulation Z

C. APR

D. RESPA

184. RESPA would prohibit which of the following acts?

A. steering

B.1 paying of kickbacks

C. blockbusting

D. redlining

185. In most states, by paying the debt after a foreclosure sale, the mortgagor has the right to regain the property. What is this right called?

A. equitable right of redemption

B. owner's right of redemption

C. vendee's right of redemption

D. statutory right of redemption

186. The lender is required, under RESPA, to provide a detailed GOOD FAITH ESTIMATE statement at the time of loan application or within three business days to:

A. the buyer.

B. the seller.

C. the buyer and seller.

D. neither the buyer nor the seller.

187. In which of the following markets may a lender sell a loan that a mortgage banker has previously originated?

A. primary market
B. secondary market
C. mortgage market
D. consumer market

188. Which of the following is considered a conventional loan?

A. FHA insured
B. VA guaranteed
C. commercial bank's ARM loan
D. contract for deed

189. Under an FHA graduated payment mortgage, which of the following fluctuates over the term of the loan?

A. interest rate
B. monthly payments
C. finance charge
D. annual rate

190. The maximum permissible loan to value ratios are:

A. based on sale price or appraised value, whichever is lower.
B. not determined by federal statute in the case of FHA loans.
C. based on the banker's competitive market analysis.

D. fixed by law for conventional loans.

191. All of the following are true of conventional loans except what?

A. They are made to the buyer without governmental insurance or guarantee.
B. The policy requirements of the lenders are not uniform.
C. The requirements to qualify are uniformly fixed by state law.
D. They require a higher down payment than non-conventional loans.

192. A buyer wants to take out an FHA loan. The broker should refer the buyer directly to:

A. any approved lending institution such as a bank or savings and loan association.
B. an FHA appraiser in the area.
C. the Federal Housing Administration Office.
D. the Federal National Mortgage Association.

193. An owner advertised Beautiful acreage; only $5,000 down; owner will personally finance down payment. Would this be in violation of the Truth in Lending Act?

A. Yes. Acreage is not exempt from Reg Z.
B. Yes--since a down payment was stated.
C. No. Owners are not covered by Reg. Z.
D. No. Brokers can advertise the down payment.

194. A mortgage company makes a number of loans to be assembled into one package and sold to permanent investors. This process is an example of interim financing to the mortgage company and is called:

A. blanket financing.
B. package financing.
C. warehousing.
D. discounting.

195. The primary purpose of Truth in Lending is to:

A. Control interest rates on behalf of the consumer.
B. Control the true costs to close a transaction.
C. Disclose the true costs of only an FHA loan.
D. Disclose the true costs of obtaining credit.

196. Why is the RESPA closing statement allowed to be examined on or before closing?

A. to allow the buyer to see costs at or before closing to see if he/she can get the loan at a cheaper price
B. to make sure the title insurance came from the right company
C. to check for mathematical errors
D. to provide for special fees to specific parties for business related to the real estate transaction

197. If a single parent is applying for a real estate loan, when would the fact have to be revealed that part of the parent's income is from child support?

A. when applying for a VA or FHA loan if the parent's income is less than $25,000
B. If more than 50% of the parent's income is from non-wage sources
C. If the parent was relying on the income for repayment of the loan
D. This type of income never needs to be disclosed. It would be a violation of ECOA.

198. When the lender under a deed of trust requires title insurance, who would be the most likely person to pay for it?

A. the mortgagee
B. the trustee
C. the trustor
D. the beneficiary

199. The Pickets are purchasing a home for $78,000 and the lender is giving them a 90% loan at 10% interest, plus a 2% loan origination fee. How much is the loan origination fee?

A. $1,404
B. $1,560
C. $1,650
D. $7,020

200. Discrimination is prohibited in lending practices under:

A. ECOA
B. RESPA
C. Truth in Lending Act
D. FNMA

201. A buyer assumes the mortgage. How is the owner relieved of the liability?

A. subject to mortgage
B. novation
C. substitution
D. graduation

202. Which type of loan will result in the largest reduction of the principal balance most quickly?

A. 10% over 30 years
B. 11% over 20 years
C. 13% over 15 years
D. 14% over 20 years

203. Who is the largest purchaser in the secondary market?

A. Ginnie Mae
B. Fannie Mae
C. FHA

D. Freddie Mac

204. Which transaction requires a securities license?

A. leasing a commercial building
B. selling a commercial warehouse
C. selling shares in Fannie Mae
D. arranging a sale-leaseback on a commercial property

205. Who is NOT an originator of primary loans?

A. savings and loans
B. credit unions
C. commercial banks
D. FHA

206. A buyer wanted to use a promissory note for consideration on the purchase of a property. Can he do this?

A. Yes. The buyer can do as he wishes since he is making the contract.
B. Yes. This is acceptable as long as the seller agrees.
C. No. Only money can be used for consideration.
D. No. Only the seller can write a promissory note.

207. If advertised alone, which would be in violation of TRUTH IN LENDING?

A. FHA financing available
B. Assumable loan
C. No down payment required.
D. easy financing terms

208. Why would a mortgagee (beneficiary) have an appraisal on the property?

A. to make sure the buyer did not pay too much
B. to determine the value of the property
C. to protect the buyer from fraud
D. to assure the property value is sufficient to cover the loan

209. In a repayment of a mortgage loan, which type of interest is used?

A. simple
B. discount
C. compound
D. floating

210. An owner was selling his own home. Can he advertise the down payment?

A. No, because it violates RESPA.
B. No, because it violates Regulation Z.
C. Yes--as long as it was listed with a broker.
D. Yes, because it was his own home.

211. Which is true about restrictive covenants?

A. They are placed by private parties in a deed.
B. They are placed by government agencies in a deed.
C. They are voidable by successive owners.
D. They are placed by government agencies in the public record.

212. Looking at shopping centers in the appraisal process, the social fiber of the community and distances from schools is called:

A. neighborhood analysis
B. market data approach
C. site analysis
D. social analysis

213. Which best describes why a buyer purchases a home using the market data approach?

A. Buyers buy on impulse.
B. Buyers buy based on how much income can be derived from other property.
C. Buyers buy after they compare the house with others.
D. Buyers buy based on current construction costs.

214. A scale drawing shows a room to be 3 inches by 4 ½ inches. Carpet, which is $15 per square yard, is to be

installed in the room. If the scale is 1 inch to 4 feet, how much would it cost to install the carpet?

A. $120
B. $202
C. $360
D. $3,240

215. A tenant leased 3000 square feet at $10 per square foot and 8% of gross income. The total annual rent she paid was $60,000. What was the gross income on which she paid percentage rent?

A. $120,000
B. $160,000
C. $300,000
D. $375,000

216. The Rose family owns a home in a semi-rural area, which is about five years old. Recently announced plans for a new regional airport will place their home directly in line with a main runway ending 1 mile before their home. If the airport is constructed, will this diminish the value of the Rose Home?

A. Yes, because of functional obsolescence.
B. Yes, because of economic obsolescence
C. No, because value would increase due to the location close to the airport.

D. No, because noise from aircraft passing overhead is not recognized as affecting property values.

217. Mrs. Jones, an appraiser, is appraising a single family residence for which she has located six closely comparable properties, all sold within the past six months. The subject property is rented for $500 per month. It is a custom-built home, approximately three years old. Mrs. Jones would probably give the most weight in her final estimate of value to which of the following appraisal methods?

A. cost approach
B. market data approach
C. income approach
D. gross rent multiplier

218. Which is the best example of functional obsolescence?

A. residential home built next to a factory
B. peeling paint
C. steep, narrow stairway in a 1 3/4 story home
D. residential home with central air conditioning

219. A real estate agent should tell the buyer, his customer, which of the following?

A. how long a property has been on the market
B. the seller's motivation for marketing his property
C. a pending or recent zoning change

D. The seller is getting a divorce.

220. A square is 1/8 of a mile by 1/8 of a mile. How many acres is this?

A. 10 acres.
B. 20 acres.
C. 40 acres.
D. 160 acres.

221. The first step in an appraisal is:

A. a market data comparison.
B. to define the problem.
C. a neighborhood analysis.
D. to gather information.

222. A recorded subdivision plat is used in the:

A. geodetic survey system.
B. rectangular survey system.
C. lot and block system.
D. metes and bounds system.

223. An appraiser is usually paid:

A. a fee based on a percentage of the appraised value.
B. a fee based on the amount of time and effort.

C. a fee agreed upon after the appraisal is completed.
D. a standard fee agreed upon by the National Appraisal Association.

224. The primary survey line running north and south in the rectangular survey system is the:

A. township line.
B. base line.
C. range line.
D. principal meridian.

225. The zoning commission of Jefferson County requires that all new construction in a specific area adhere to a specific type of architecture. What type of zoning is this?

A. bulk
B. incentive
C. directive
D. aesthetic

226. The appraisal approach most likely to be used in valuing a public library building would be:

A. market.
B. cost.
C. income.
D. residual.

227. Physical deterioration is considered curable whenever:

A. It is caused by lack of maintenance.
B. It does not result in loss of economic utility.
C. It costs less to correct than the resulting value increase.
D. It can be repaired regardless of the cost.

228. The economic life of an investment can be described as:

A. the remaining chronological life of the improvements.
B. the time over which value generated exceeds cost of operation.
C. the time when yield is attributable to the land itself.
D. the actual age of the property.

229. When an appraiser correlates the three approaches into a final estimate, he:

A. averages the estimate.
B. accords the greatest weight to the median value.
C. selects the estimate nearest that desired by the employer.
D. reconciles the differences according to the type of property being appraised and the quantity and quality of data available.

230. Apartment houses in an area were selling for $100,000 and a buyer offered $100,000 for an apartment building. The buyer is operating on the principle of:

A. highest and best use.
B. conformity.
C. substitution.
D. increasing returns.

231. A feature found in a comparable property that is not present in the subject property will result in a:

A. a reduction adjustment to the comparable's selling price.
B. an increase adjustment to the subject property's selling price.
C. the reduction adjustment to the subject property's selling price.
D. an increase adjustment to the comparable's selling price.

232. Economic obsolescence in a property is generally:

A. a result of poor maintenance.
B. due to architectural faults.
C. a type of depreciation that is incurable.
D. caused by the aging process.

233. When an appraiser uses the phrase effective age, he is referring to:

A. the number of years since the improvements were made.
B. the age of the property based upon its condition.
C. the estimated total life of an improvement.
D. the number of years during which the property will yield a worthwhile return on the investment made.

234. The Adams family purchased the largest and most expensive house in a new subdivision. Five years later, when they were ready to move, they discovered the monetary value of the home had gone up proportionately less than the other houses in the neighborhood. This phenomenon is an example of the principle of:

A. diminishing return.
B. change.
C. regression.
D. substitution.

235. In valuing a single family residence by the comparison approach, an appraiser would make adjustments to:

A. the comparable properties.
B. the subject property.
C. both the comparable and the subject property.
D. current properties being offered for sale.

236. An owner was building a house for himself. Due to personal preference, he decided not to put in a bathtub. This would result in:

A. physical deterioration.
B. external obsolescence.
C. functional obsolescence.
D. social obsolescence.

237. How does one determine the gross rent multiplier?

A. Property value divided by the capitalization rate.
B. Property value divided by the monthly rent.
C. Property value divided by the net income.
D. Property value divided by the gross income.

238. Restrictive covenants that run with the land:

A. are no longer effective when the title is transferred.
B. apply only until the developer has conveyed the title.
C. can be removed by a court of competent jurisdiction.
D. apply to and bind all successive owners of the property.

239. In doing a market analysis, an appraiser found a recently sold property where the owners had just gone through a divorce. The property had been listed for $60,000 for 3 months but was purchased for $40,000 by one of the spouses. Should the appraiser use this as a comparable?

A. Yes. You would use the actual sale price of $40,000.
B. Yes--because it was a comparable type property.
C. No--because it had only been listed for 3 months.
D. No--because of the divorce it was not an At arms' length transaction

240. For the past 30 years, the Ls have operated a neighborhood grocery store. Last week the city council passed a zoning ordinance that prohibits packaged food sales in the area where the Ls' grocery store is located. The store is now an example of a/an:

A. illegal enterprise.
B. nonconforming use.
C. violation of eminent domain.
D. variance of the zoning laws.

241. Marian Kent, a real estate salesperson, is developing a web site to promote her services. What, if anything, must she specifically include in the content of her web site?

A. Name and location of her employing broker's office and a list of states in which she is licensed
B. Name of her employing broker's firm and a list of states in which she is licensed
C. Name and location of her employing broker's office and the specific period for which her real estate license is valid
D. No specific disclosures are required.

242. What is the official view of listings based on net price?

A. They are lucrative and preferable to other types of listings that limit commissions.
B. They are allowable only with the permission of the Kentucky Board of Real Estate Brokers and Salespersons.

C. They are only legal in Kentucky if the seller gives written consent after receiving information clearly delineating the advantages and disadvantages of such a listing.
D. They are illegal in Kentucky.

243. How are commissions regulated in Kentucky?

A. Commissions are regulated by the Kentucky Board of Real Estate Brokers and Salespersons.
B. Commission guidelines are established by local groups of brokers.
C. Commissions are set by law.
D. Commissions are fully negotiable between brokers and clients.

244. When must funds received on behalf of a buyer be deposited in an escrow or trust account?

A. Within 3 days of the tendering the offer
B. Within 2 banking days of receiving all signatures on the contract
C. Within 5 business days of tendering the offer
D. Within 3 business days of finalizing all signatures for the contract

245. Lewis Oakley, a broker, receives an earnest money deposit from Rich Munroe for an offer on a house. What must Lewis do with the money?

A. Open an escrow account designated specifically for the Munroe transaction.

B. Deposit the money into the brokerage's existing non-interest-bearing escrow account for all such transactions.

C. Hold the deposit in a safe place at the brokerage office until the offer is finalized.

D. Deliver the money to the seller's attorney for safekeeping until the closing.

246. What is accepted practice for managing an escrow account?

A. Escrow accounts are reserved solely for the brokerage's operating expenses.

B. The brokerage must keep a journal detailing all account activity and a ledger detailing each transaction.

C. Escrow accounts must be opened at an institution other than the broker's personal bank.

D. The name of the account must be specified as Escrow Account on all account materials to specify its purpose.

247. Which of the following activities may be performed by brokers and salespeople who are not lawyers?

A. Explaining the legalities specific preprinted contract clauses to a buyer or seller

B. Adding additional language to a preprinted contract that more specifically reflects the nature of the individual transaction

C. Completing blanks on preprinted form contracts

D. Completing a bill of sale after finalization of the contract

248. Which of the following is NOT a required element for a written listing agreement?

A. A provision requiring the party signing the listing agreement to cancel the agreement in writing on or after the date set for expiration
B. Legal description of the property
C. Fair housing statement that prohibits discrimination on the basis of religion, race, color, national origin, age, sex, disability, familial status, or marital status
D. Definite expiration date of the listing

249. In Kentucky, which of the following need NOT be included in a listing contract?

A. Fair housing language
B. Signatures of title holders
C. Disclosure of all sources of compensation
D. Disclosure of any known material defects

250. What obligation does a licensed broker or salesperson have upon obtaining a listing?

A. Aggressively market the listing as widely as possible.
B. Establish a listing file with a unique number.
C. Communicate and cooperate with other brokerages wishing to participate in the marketing of the listing.

D. Provide the signers of the listing with a legible, signed, true, and correct copy of the listing.

251. Within what period of time must a housing discrimination charge be filed with the Kentucky Civil Rights Commission?

A. 30 days
B. 180 days
C. 1 year
D. 2 years

252. With which agency or individual may a person file a complaint regarding fair housing practices?

A. With HUD or the Kentucky Civil Rights Commission
B. With the board of REALTORS®
C. With the named licensee's office
D. With the Kentucky Board of Real Estate Brokers and Salespersons

253. What is the legal view of a clause added to preprinted contracts in Kentucky?

A. As long as the language does not directly involve the conveyance of title to real property, the real estate broker may add a requested clause.
B. Only a licensed attorney may write the language for inclusion of a clause in a real estate sales contract in Kentucky.

C. As long as the clause is a substantive clause and not frivolous, it may be added to the contract.
D. Preprinted contracts must be used only as provided because they have been approved by the state board for general usage.

254. From whom may a Kentucky real estate salesperson collect compensation?

A. From either a buyer or seller
B. Only from the employing broker
C. From any party to a transaction or their designated representative
D. From any licensed real estate broker with whom the salesperson worked

255. When may a salesperson be licensed under more than one broker simultaneously?

A. Never
B. Only with the written permission of the board
C. Only with the written consent of the brokers for whom the licensee is working
D. Only for supervision purposes when the licensee has offices in brokerage firms located in separate, non-adjacent counties

256. Gail has decided to leave her employing broker and work for a new employing broker in a larger brokerage. Which of the following steps must Gail take to notify the board?

A. When she renews her license, she may petition the board to transfer her license to a new employing broker.
B. She should prepare an official letter of termination that her current broker can forward to the board.
C. She must return her license to the board, along with a letter of termination.
D. Nothing; it is the current broker's responsibility.

257. Mikhail Rubynov is a sole proprietor whose license has been suspended for two years due to mismanagement of client records. How will Mikhail's associated brokers and affiliated salespeople be impacted by his suspension?

A. Their licenses will be suspended for the same period of time.
B. Their licenses are revoked pending review.
C. Their licenses are suspended until they find new employing brokers.
D. Their licenses are not affected by the broker's suspension.

258. When a broker's license is suspended, his salespeople's and affiliate's licenses are suspended pending their affiliation with a new qualified broker or until the broker's license is reinstated.

A. Yes, she may accept the money if more than 30 days have passed since the closing.
B. Yes, she may accept the money because she is licensed as an associate broker.

C. No, she may not accept the money if it comes from any party other than her employing broker.

D. No, she may not accept the money because she has already collected a fee for the transaction and this would be considered double billing.

259. What information must a broker supply to be eligible for a license for a branch office in a town 40 miles away from the home office?

A. Nothing; a branch office is not allowed to exist more than 25 miles from the main office city limits.

B. A letter from the board giving consent for the branch office.

C. A unique name for the branch office that does not imply a relationship with the home office

D. The name of a broker associate who will act as branch manager.

260. To ensure entitlement to a commission, a broker must have all of the following essential components EXCEPT:

A. A binding contract

B. A ready, willing, and able buyer

C. A signed listing agreement

D. A closing

261. Joe Crouch, a Canton Broker, has three different trust accounts. Hans Hergesheimer, another Broker in town, tells Joe that he thinks he can only have one according to

Kentucky law. Joe says he needs them, and that it is not illegal for a Broker to have more than one. Which of the following is true of this situation?

A. Joe can only maintain a single trust account in Kentucky.
B. Joe can only maintain two trust accounts as long as the Department approves it.
C. Brokers in Kentucky may maintain more than one trust account if they want to, as long as all trust fund provisions are followed.
D. Both A and B.

262. What stipulation governs the inspection of records and escrow accounts in real estate offices?

A. The records need to be made available only to a CPA who makes an appointment for inspection.
B. The records will be opened to a state designee during the office's normal business hours.
C. The records should be available for inspection upon 48 hours' notice from the proper authority.
D. The records must be shown to a designee of the state at the designee's convenience.

263. An investment specialist introduced a broker to a young couple looking to relocate to Kentucky and purchase a starter home. This meeting eventually turned into a sale for the broker. How soon may the broker reward the investment specialist for the lead?

A. The broker may not pay the investment specialist for the lead.

B. The broker may pay the investment specialist only after completion of the transaction.

C. The broker may pay for the lead only after the offer has been signed by both parties.

D. The broker may pay for the lead as soon as funds are disbursed from the escrow account.

264. The laws and regulations set forth in Article 6 do not pertain to which of the following circumstances?

A. False advertising

B. Failure to pay a commission to a cooperating broker

C. Demonstration of incompetence

D. License fraud

265. Floyd Hoopeston has lived in his condominium from May through November in each of the six years since he bought the new construction. He has recently decided to make his southern migration permanent and has just signed a contract with a buyer, Tracy Li. Under which circumstances does Tracy have the right to cancel the signed contract?

A. Within 5 days of execution of the contract

B. Within 5 days of receipt of resale documents

C. Within 10 days of receipt of resale documents

D. The contract may not be canceled in this situation

266. Of the following scenarios, which would NOT result in licensing proceedings against a salesperson?

A. A licensee accumulates offers on a house and presents them to the seller in a single bundle.
B. A licensee accumulates offers on a house and presents the best offer to the seller.
C. A licensee fails to submit an offer to a seller who is already under contract.
D. A licensee presents accumulated offers to a seller on a weekly basis.

267. What heading should a preprinted offer to purchase display if it is intended to become a binding contract?

A. Offer to Purchase
B. Standard Purchase Offer and Contract
C. Real Estate Sale Contract
D. No particular heading is required.

268. Which of the following is true of a broker's commission in a real estate sales transaction?

A. The commission, which is negotiable between broker and seller, must be stipulated in the listing agreement.
B. The commission will be decided through mediation by the department if any dispute exists.
C. Commission funds are due at closing, payable by cash or cashier's check only.

D. Published rates set by the agreement of local brokers delineate standard commission rates by which all brokers must abide.

269. Jesse Waters, a top-rated broker, wants to earn the listing for the Millers' house but is competing with a number of other brokers for the listing. After considering the situation, Jesse entices the Millers to list their house with him based on the following guarantee: If the property does not sell within 90 days, Jesse promises to buy it. Given this advertising, Jesse must take all of the following steps EXCEPT which one?

A. Market the property as he would in any other circumstances, special agreement notwithstanding
B. Demonstrate financial capability to purchase the property if not sold after 90 days
C. Review the written details of the plan with the Waters before they sign the contract
D. Purchase the Waters' property at the established price before the 90-day period concludes

270. What is the age of legal competence in Kentucky?

A. 16
B. 18
C. 21
D. 18, unless emancipated or married at a younger age

271. Which of the following legal agreements need NOT be set forth in writing?

A. Exclusive-right-to-sell agreement
B. Multiple listing
C. Exclusive-agency listing
D. Open listing

272. All of the following are protected classes under Kentucky fair housing law EXCEPT:

A. Disability
B. Race
C. Sexual preference
D. Ancestry

273. What ceiling is specified for interest rates on properties financed by sellers?

A. 8 percent
B. 11 percent
C. 15 percent
D. None exists

274. Does Kentucky Law require a landlord to allow a visually impaired girl with a guide dog to reside in an apartment complex with a no pets policy?

A. Yes, Kentucky law prohibits a landlord from refusing to rent the apartment to a visually impaired person on the basis of a no pets policy.

B. Yes, but the visually impaired tenant may be required to pay a special damage deposit upfront.

C. No, since a no pets policy can be enforced if applied to all circumstances equally, the visually impaired person will not be allowed to rent a unit in the complex.

D. Kentucky law does not provide guidance on the issue of working dogs to support people with disabilities.

275. The person ultimately responsible for preparing documents for a closing would be which of the following individuals?

A. The attorney for the seller
B. The listing broker
C. The lender
D. The salesperson facilitating the transaction

276. Whose responsibility is it to file a 1099 for real property transactions?

A. The closing agent
B. The title company
C. The lender
D. The listing broker

277. Which of the following actions does not lie within the realm of responsibility of a broker preparing for a closing?

A. Oversight of the inspections
B. Delivery of documents and escrow monies to the appropriate attorney
C. Review of closing procedures with both parties to a transaction
D. Completion of required title searches

278. What constitutes a tract per the Land Division Act?

A. The land an individual owned prior to March 31, 1997
B. The sum total of contiguous property purchased after March 31, 1997
C. Two or more parcels with a common property line, if in existence prior to March 31, 1997 and still under the same ownership
D. Four parcels of land fronting on a major road

279. What is the allowable depth-to-width ratio for a created parcel of land smaller than ten acres?

A. The depth may not exceed 3 times the width, with certain exceptions.
B. The depth may not exceed 4 times the width, with certain exceptions.
C. The depth may not exceed 4 times the width, with no exceptions.

D. Depth-to-width ratios only apply to parcels of land that exceed 10 acres.

280. Russ Hayworth owns 15 acres of undeveloped land which he has decided to sell. Gene Lowes, a buyer, agrees to purchase 100% of the land at an agreed-upon price. If this land is transferred in a single action, what must the mandatory clause on the deed specify?

A. No clause is required.
B. The clause must give Gene Lowes the right to make All divisions under section 108 of the Land Division Act.
C. The clause must stipulate the exact number of division rights being conveyed to Gene Lowes.
D. The clause must specify general right to divide without inserting the number of division rights passed to Gene Lowes.

281. Blaise Wilkes owned a ranch on which valuable minerals were discovered in 1976. Subsequently, he has sold the property but retains ownership of the mineral rights. Which of the following is true?

A. Blaise must record his ownership of mineral rights every 20 years
B. Blaise need only record the mineral rights when first acquired in 1976; they are granted in perpetuity.
C. Blaise must have recorded the rights when he sold his property and wished to retain ownership of the mineral rights.
D. Once property has been transferred to a new owner, Blaise may not retain ownership of mineral rights to the property.

282. By when must all condominium documents be delivered to the purchaser in a new construction condominium sale?

A. Prior to the contract becoming binding
B. Within 5 business days of the seller's acceptance of the purchaser's offer
C. Prior to accepting the purchaser's offer
D. At least 48 hours prior to the closing

283. Which of the following is NOT required of a Kentucky broker who promotes the sale of land located in another state?

A. Adherence to all restrictions and conditions stipulated by the real estate department
B. Reimbursement of any travel expenses the real estate department incurs while investigating the promotion
C. Disclosure of all details about the property to the real estate department
D. Licensure in both Kentucky and the state in which the property is located

284. What is the principal method of describing property in Kentucky?

A. Rectangular survey system
B. System of metes and bounds
C. Grid of meridians

D. Colonial block grant system

285. In which circumstances are subdivision developers regulated by the Interstate Land Sales Full Disclosure Act?

A. If 25 or fewer lots are sold outside Kentucky's limits
B. If 25 or fewer lots are sold within Kentucky's limits
C. If 25 or more lots are sold outside Kentucky's limits
D. If 25 or more lots are sold within Kentucky's limits

286. What type of activity performed without a permit in a designated wetlands area would violate Kentucky's Wetland Protection Act?

A. Constructing a boardwalk along a riverfront
B. Planting a vegetable garden on a half acre of land
C. Installing an in-ground swimming pool
D. Relandscaping an area previously overgrown with vegetation

287. Which of the following legal descriptions of property is not valid in Kentucky?

A. Torrens registration
B. Metes and bounds
C. Recorded plats
D. Rectangular survey system

288. Where would a property be located in relationship to the intersection of the base line and the principal meridian if its location is described as the southeast quadrant of Section 5, Township 5 South, and Range 2 East?

A. Northwest of the initial point
B. Northeast of the initial point
C. Southwest of the initial point
D. Southeast of the initial point

289. Of the following descriptions of property, which is NOT considered legal in Kentucky?

A. Lot 5, Block 7 of Whitehall Subdivision, Alcona County, Kentucky
B. 2340 Oak St., Grand Rapids, Kentucky
C. A parcel beginning at the northwest corner of Section 4, T2N, R2W bounded on the east by Wild Rd, on the south by Worthington Court, and on the west by Jack Rabbit Crossing.
D. Section 3 of T2N, R4S

290. How does one acquire land by adverse possession?

A. Use the land with owner's permission
B. Use the land for a period of 30 years
C. Use the land furtively to avoid detection
D. Use the land without permission

291. The Simsons hope to acquire an easement on their neighbor's property. Their neighbor's property has a woods that borders a public lake on which they frequently sail in warm weather. The Simsons have been hauling their speedboat through their neighbor's woods for 5 years; how much longer must they continue this pattern of use in order to obtain an easement?

A. 5 more years
B. 10 more years
C. 15 more years
D. 25 more years

292. What must a property owner do to prevent someone from acquiring an easement to cross his or her land?

A. Post a No Trespassing sign
B. Write a letter denying permission to cross the land
C. Follow procedures outlined in the Kentucky statutes
D. Write a letter granting permission to cross the land

293. What is the minimum age at which an individual may enter a legally enforceable contract?

A. 16, if married or emancipated; otherwise 18
B. 17, if married or emancipated; otherwise 18
C. 18, with no exceptions
D. 21, with no exceptions

294. Alyssa, a college student, found the perfect apartment just at the edge of campus. She has two years until graduation and asked the landlord to give her a lease for the full two-year period in exchange for a small discount on rent. What type of lease may the landlord record for Alyssa's extended lease term?

A. A notice of lease
B. A lis pendens
C. A rent supplement notice
D. A notice of constructive occupancy

295. Sherry and Bill Vaughn signed a lease with a provision to waive their rights to the security deposit. Which of the following is true of the provision?

A. The provision is unenforceable, but the lease is still valid.
B. The provision is unenforceable, so the lease is invalid.
C. The provision is enforceable because the contract is signed.
D. The provision is enforceable only for the initial term of the lease.

296. Michael Laughlin skipped out before paying July's rent on a lease that expired at the end of July. Which of the following actions may the landlord take?

A. The landlord may confiscate the tenant's belongings.
B. The landlord may extend the lease automatically because the tenant left without notice.

C. The landlord may keep a portion of the security deposit to cover the rent owed.
D. The landlord may do nothing because the lease is terminated as of the date the tenant vacated the premises.

297. Rachel Carson has been evicted from her apartment for continual violations of the apartment's no pets rule. If she does not remove her belongings, under summary process, what course of action is available to the landlord?

A. The landlord may sell the belongings and keep the proceeds.
B. The landlord may summon the sheriff to place the belongings on the street.
C. The landlord may keep the belongings for personal use.
D. The landlord may deliver the belongings to the town dump.

298. Which of the following rules applies to security deposits?

A. Landlords may only collect security deposits for residential units.
B. A landlord may apply a security deposit at the end of a lease period to cover rent owed by a tenant.
C. A landlord must return the security deposit to the tenant within 30 days of the end of the lease unless property has been damaged.
D. Security deposits must be placed in an interest-bearing account, and tenants must be paid accumulated interest when their security deposit is returned at the end of the lease period.

299. Jacob Frost has established a year-to-year tenancy with his landlord over the past 5 years. Now, the landlord wishes to terminate the year-to-year tenancy and convert the apartments into a new form. What notice is the landlord required to provide Jacob?

A. 1 week
B. 30 days
C. 3 months
D. The number of days equivalent to the basis on which rent is paid

300. Maxim Apartments charges $450 monthly rent for each of their studio units. What is the maximum amount that the landlord may require for a security deposit according to the Kentucky Security Deposit Act?

A. $450.00
B. $675.00
C. $900.00
D. $1,350.00

REAL ESTATE MATH EXAM

1. The fastest way to calculate one month's interest on a real estate loan with an interest rate of 7.2% interest per annum is to multiply the principal balance by:

A.   0.006
B.   0.6
C.   7.2% and divide by 12
D.   12 and divide by 7.2%

2. A duplex with a fair market value of $20,000 and an outstanding loan balance of $12,000 was exchanged for a four-plex with a market value of $35,000 and an outstanding $18,000 loan balance. The owner of the duplex would pay in cash or secondary financing

A. $6,100
B. $8,100
C. $9,100
D. $15,100

3. Mr. Brown, licensed broker, took an offer from Mr. Green on land for $6,000 with the following terms: $2,000 down and purchase money trust deed and note for the balance, payable $70 per month including interest at 7.2%. If the offer was accepted by the seller, what is the balance of the loan after the first 3 months payment?

A. $3,186
B. $3,467

C. $3,861
D. $3,790

4. After subtracting $140.00 escrow fees and 6% commission on gross sales price, a seller receives $13,584.00. What is the selling price?

A. $12,770
B. $14,440
C. $14,540
D. $14,600

5. Keith Johnson purchased a property at 20% less than the listed price and later sold the property for the original listed price. What was the percentage of profit?

A.   10%
B.   20%
C.   25%
D.   40%

6. Lots "A", "B" and "C" sold for a total price of $39,000. If lot "B" was priced at $6,400 more than lot "A", and lot "C" was priced at $7,100 more than lot "B", the price of lot "A" was:

A. $13,000.00
B. $6,366.67
C. $5,433.33
D. $4,633.00

7. Assume a real estate salesman sold a residence for $31,000. If the broker's commission was 6% and the salesman was to receive 45% of the total commission for selling the property, the salesman would receive:

A. $837.70
B. $959.95
C. $1,860.00
D.   None of the above

8. Smith and Allen wish to exchange real property. Smith owns a property valued at $150,000 against which there is a $35,000 trust deed. Allen owns property worth $105,000 on which there is an existing first trust deed of $25,000 and a second trust deed of $20,000. Allen has $15,000 in cash which he is willing to pay towards the exchange. If Smith is willing to accept a second trust deed and note from Allen in order to effect the exchange, the amount of the note would be:

A. $20,000
B. $40,000
C. $50,000
D. $70,000

9. An apartment house property costs $240,000 and this price has been verified to be an accurate estimate of the property value. In comparable circumstances it is also verified that the owner may use a 10% capitalization rate to the purchase price in determining his net income. Should there be a 10% increase in rental income with no increase in the owner's expense and should the capitalization rate of the

property be increased to 12%, what would be the estimated value of the property be?

A. $220,000
B. $240,000
C. $264,000
D.   None of the above

10. Able purchased a $15,000 home. His down payment amounted to 6 2/3% of the purchase price; the balance was carried as a first trust deed bearing interest at 8.4% per annum. The principal is to be repaid at $50.00 per month. A three-year insurance policy costs $72.00; the property taxes are $360.00 per year. Able is required to make a proportionate monthly payment to a loan trust fund for these items. The total amount of the first monthly payment most nearly would be:

A. $267
B. $182
C. $186
D. $188

11. A husband and wife own a vacation home in the mountains. The annual taxes on the property are $400.00. Since the total taxes cannot exceed 1% of the full cash value of the property, the "full cash value" of the property would be:

A. $10,000
B. $20,000
C. $40,000

D. $80,000

12. A house sold for $16,350, which amount was 9% more than the cost of the house. The cost of the house was:

A. $14,878.50
B. $15,000.00
C. $16,000.00
D. $17,821.50

13. The Southern Pacific Railroad Company sold ABS Developers three sections of land that had been divided into 20 acre parcels. 16 sold at $4,000 each and the remainder sold at $5,000 each. Which of the following was most nearly the total amount realized by the seller?

A. $350,000
B. $358,000
C. $475,000
D. $500,000

14. An acre is to be divided into four equal lots. If the lots are parallel to each other, rectangular, and 200 feet deep, the width of each lot would most nearly be:

A.   15 feet
B.   55 feet
C.   200 feet
D.   218 feet

15. A prospect is considering the purchase of an income property which has an operating statement showing

$94,500.00 deducted from gross income to arrive at the net income. The deductions amount to 60% of the gross income. If the prospect wants a 12% return on the purchase price of any investments he makes, what should he pay for the property?

A. $81,000
B. $196,000
C. $504,000
D. $720,000

16. Richard Rock sold his residence which was unencumbered. Total deductions in escrow amounted to $215.30 in addition to a broker's commission of 6% of the selling price. The selling price was the only credit item. Richard Rock received a check for escrow amounting to $15,290. The selling price was most nearly:

A. $16,200
B. $16,266
C. $16,430
D. $16,495

17. Mr. and Mrs. Smith acquired a home in 1977 for $48,000. In 1987 they sold it for $60,500 and moved into an apartment unit. During the ten year period of ownership, permanent improvements totaling $12,750 were made to their house. If Mr. Smith's income consists entirely of wages, how would the sale affect his 1987 federal income return?

A.   No affect
B. $125.00 loss

C. $250.00 loss
D. $12,500 gain

18. Eddie Ronquillo sold his house and took back a note for $4,200 secure a second deed of trust. He promptly sold the note for $2,730. This represents a discount of:

A.   28%
B.   35%
C.   55%
D.   65%

19. An owner depreciated the improvements based on a cost basis of $160,000 using the straight line method. Improvements are depreciated 37.5% to date and the remaining economic life is estimated to be 15 years. Which of the following is correct? The:

A.   Rate of depreciation exceeds 4% per annum
B.   Time of depreciation to date is over ten years
C.   Value of the building is $120,000
D.   Rate of depreciation cannot be determined from the data given

20. What is the monthly return on an income property with a 6 1/2% return on its value of $46,500?

A. $251.88
B. $302.50
C. $151.25
D. $3,630.00

21. Andrew Blacker was the owner of a straight note with an annual interest rate of 8.4%. In 5 years, he had received $5,460 in interest. What was the principal amount of the note?

A. $1,092
B. $13,000
C. $6,500
D. $3,250

22. The Phillips sold their home for $36,850, which represents a 17% profit over the original price. What was the original price?

A. $31,495
B. $35,000
C. $53,540
D. $19,850

23. If a building's costs increased 20 percent, the value of the investor's dollar has decreased by:

A.   16 and 2/3%
B.   20%
C.   25%
D.   33 and 1/3%

24. One month's interest on a 5 year straight note amounted to $225.00. At a 7 1/2% per year interest rate, what was the face amount of the note?

A. $2,700

B. $1,688
C. $36,000
D. $44,000

25. Escrow closed May 1 with interest on a $4,415 second trust deed paid to June 1. The interest rate is 7 2/10%. What is the debt to the buyer, if the buyer assumes the loan?

A. $22.09
B. $26.49
C. $4,415.00
D. None of the above

26. A man owns an apartment building with 20,000 square feet of living space and wants to carpet 60% of the area. If the carpet costs $6.00 a square yard, what is the total cost of the carpeting?

A. $3,996
B. $4,000
C. $7,998
D. $24,000

27. One month's interest on a straight note amounted to $45. At 4 1/2% per year, what was the face amount of the note?

A. $2,025
B. $1,200
C. $12,000
D. $24,000

28. If the interest is paid at a rate of $60 per month and the rate of interest is 8% per year, what is the principal amount of the loan?

A. $5,760
B. $8,560
C. $9,000
D. $90,000

29. Mr. Morton paid $945 interest on a straight note loan of $7,000, at a rate of 9%. What was the term of the loan?

A.   18 months
B.   36 months
C.   48 months
D.   60 months

30. A man paid $140 in interest for a 90 day period on a $7,000 loan. What was the interest rate on the loan?

A.   6%
B.   8%
C.   10%
D.   11%

31. A rectangular parcel containing 540 square yards which has a frontage of 45' would be how many feet deep?

A.   54' deep
B.   108' deep
C.   270' deep
D.   540' deep

32. How many acres are contained in a parcel of land 1,320' by 2,640'?

A.   40 acres
B.   60 acres
C.   80 acres
D.   120 acres

33. If $150 interest is paid in 8 months on a straight note loan of $2,500, what is the annual rate of interest?

A.   9%
B.   10%
C.   11.50%
D.   12%

34. A parcel of land 1/4 mile by 1/4 mile is how many acres?

A.   Ten acres
B.   Twenty acres
C.   Forty acres
D.   Eighty acres

35. A man bought a home for $31,680 and now wishes to sell. He is informed that the cost of selling will amount to 12% of the selling price. He wishes to sell at a price so as not to have a loss. How much would the home have had to appreciate in order to offset the selling costs?

A. $1,080
B. $2,160
C. $4,320

D. $5,400

36. A building that has interior dimensions of 26' x 30' and has 6" walls would cover how much square footage of land?

A.   58
B.   428
C.   837
D.   3,680

37. A rectangular parcel of land measures 1,780' x 1,780' and contains how many acres?

A.   73
B.   316
C.   632
D.   1,780

38. A borrower paid $120 interest on a 90-day straight note. The principal was $6,000. What was the interest rate?

A.   6%
B.   7%
C.   8%
D.   9%

39. A man borrowed $750 on a straight note at an interest rate of 7.2%. If his total interest payment was $67.50, the length of the loan was?

A.   Twelve months
B.   Fifteen months

C.   Twenty four months
D.   Thirty months

40. A house sold for $16,350 which was 9% more than its original cost. What was the original cost?

A. $15,000
B. $20,000
C. $25,000
D. $30,000

41. A homeowner sold his house for $23,000. This selling price represented a 15% profit over what he had originally paid for the house. What was the original price of the home?

A. $15,000
B. $20,000
C. $25,000
D. $30,000

42. Assume that a second trust deed of $1,000 was to be paid in annual installments of $300 plus 6% interest, with a balloon payment of the balance at the end of the third year. The remaining balance of the principal after the second annual installment was paid would be:

A. $400.00
B. $424.00
C. $505.60
D. $520.00

43. Mr. John listed his home with Broker Bob for $35,000. The broker was to receive a commission rate of 6%. The

broker brought an offer at 10% less than the listed price. The owner agreed to accept the offer if the broker reduced his commission by 20%. If they all agree to these terms, what amount of commission would the broker receive?

A. $812
B. $1,012
C. $1,312
D. $1,512

44. A man had an income property which suffered a $300 monthly loss of net income when a freeway was built nearby. At a capitalization rate of 12%, how much did his property lose in value?

A. $20,000
B. $30,000
C. $40,000
D. $50,000

45. Kent was the owner of a straight note with an annual interest rate of 8.4%. In five years he had received $5,460 in interest. The principal amount of the note was most nearly?

A. $12,000
B. $13,000
C. $14,000
D. $15,000

46. An investor owns a 20-unit apartment house. When compared to comparable apartment properties he loses $200 net income a month because his property is located next to a

busy freeway. Appraisers are using a 12% capitalization rate for this neighborhood of income properties. The subject property has suffered a loss in value in the amount of:

A. $20,000
B. $25,000
C. $30,000
D. $35,000

47. In order to earn $208 per month from an investment that yields a 6% return you would have to invest approximately:

A.   12480
B. $20,800
C. $24,960
D. $41,600

48. A man bought two 60 foot lots for $18,000 each and divided them into three lots which he sold for $15,000 each. What was his percentage of profit?

A.   15.00%
B.   25.00%
C.   28.00%
D.   30.00%

49. If a man paid $50,000 for a business which gave him a 6% return on his money, how much did he make during the first year that he owned it?

A. $1,500
B. $3,000

C. $4,500
D. $6,000

50. An investor was going to have a building constructed which was to cost $150,000 and could, when completed, be leased for $2,500 per month. The annual operating expenses for the property would be $6,000. The amount he could invest in the land to realize a 12% return would be:

A. $50,000
B. $75,000
C. $100,000
D. $150,000

51. An investor purchased property for a total price of $72,000, paying $20,000 down and financing the balance of $52,000 using a straight note. If the investor eventually sold the property after it had doubled in value and had made no principal payments on the loan, each dollar invested would show a return of:

A. $2.00
B. $4.60
C. $5.60
D. $8.70

52. Which of the following contains the largest area?

A.   4 square miles
B.   5,280' X 10,560'
C.   2 sections

D. 1/10 of a township

53. Harris obtained a loan in the amount of $20,000 and paid the mortgage lender four discount points and an origination fee of 2%. If the payments on the loan were $163.00 per month, including 8% interest and the average balance over a five year period was $18,500, the gross amount earned by the lender is the 5 years was most nearly:

A. $5,100
B. $6,000
C. $7,400
D. $8,600

54. An individual who receives $225 per month on a money market savings account that pays 7 1/2% per year, has invested which of the following amounts?

A. $12,500
B. $27,000
C. $36,000
D. $48,000

55. A seller took back a second trust deed and note in the amount of $11,400 payable $240 per month, including interest at 7% per annum. If interest on the note begins July 15 and the first payment is made on August 15, the amount of the first payment that is applied to the principal is:

A. $66.50
B. $79.80
C. $173.50

D. $240.00

56. Humphreys sold his residence which was unencumbered. Total deductions in escrow amounted to $215.30 in addition to a broker's commission of 6% of the selling price. The selling price was the only credit item. Humphreys received a check from escrow amounting to $15,290. The selling price was most nearly:

A. $16,200
B. $16,266
C. $16,430
D. $16,495

57. Ms. Rodgers sold her house and took back a note for $4200 secured by a second deed of trust. She promptly sold the note for $2730. This represents a discount of:

A.   28%
B.   35%
C.   51%
D.   73%

58. After subtracting $140 escrow fees and 6% commission on gross sales price, a seller receives $13,584. What is the selling price?

A. $12,770
B. $14,440
C. $14,540
D. $14,600

59. A man purchased a property at 20% less than the listed price and later sold the property for the original listed price. What was the percentage of profit?

A.   10%
B.   20%
C.   25%
D.   40%

60. Escrow closed May 1st with interest on a $4415 second trust deed paid to June 1st. If the interest rate is 7.2%, the debit to the buyer, if the buyer assumed the loan, would be:

A. $22.09
B. $26.49
C. $4,415.00
D.   None of the above

61. A board foot of lumber could be obtained from a piece of lumber that is:

A.   6" X 6" X 1"
B.   6" X 12" X 1"
C.   12" X 1" X 1"
D.   6" X 12" X 12"

62. Assume that a second trust deed of $1000 was to be paid in annual installments of $300 plus 6% interest, with a balloon payment of the balance at the end of the third year. The remaining balance of the principal after the annual installment had been paid was:

A.	$400
B.	$424
C.	$506
D.	$520

63. Assume a real estate salesman sold a residence for $31,000. If the broker's commission was 6% and the salesman was to receive 45% of the total commission for selling the property, the salesman would receive:

A.	$837.70
B.	$959.95
C.	$1,860.00
D.	None of the above

64. If Broker Christianson brought in an offer of 10% less than the listing price of $15,300 and the seller would agree to the price if the broker would accept a 20% reduction of his commission, the broker's commission would amount to:

A.	$660.96
B.	$689.85
C.	$735.84
D.	$827.82

65. A man enters into a lease agreement on a grocery store with the following terms: $350 minimum monthly rent or 5% grocery sales, 7% of meat sales, 6% of deli sales, and 8% of produce sales, whichever is greater. The grocery sales were $27,000 annually, meat sales $500 per month, deli sales $300 per month and produce sales $3,000 annually. What was the annual rent on the store?

A. $3,180
B. $4,200
C. $4,386
D. $5,120

66. A building was insured for $19,500 at a rate of .18 per hundred. If the three year policy was 2 1/2 times the one year rate, what amount per month should be added to the monthly payments to properly cover the insurance cost?

A. $7.31
B. $2.92
C. $2.44
D. $1.46

67. What is the annual interest rate on a $16,000 loan when the interest payments are $160.00 per quarter on the full amount? At least:

A. 3%, but less than 4%
B. 4%, but less than 5%
C. 5%, but less than 6%
D. 6%, but less than 7%

68. A homeowner sold his house for $23,000. If the selling price represented a 15% profit over what he had originally paid for the house, the original price of the home was:

A. $19,550
B. $20,000
C. $27,000

D.   None of the above

69. An owner of a section of land dedicates an easement for a road along the south side of his section. The easement contained 3 acres. The width of the road was approximately:

A.   Twenty feet
B.   Thirty feet
C.   Forty feet
D.   Fifty feet

70. There are five units in a condo. Smith paid $12,600, Jones paid $13,500, Kahn paid $13,750, Poe paid $14,400 and Clark paid $15,250. If there was an $1800 annual maintenance fee and each owner was to pay his proportionate share based upon the ratio of his unit purchase price to the total purchase price of all units, the monthly share of Smith's unit would be:

A. $8.00
B. $27.00
C. $32.40
D. $36.00

71. A property in probate was offered for sale and an offer of $12,000 was received. If anyone else wishes to bid on the property at the time of the confirmation, the initial minimum overbid must be:

A. $12,000
B. $13,000
C. $13,100

D. $13,500

72. The total number of lineal feet on one side of a Section is:

A.   1,000
B.   2,640
C.   5,280
D.   43,560

73. Arnold held a straight note which carried an annual interest rate of 8.4%. If in five years he had received $5,460 in interest, the principal amount of the note was:

A. $10,000
B. $11,500
C. $13,000
D. $15,000

74. Escrow companies normally base their prorations on an escrow year of:

A.   350 days
B.   355 days
C.   360 days
D.   365 days

75. Eddie Ronquillo sold his home for $17,200. If this represents 9% more than what he paid for it, the cost of the home was most nearly:

A. $15,424
B. $15,500

C. $15,800
D. $16,000

76. An individual borrowed $750 on a straight note at an interest rate of 7.2%. If the total interest payment on the loan was $81.00, the term of the loan was:

A.   15 months
B.   18 months
C.   21 months
D.   24 months

77. The Richard Rock sold his home and had to carry back a second trust deed and note of $5310. If he sold the note for $3823.20 before any payments had been made on the note, the rate of discount amounted to:

A.   25%
B.   28%
C.   54%
D.   72%

78. A real estate syndicate paid $193,600 for a lot on which they planned to build a high rise apartment. If the lot was 200 feet deep and they paid $4.40 per square foot, the cost per front foot was:

A. $220
B. $440
C. $880
D. $960

79. A rectangular parcel of land that measures 220' X 330' contains most nearly:

A.   1 1/4 acres
B.   1 3/5 acres
C.   1 2/3 acres
D.   2 acres

80. A borrower signed a straight note for a term of eight months in the amount of $2500. If she paid $150 in interest on the loan, the interest rate was:

A.   8%
B.   9%
C.   9%
D.   10%

81. An income property was appraised for $100,000 based on a 6% capitalization rate. If an investor used an 8% cap rate, the value of the property would be:

A. $60,000
B. $75,000
C. $80,000
D. $90,000

82. If a note in the amount of $22,250 specifies monthly payments over a period of 30 years at 6.6% interest per annum, what is the first month's interest payment?

A. $111.25
B. $122.38

C. $130.71
D. $140.50

83. If Haeli McDonald paid a commission of 6% of the selling price of a property valued at $54,375, the selling broker would receive:

A. $4,275.00
B. $3,375.00
C. $3,262.50
D. $3,191.50

84. A bank agreed to lend the owner of a piece of property a sum equal to 66 2/3% of its appraised valuation. The interest rate charged on the amount borrowed is 5% per annum. The first year's interest amounted to $200.00. What was the valuation placed upon the property by the bank?

A. $3,000.00
B. $4,000.00
C. $5,333.33
D. $6,000.00

85. A married couple purchased a property for a total price of $18,000, paying $5000 down and having the seller take back a first trust deed in the amount of $13,000. The terms of the $13,000 trust deed called for no payments in the first year. If at the end of the first year, they were to sell the property at twice its original cost, their original dollar is now worth:

A. $2.00

B. $4.60
C. $7.20
D. $8.00

86. If a borrower pays $1650 interest per quarter on a straight note of $60,000, the interest rate would be:

A. 8.50%
B. 9.00%
C. 10.50%
D. 11.00%

87. Maria Watson sold a residence that was free and clear of all liens and received a check for $30,580. If closing costs of $430.60 had been deducted as well as the broker's 6& commission, the actual selling price would have been most nearly:

A. $31,590
B. $31,825
C. $32,885
D. $32,990

88. The number of townships in a tract of land that is 28 miles square is most nearly:

A. Eleven
B. Seventeen
C. Twenty two
D. Fifteen

89. Clever executed a promissory note in the amount of $7000. If the note called for the payment of interest only and Clever paid off the entire sum in 90 days together with interest of $210, the interest rate on the note was most nearly:

A. 9%
B. 10%
C. 11%
D. 12%

90. Broker Thomas is listing a property owned by Gibson. Gibson has advised Thomas that he wished to realize $37,000 cash from the sale after paying Thomas a 4% commission and paying $600 in closing costs. To accomplish this and assuming that the property is free and clear, the selling price must be at least:

A. $37,856
B. $38,480
C. $39,110
D. $39,167

91. The interest rate on a straight note in the amount of $27,000 that calls for interest payments of $573.75 each quarter would most nearly be:

A. 6.6%
B. 7.2%
C. 8.6%
D. 9.2%

92. A commercial office building yields an annual net income of $174,000. If an appraiser applied a capitalization rate of 8% to the property, the market value of the property would most nearly be:

A. $1,392,000
B. $1,666,000
C. $1,932,000
D. $2,175,000

93. An individual who receives $225.00 per month on a money market savings account that pays 7.5% per year, has invested which of the following amounts?

A. $125,000
B. $27,000
C. $36,000
D. $48,000

94. A holder of a second trust deed and straight note with a face amount of $3740 sold it for $2431. This amounted to a discount of:

A.   26%
B.   35%
C.   45%
D.   55%

95. A seller took back a second trust deed and note in the amount of $11,400, payable $240 per month, including interest at 7% per annum. If interest on the note begins July 15 and the first payment is made on August 15, the amount

of the first payment that is applied to the principal is:

A. $66.50
B. $79.80
C. $173.50
D. $240.00

96. A homeowner made a regular monthly payment of $550 on her home loan. Out of the total payment, the lender deducted the interest that was due for the month and applied the remaining balance of $43.85 to the principal. If the outstanding balance of the loan was $56,500, the interest rate on the load was most nearly:

A.   8.50%
B.   9.25%
C.   10.75%
D.   12.50%

97. A square parcel of land that is 1780' X 1780' contains most nearly:

A.   27 acres
B.   54 acres
C.   65 acres
D.   73 acres

98. An investor purchased two lots and paid $18,000 for each one. Since each lot had a 60' frontage he was able to subdivide the combined parcels in 3 lots with equal front footage. If the 3 lots sold for $15,000 each, his rate of profit on his investment was:

A.   20%
B.   25%
C.   33%
D.   40%

99. A one acre parcel of land that is square is divided into four lots of equal size. If the lots are rectangular, parallel to each other and are 240' deep, the width of each lot is most nearly:

A.   45.4'
B.   90.8'
C.   181'
D.   240'

100. Natalie Johnson owns a $100,000 property based on a 6% capitalization rate. If due to changes in economic conditions investors now require a higher capitalization rate or 8%, what would the value of the property be using the same dollar income?

A. $90,000
B. $75,000
C. $80,000
D. $60,000

SECRETS TO PASSING THE REAL ESTATE EXAM

Studying by itself is not always enough. Learning good examination habits and techniques is also important. Good "examinationship" will mean extra points for you.

Knowing how to take an examination can make the difference between passing and failing. Many people fail the real estate exam before they enter the examination room. Be prepared and be confident.

Don't study late the night before your examination. If you have done your preparation, the few extra hours of rest will mean more in being fresh for the examination.

Avoid the use of amphetamines. They frequently give a false sense of understanding.

They cause students to jump at an answer without carefully weighing alternative possibilities.

Allow yourself plenty of time to get to the examination location. Plan for traffic problems, parking, etc. Murphy's Law states: "Whatever can go wrong, will go wrong!" and O'Brian's Law states: "Murphy was an optimist!"

People are nervous at test time. Avoid pre-examination socializing. Talking with a group of nervous people will only tend to heighten your anxiety. Fear is contagious. Don't listen to the "expert" who knows the ropes simply because he has taken the exam several times.

He is obviously doing something wrong. Remain calm and confident. This is key!

Take a seat as far forward in the examination room as possible. You are less likely to be distracted by students moving in front of you.

The Department of Real Estate allows the use of non-programmable electronic calculators. Make sure you have one and you fully understand its operation. Go through sample problems with it in advance. Some calculators will give wrong answers when the batteries are low. Remember "Murphy": Have new batteries in your calculator.

Bring several sharp pencils to use for the examination. However, if the state supplies you with a pencil, USE IT, not your own. The test is electronically scored and your own pencil mark may not register. Different pencil manufacturers use different types of graphite in their pencils.

Pay attention to all instructions given by the examination tutor as well as those written on the examination.

If you are right-handed, place the examination answer sheet to the right of the examination booklet. If you are left-handed, place the answer sheet to the left. This way your arm does not crowd over the examination booklet while answering a question. Not only will it save time in finding your place, but it will also reduce the possibility of answering a question in the wrong section of the answer sheet. You DO NOT want to suddenly find yourself out of sequence by marking the answer to question 100 in the section for question 99 and find out you have been marking the wrong section for the past 15 questions.

Frequently among the first few questions it seems that there are some of the most difficulty. Physiologically it will throw you off pace and the Department of Real Estate has coldly done this on purpose. What you will want to do is skip the first 5 questions and start with question number 6. Once you have finished all the questions, then go back and do questions 1 through 5. Also, you will want to skip all the math questions in your first run through. You will want to wait to answer any math questions until the very end. This reason for this is that the brain takes about 10 to minutes to completed go from a comprehensive thinking to analytical mathematical thinking. Your exam will be timed and you will only have about a minute and a half for each question. So your time will be valuable.

Here is a run down of how you should approach the exam process:

You will be allowed one sheet of scratch paper. On this sheet make 3 columns labeled A, MATH and GUESS. Write the numbers 1, 2, 3, 4, 5 in column A and draw a line under number 5. These are the first 5 questions you are going to skip and come back to. Remember we mentioned this earlier in the beginning of this book. On this first run through you are NOT going to guess at any questions. Start with question number 6. Let's say you know the answer and you answer it correctly. Then go to the next question, number 7. You do not know the answer right away and it might cause you to think about it for awhile.

Remember time is valuable. Write the number 7 on your sheet of scratch paper in column A with the other numbers. You will come back to this later. You go on to question number 8. This one you know, and answer it correctly. You continue on answering correctly until you come to question number 15. It is a math question. Place this in the MATH column and any other math questions you come across on this first run through. From now on in this first run through you will place all questions you do not know right away in the column A, any math questions in column labeled MATH. The column labeled GUESS will be for the second run through. Your scratch paper should now look like the image on the next page.

A	Math	Guess	
1 2 3 4 5	15		
7			

Continue with your first run through of the exam, placing math questions in the MATH column and unknown questing in column A until you get to the end. You will find that there will be very few math question on the exam. They do not weigh very heavily on the exam.

Now you are ready for the second run through. Look at your scratch paper. Go to column A and start with the first question below the line under the number 5. This question has now had some time to incubate in your mind, or there was another question like it in the exam that you answered correctly. You now know the answer and answer it correctly.

Cross out the number 7 and go to the next one in the column. Continue until you come across one in this column that you still do not know or absolutely have not clue. Let's say it was question number 37. Cross out number 37 and place it in the GUESS column.

Continue on this second run though. Answering the ones you now know and crossing them out, and placing the ones that you still do not know in the GUESS column until you reach the end again. Your scratch paper should look something like the image on the next page.

A	Math	Guess	
1	15	37	
2	21		
3	35		
4	45		
5	67		
~~7~~			
~~18~~			
~~26~~			
~~37~~			
42			
63			

Now for the third run through. Go back to column A and answer the first 5 questions. Do the same as before. The ones you do not know place them in column labeled GUESS.

Once you have gone through the first 5 you are now ready to go on to the MATH column.

Do the same with this column. If you absolutely do not know one of the math questions, place it in the GUESS column. Your scratch paper should now look like the one on the next page.

A	Math	Guess	
~~1~~	~~15~~	37	
2	~~21~~	4	
3	~~35~~	21	
~~4~~	~~45~~		
~~5~~	~~67~~		
~~X~~			
~~18~~			
~~26~~			
~~37~~			
42			
63			

Now you are ready to attack the GUESS column. First go to the math question. If the math question has answers that look like the ones below, you will see that nothing in residential real estate costs $36.00 and hardly anything in residential real estate costs $360,000,000.00. So, you can eliminate A and D. This leaves B and C and a 50/50 chance at getting it correct. Take a look at the question once more. Look at the numbers that are being used in the question and the type of question it is. Is the math question about commission or annual interest? If so, the answer may be C. Or, is the math question about fees, penalties, monthly payments, monthly savings, or monthly interest? If so, then the answer to this question is probably B.

A. $36.00
B. $360.00
C. $3600.00
D. $360,000,000.00

Finally, finish the GUESS column with the comprehensive questions you had no clue about. Can you play the elimination game with those and give yourself a 50/50 chance on those too? If so, great! But still do not answer it. Locate the question on your answer sheet. Look at the answers you bubbled in for the 3 before it and the 3 after it. Does there seem to be a pattern? In the Department of Real Estate's exam there are patterns and they usually happen in 4's. If you see that there is a pattern of 4 with the answers like the ones below, continue that pattern.

35. B
36. B
37. (this one you did not know and is in your GUESS column)
38. B
39. C

So, for number 37 you will mark it B. If you do not see a pattern, and you cannot eliminate to make a 50/50 chance, do as the old college saying goes, "if you don't know it, mark it C". You will be amazed at how many question on ANY exam has the letter C as the answer.

So, now you have the tools to take your exam with even more confidence knowing that you have a better chance at passing your exam than anyone else there in the exam room.

Many people consider the examination which they took to become a real estate license tougher than any examination they ever had in college. You can see that there are hundreds of unfamiliar terms and phrases too be learned which cover a wide spectrum of areas.

Do not be intimidated by the size of the task before you. You do not need to have an exceptional intellect or memory to pass your examination. What you must have is dedication to continue with your studies and plan to get the most of your study time. As said before, confidence is the key.

Many students are discouraged because of confusion. During your first few lessons, confusion is the normal situation not the exception. Many students have stated that they are confused and unsure until they start their reviews. Then things start to clarify and make sense.

Teenagers and octogenarians have passed real estate examinations, and you can too. A positive attitude and learning how to study and take an examination can mean your success.

CLOSING

The Department of Real Estate or Real Estate Commission regularly changes the real estate exam. However, they do not write new questions for each new exam. The state keeps a test bank of real estate questions. Each real estate exam is composed from this bank of questions. Questions are dropped from the bank that are either seldom answered correctly or nearly always answered correctly. Consequently, the majority of the questions are repeated again and again. Often questions will be changed slightly to call for a "negative" rather than a "positive" answer. Other times the question will remain the same, but the answer will be worded differently. The questions offered in this Real Estate Exam Prep book are questions from this "test bank". Studying these questions and answers (with explanations) is a great way to familiarize yourself with the examination you will receive by the Department of Real Estate or Real Estate Commission, and will substantially increase your odds of passing the exam on the first try.

As mentioned before, confidence is the key. What better why to give yourself confidence than to have this book along with the questions and answers BEFORE you take the exam. Knowing exactly what to expect on the day of your exam will boost your confidence level.

Thank you again! We hope this book will give you the confidence needed to pass your real estate exam and become a successful real estate agent.

Limits of Liability

Made in the USA
Las Vegas, NV
14 October 2021